Another Family Reunion Novel
in the Wisdom of the Ancestors Series
— Book 19 —

A *Forever* KIND OF LOVE

ALEX-MONT KIDS SAGA, Episode 2

ANN JEFFRIES

Praise for
A Forever Kind of Love
The Alex-Mont Kids Saga: Episode 2

"Ann Jeffries creates a beautiful love story of two young people falling in love...learning from the example of family and friends surrounding them. Presenting her second episode in the Alex-Mont Kids Saga, A Forever Kind of Love, Jeffries engages the hearts of all through her characters."
–Bella Fayre, Author, *Legacy of the Lost*

"A heartwarming story, masterfully told. I think a lot of people would love to have the life Brian and KiLe share."
–Michael Minton, Author, *A Wind in the Pines*

"A beautiful novel that resonates with people who display deep moral virtues. Ann Jeffries' writings compel you to believe the characters are reaching out and speaking directly to you. Bravo, Ann, on accomplishing another stunning novel in the Wisdom of the Ancestors series."
—Debra Geiman Colletti, Author, *Bittersweet*

"There's a skill in writing a story that makes you lose yourself in the pages. Ann Jeffries has that skill. Another winner from an author I can't get enough of."
–J. A. Meinecke, Author, *A Woman To Reckon With*

"In the continuing saga of Ms. Jeffries' 'Wisdom of the Ancestors' series, the author has another winner. She weaves a tale of romance with a smattering of suspense that will leave the reader wanting more from this author.
–Nancy Engle, Author, *Reunions Can Be Murder*

Copyright © 2020 by Ann Jeffries
www.annjeffries.net
All rights reserved
Printed and Bound in the United States of America

Published and Distributed By
New View Literature
820 67th Avenue N, #7603
Myrtle Beach, South Carolina 29572
annjeffries@newviewliterature.com
www.newviewliterature.com

Editorial Services:
Laurie D. Willis of Laurie's Write Touch!

Jessica Tilles, TWA Solutions
Cover and Interior Design

ISBN: 978-1-941603-23-9 Print
ISBN: 978-1-941603-24-6 eBook
Library of Congress Control Number: 2017903340

First printing April 2020

This is a work of fiction. Names, characters, business, places, events and incidents are either the products of the author's imagination or used in a fictitious manner. Any resemblance to actual persons, living or dead, or actual events is purely coincidental.

No part of this book may be reproduced, stored in a retrieval system or transmitted in any form or by any means without the prior written permission of the publisher—except by a reviewer who may quote brief passages in a review to be printed in a newspaper, magazine or journal.

For inquiries, contact the publisher.

Acknowledgments

I bow in humble gratitude to:

The Creator

My Ancestors

Jessica Tilles, TWA Solutions

The Carolina Forest Authors' Club

Kelley Hazen, Storyteller Productions

Laurie D. Willis of Laurie's Write Touch!

The Carolina Forest Library, Horry County, SC

Charles Engle, Computer Wizard

Faithful Family, Friends, and Fans

The struggle for literary perfection continues and will never cease.

I remain faithfully yours,

Ann Jeffries

Ann Jeffries Titles
In the Family Reunion—Wisdom of the Ancestors Series

In Print and E-book formats
Southern Exposures
Another Point of View
Northern Exposures
Uncommon Choices
An Unguarded Moment
Moments to Remember
The Better Part of Valor
Walking On Uneven Ground
Ask Me No Questions...I'll Tell You No Lies
Touch Me in the Morning
All Goodbyes Aren't Gone
A Different Frame of Mind
Judicial Indiscretion
Crystal Clear Persuasion
Sweet Justice
Bittersweet Memories
All in the Family
An Ulterior Motive

In audiobook format:
Southern Exposures, Producer Ginger Walton
Another Point of View, Producer Glen Pavlovich
Northern Exposures, Producer CJ McAlister
Uncommon Choices, Producer Kelley Hazen
An Unguarded Moment, Producer Richard Dennis Johnson
Moments to Remember, Producer Richard Dennis Johnson
The Better Part of Valor, Producer Richard Dennis Johnson
Walking on Uneven Ground, Producer Richard Dennis Johnson
Ask Me No Questions...I'll Tell You No Lies, Producer Pam Dougherty
Touch Me in the Morning, Producer Ginger Walton
All Goodbyes Aren't Gone, Producer Julian Thomas
A Different Frame of Mind, Producer C. J. McAllister
Judicial Indiscretion, Producer Kelley Hazen
Crystal Clear Persuasion, Producer C. J. McAllister
Sweet Justice, Producer C. J. McAllister
Bittersweet Memories, Producer Richard Dennis Johnson
All in the Family, Producer Kelley Hazen
An Ulterior Motive, Producer Kelley Hazen

"If you let me, I would show you the love you have never known, a forever kind of love."
—Kim Morrison

"We have that forever kind of love, something felt once in a lifetime." —Marcquiese Burrell

"I still want you to be with me. I still want you to dream with. I'll never, ever give up on us 'cause we've got a forever kind of love."
—John Derek Hamilton

"The forever kind of love is full of plans, holding hands. When I look at you, I can see it. It's that forever kind of love."
—Keeley B

"He reads your feelings as easily as a book and can tell what you're thinking with just a quick look. That's a forever kind of love."
—Codey

I can't wait to look at someone and know we have a forever kind of love."
—Rose, Thirteenpurpleroses

CHAPTER 1

Brian Alford Montgomery quickly and expertly rode his favorite stock horse, Lucky, cutting back and forth around the perimeter of the herd of Black Angus cattle and then pulled to a smooth halt. Waiting while the other ranch hands corralled the herd in the pens, he then leaned down to close and lock the gates. It had taken all morning from four-thirty and a little into afternoon to round up the herd of cows on the sprawling Alexander-Montgomery (Alex-Mont) Ranch. He was pleased that his two, black, eight-month-old Labrador Retrievers, Starsky and Hutch, were learning their roles in helping with the round-up.

Alex-Mont's cattle were not headed for slaughter. Rather, they were bred for domestic and foreign markets to improve the bloodlines cultivated on other farms. Doc Peterson, the veterinarian, and the doctor's helpers were there to inspect the herd and administer an antibiotic indicated for the treatment of bovine respiratory disease and foot rot for cattle at high risk for developing the ailments.

Brian didn't believe that any of his herds were affected, but he was taking no chances. He shipped his stock worldwide and would continue to ensure and certify that his cattle were disease-free. There had been an outbreak of the diseases in Texas and Wyoming. Nothing east of the Mississippi River anywhere near his family's Maryland, Pennsylvania, and South Carolina ranches, but he had recently, within the last year, purchased more short-horn bison stock from other places in the Rocky Mountains. This was the third year he would be cultivating a herd of American buffalo at his ranch in the Pocono Mountains of Pennsylvania. The buffalo were in high demand and garnered higher stud fees on the open market.

His herds of Black Angus cattle in South Carolina and Pennsylvania were being checked and inoculated, as well. For now, while the doctor began his examinations and the ranch hands ran the cows through the pens for a headcount, they didn't need him. So, he decided he could leave them to this task and get some paperwork done. Raising his hat, he waved it, signaling his departure and received acknowledgments from the men and women working the cattle.

Placing his hat firmly on his head again, Brian whistled for Starsky and Hutch. The dogs stopped playfully tumbling over each other in the mud and came on the fly. "Let's go, Lucky," he said, patting his mount's long neck. The horse responded with little or no provocation and headed across the open acreage, which was still sufficiently covered with a blanket of snow from a recent storm. They headed to the barn and horse corral at a pretty good clip with the dogs racing like wild things ahead. "Ah, you want to run, do you?" Brian said to Lucky and detoured; he headed to one of the bridle paths, which led to a quarter-mile race track. The dogs sniffed the ground and trees and then marked their territory.

Other ranch hands were putting the Alex-Mont thoroughbreds through their paces on the snow-cleared track in preparation for the upcoming Native Dancer Stakes. The American Thoroughbred horse race was run annually at Laurel Park Racecourse in Laurel, Maryland, not far from the Alex-Mont Ranch. Since the race is open to horses aged three and older and is contested on dirt tracks over a mile distance, Alex-Mont Ranch had seven entries scheduled to participate. Although the seventy-five thousand dollars winner's purse was attractive, Brian felt that the trophy alone would be more beneficial to Alex-Mont's reputation for quality thoroughbreds. The notoriety would cause the stud fees to double the winner's purse per horse. Brian didn't make a practice of studying data or other information on the competing horses, but he knew his thoroughbreds would win, place, or show against the rest of the field. He looked forward to the challenge.

"Stay," he ordered his dogs once he reached the race track before taking Lucky around the oval giving him his head. He leaned low over Lucky's head and nearly lost his Stetson, but Lucky flew as if he had wings. Brian loved the feel of the chilled wind racing past. He then took Lucky around the track again, this time for a cool-down trot before heading back through a different bridle path to the horse barn. He slowed, allowing more time for Lucky to cool down while letting his dogs sniff, explore, and mark their territory before racing on. When he reached the first barn, a number of ranch hands stood waiting.

"You made good time, Brian," commented one of the horses' handlers when Brian brought Lucky to a stop and smoothly slid from his saddle. "Mary Todd was surprised and called ahead to tell me about it."

"Lucky wanted a run today." Brian handed over the reins before inspecting Lucky's shoes. "Give him a good wash and rub down and the dogs, too," he said once he finished his inspection. Brian loosened and removed the saddle from Lucky's back and slung it over his shoulder, holding it by the saddle horn. The blanket he left in place to keep him warm until his bath.

Lucky nosed Brian's pocket, causing him to laugh.

He reached into his deep, buckskin coat pocket and pulled out a few apples he had left. "Ah, so you think you deserve a treat, do you?" He rubbed the horse's long neck. "Now, you want to eat the last of my lunch?"

Lucky nodded his head as if he understood the question and then neatly nipped the apples out of Brian's open gloved palm.

"Well, I guess you have earned it today, boy." Brian gave Lucky another brisk rub and pat before turning him over to a ranch hand. With Starsky and Hutch playfully leading the way, Brian walked into the barn's tack room to store his saddle. Resolved that he didn't have time to tend to his gear today, he allowed a couple of the stable boys, who were eager to do it for the extra pocket change he would pay them, to take over the task. He left the saddle with them and dug out a couple of raw bones for his dogs. When he pulled off his gloves, he tucked them into his coat pocket. Pulling off his Stetson, he ran his fingers through his hair and knocked the dust off his jeans and coat with his hat. He needed a haircut he knew, but that, too, would have to wait a few more days. For now, once he reached his cabin, he was looking forward to a long, hot shower. After he washed his hair and then dried it, he would simply tie it together at the nape of his neck the way his dad usually wore his hair. Smiling, he thought that they had that in common. When he got to Pennsylvania, Brian decided that he'd ask his grandaunt, Althea Hardyston, to give him a trim.

As Brian walked toward his cabin, located in the woodland area of the ranch by a stream, he rolled his broad shoulders, stretched his arms over his head, and behind his back to work out the kinks. He'd been up and in the saddle since early morning gathering the cattle with his ranch hands, roping and then pulling some of the heavy bovines out of muddy gullies and bogs. The remaining snowfall and ice hampered their tasks in some areas.

It was now well past lunchtime. He needed a shower to wash away the grime, his fatigue, and something to fill his empty belly other than the apples he fed to Lucky.

Ranch work was a hard, never-ending process. He usually worked from can't-see-in-the-morning-until-can't-see-at-night, putting in twelve to fourteen-hour days. There were times he'd been up all night for the birth of some of the prized animals, but he loved his ranch life and wouldn't have it any other way. Still, it was also a business and it had to be run efficiently with an eye on the bottom line. They had cattle, buffalo, thoroughbred and stock horses, pigs, chickens, turkeys and all manner of other farm animals that were more his siblings' pets than livestock for sale.

The ranch housed other businesses as well. Their glass-enclosed hydroponics gardens spanned many acres and operated twenty-four seven, three-hundred-sixty-five days a year. The production of fresh fruits, vegetables, and flowers was in high demand by boutique stores and high-end restaurants throughout the region. They also raised and harvested fish, crustaceans, mollusks, aquatic plants, algae, and other aquatic organisms in the largest indoor aquaculture in the state. Although he wasn't a particular fan, their snails were in high daily demand by restaurants for *Escargot*. Their facilities cultivated both freshwater and saltwater crustacean populations under stringently-controlled conditions.

Nothing went to waste on any Alex-Mont property. They worked everything possible, all trash into compost and reintroduced it into improving the soil. Their exterior gardens were a showplace often photographed for magazines. Brian set aside special raised gardens in a greenhouse for his siblings to grow anything they chose. As a result, there was a wide array of edible herbs, vegetables, fruits, and flowers. Each child from the toddlers to the teens and young adults—stairsteps all—had his or her own five-by-five-foot or more space to cultivate. Some added toys, like an old wooden train with tracks curving among the plants, while others added wrought-iron or glass art. His siblings were quite a creative bunch and constantly surprised him with their ingenuity.

Although the ranch operated diverse businesses year-round, the crew of ranch hands, no matter the task, was second to none when it came to getting the job done. They worked just as hard as he did every day. He didn't tolerate slackers on his teams, and the ranch hands appreciated that everyone pulled his or her own weight, including him. He wasn't the type of manager who sat back on his laurels and let others do the tough stuff. He was always an extra pair of hands when needed for any undertaking. That was the way he and his siblings were raised. They stepped up and did whatever task came next on the energetic working ranch.

The Maryland Alexander-Montgomery Ranch consisted of thousands of acres surrounded by state and federal parklands that he tended to. Most of their ranch land was still forested with natural lakes, ponds, and streams they left undisturbed except for the hiking trails, bike routes, and bridal paths he and his thirty-plus siblings forged from the time they were adopted, most as toddlers, and came to live on the property.

For the most part, their hydroponics farms of fruits, vegetables, and flowers and the aquaculture were very profitable. Their livestock was gaining in profitability by leaps and bounds year after year. Not that his family depended on the revenue from breeding farm animals, the hydroponic farming or aqua breeding to survive. Actually, the ranch was more of a lucrative hobby to appease his dad's desire to be a rancher and his mom's love of farm life. It also fed the family and the people who lived and worked there.

His dad, nearly seven-foot-tall and a former professional basketball icon, Charles Patrick Montgomery, known far and wide as "Chuck," grew up on a farm in the Pocono Mountains of Monroe County, Pennsylvania. After he retired from professional sports, he became an emergency room doctor. Now he and other doctors were owners and operators of Physicians Hospital, a not-for-profit, one-hundred-bed facility, located in the rural Maryland countryside a few miles from the ranch where they lived. Dr. Montgomery loved everything about ranch life. Still, he also loved the practice of medicine and saw patients at his office and clinic across the single-lane country road from the ranch. He also still attended his long-time patients at Georgetown Medical in nearby Washington, DC, where he was at one time the head of emergency medicine.

Because it was his birthday, Chuck didn't have office hours today. Still, he was out early this morning at the hospital to see his patients before his planned mini-birthday vacation. Otherwise, he, too, would have been with Brian and the other ranch hands on the cattle round-up this morning.

Brian's mom, Vivian Alexander Montgomery, a U.S. Supreme Court Judge, an Olympic gold medalist in basketball, and one of the wealthiest women in the world, enjoyed ranch life, too. She was also raised on a farm in Goodwill, Summer County, South Carolina, and loved living on the ranch. It wasn't a difficult commute for her from the rural area into Washington, DC, to the U.S. Supreme Court building on Capitol Hill. His parents and siblings, who were of school age, made the round trip daily. The little ones, still under school age, attended preschool activities with the children of the ranch hands at a facility on the Alex-Mont Ranch. None of his siblings objected to living in the rural area of the county. They had everything they needed there on the ranch in a fun-filled, stress-free environment.

After he finished college and grad school at UPenn, Brian took over management of the three ranches fulltime from his dad. It was what he always wanted to do and his parents trusted him to do a good job.

As a part of his many duties, Brian managed the nursery and preschool campus in a protected and secluded spot on the ranch where the children had access to a petting zoo, Shetland ponies, and plenty of playground equipment and space. Some of the children's parents worked or volunteered at the school, along with the professional teachers and counselors he hired who were paid for their educational service.

Two men and one woman worked as cooks in the school kitchen and the main mansion, while three others cleaned the common areas. The ranch hands chose to combine their resources and had their own communal meals prepared in the ranch community center by the workers' spouses. The community center also housed a movie theatre, library, beauty and barber salon, and recreation room. There was even a workout room with equipment, an indoor exercise pool, and a sauna.

Brian also managed the housing for the ranch hands and those who had families. Most of the people who lived on the Alex-Mont properties, both men and women, came to him by way of a family homeless shelter in Washington, DC. Recently, more male and female military veterans were turning up at the shelter, some with families and others without. Through careful screening, some were offered an opportunity to work in the pastoral lands of the ranch in Maryland or at the ranch in Monroe County, Pennsylvania or Summer County, South Carolina. All of the hands were paid a fair wage, lived rent-free in comfortable ranch housing and had full medical, optical, and dental benefits as a part of their employment package. Some had been on the ranch since its inception while others, once they got their feet under them, were able to move on to other endeavors.

His family supported continuing education for all of their employees. Many took advantage of that benefit at the nearby junior college or at one of the many state university campuses in the Washington, DC, metropolitan area. As a result, several ranch hands were competing for advanced degrees outside the area and would be leaving after graduation. That would open slots to hire five more ranch hands in Maryland, three in Pennsylvania and two in South Carolina, so he'd be visiting the homeless shelter again soon.

Claudia Shaffer, a widowed, female military veteran with two small children, hailed him as he was heading for his cabin. Brian turned to meet her halfway mindful of the prosthesis replacing her lower left leg.

"What's up, Claudia?"

"We've got a fox in the area again. My dogs sniffed it out, but it got close to the chicken coop before the dogs alerted."

"Okay, pick a few hands to go with you to capture the animal. Doc Peterson is over on the north pasture of the ranch examining the cattle. Once you've captured the fox, cage it, and take it to the doctor so it can be checked for disease. If Doc says it's okay, have him tag it. If you catch it before I leave, I'll take it up to Monroe County and set it loose up in the mountains when I go up early tomorrow morning."

"Yes, sir," she said and started away.

"Claudia," Brian called after her, "be sure to check the sex of the fox and, if it's a female, have Doc make sure it hasn't left a litter somewhere.

If so, you'll have to put a locator device on it to track it back to its lair to rescue the pups. Also, you and your dogs are doing a fine job for us, but if you don't stop calling me 'sir,' I'm not going to be happy."

She smiled at him, saluted, and said, "Thanks, Brian," with a cheeky grin. She was a former Army Ranger who worked with bomb-sniffing dogs in Afghanistan. She was injured and lost her lower left leg below the knee when a bomb exploded, killing her dog. At about the same time, her husband, an accountant, was killed on his way to work in Washington, DC, when a train he was on derailed in the northern Virginia countryside. They had no close family to help her with their two young boys while she recuperated and tried to recover from the loss of her husband.

However, a Montgomery family friend, Dr. Mark Brooks, a physician with Doctors Without Borders, stationed at the Landstuhl Regional Medical Center located near Landstuhl, Germany, tended to the young woman's injuries. The hospital serves wounded soldiers coming from Iraq and Afghanistan. When Dr. Brooks heard about her husband's death, he cut through all of the military's red tape. He arranged to have her boys brought to Germany via private jet.. That was better than having them placed in foster care until Claudia could be released from the hospital. The boys were enrolled in a preschool at the hospital facility where Claudia was convalescing.

Service dogs were also cared for at the facility in Germany. So, since Claudia had experience working with dogs, she was asked to provide assistance during her convalescence. It was a good connection, since neither she nor the dogs would see further military service. In addition, the dogs needed to be retrained. It was Dr. Brooks' idea to contact his pal, Dr. Chuck Montgomery, to determine whether Chuck had a place for Claudia, her sons, and the former service dogs on his ranch. When his dad discussed it with him, Brian readily agreed. Now Claudia had three dogs that she retrained to provide security for the ranch. Because it was so large, she was awaiting the delivery of two more dogs to work into her canine security team.

Dr. Brooks visited the ranch a few times to check on Claudia's progress and her sons. The young family was flourishing in the ranch environment. The boys were in the ranch school, but Brian suspected Dr. Brooks' interest in Claudia went beyond the doctor-patient relationship. Claudia, a strong-minded, attractive young woman, didn't let her injury become an impediment. Brian taught her to ride a horse when she made the rounds of the ranch with her dogs or she'd take one of the Jeeps or an ATV. The dogs were equipped with motion-sensitive video cameras, which alerted whenever they were on the move. Reporters had been caught trying to enter the ranch to get pictures of the family or interview the workers. In everyone's view, Claudia and the dogs were vital assets to the security of the ranch's operation. Brian needed to decide whether to replicate this security measure at the ranches in Pennsylvania and South Carolina. So far, his thoughts were favorable.

After Claudia, he was waylaid twice more by ranch staff members returning in the ranch's delivery trucks before he made it to his cabin. Once inside, he took time to hang his Stetson on the hook beside the door and empty his pockets into the wooden bowl he carved from a tree burl when he was nine years old. Placing his sunglasses on the credenza, he plugged in his iPhone to recharge. The rest of his clothes, he started stripping off on his way to his bedroom shower.

Only momentarily did he stop to turn on his audio system to listen to his cousins' yet-to-be-released CD and dump a frozen bag of beef stew into a small crockpot to heat while he washed. Thanks to his tankless water heater and geothermal system, the shower instantly yielded invigoratingly hot water from all directions as if he were in a car wash. He sang along with what he knew would be another one of Ivy's top hits. He stood still and let the water pummel his body from several directions for a few moments before he washed his hair and lathered his body.

He didn't know how he let Whitney and her younger triplet sisters talk him into singing background for them on three of the CD's cuts. His musically-inclined family's sound studio and recording equipment on the lower level of the mansion were in constant use. Whitney actually recorded some of the cuts there using family members as the technicians. Now she coerced him to singing several songs at her wedding. He was in a glee club in high school and college and occasionally enjoyed singing with his sibs, Whitney, and his Montgomery cousins in Pennsylvania. Although he never planned to make a career in music, he was proud of his cousins' success and would do anything to help.

Brian sat on the shower bench to clean and clip his nails before resting his head back against the shower wall and closing his eyes while the water beat down on his body. The skylight above his head reminded him that although he would relish a longer shower, it was getting late, he had more to do that day, and he was hungry. He couldn't laze around or even take a break.

He knocked off work early today because later tonight, his parents would be celebrating his father's birthday. The place would be packed with family and friends. Tomorrow, his parents were scheduled to fly to their island home in Bimini and he was planning to check on a laundry list of things at the ranch in Monroe County, Pennsylvania. Both sets of grandparents were already at the mansion and would stay with his siblings until his parents returned the following weekend.

He wasn't sure when he would be back in Maryland, but he was planning to be in Pennsylvania for only a few weeks. Three at the most. Since he was arranging to leave early the next morning, he needed to do laundry and to pack his clothes before he left for the party. He didn't need much. He kept clothes in all three ranch locations. Still, he hadn't found time to clean his place or do his laundry in more than a week. He could have had someone come in to do the work for him, but he liked to do things for himself. He couldn't leave before performing those tasks.

After turning off the shower, he grabbed a rug-sized towel to dry his hair and body before heading for the kitchen area. He was still singing along with the music, but was brought up short when he pulled the towel away from his head and face. He spotted a small person sitting on the floor crying. With her back to his front door and her arms around her up-drawn legs, her forehead was resting on her knees.

CHAPTER 2

KiLe Hakamora couldn't believe her eyes when she entered the side door of the Alexander-Montgomery mansion's ballroom. There, in a corner behind the stage, she found her boyfriend of two years, Payton Bradshere, with a relatively new member of their band, Stephany Thomas' hand inside his pants and one of his hands under her minuscule skirt. Stephany's long, right leg was hiked up around Payton's thigh. He had her pinned against the wall and was breathing as if he were a long-distance runner breaking speed records for the gold. They were in a serious lip lock tickling each other's tonsils and going at it like two wrestlers in the heat of a championship match. The two were in such a deep fog it took moments before the closing of the heavy door behind KiLe alerted the lovers they weren't alone.

When they spotted her, they sprang apart. "KiLe," Payton began, as he moved toward her while stuffing his member back into his Jockeys. She turned and ran through the double doors Chet Powell, another Changeling band member, had propped open to bring in the band's equipment.

She didn't mean to bowl Chet over in her blind dash, but she was so hurt, embarrassed, and humiliated she didn't know what she was doing. She could hear Payton calling her name as he gave chase. She had a head start and kept running as fast as her short legs and tennis shoe-clad feet could carry her. She ran into the woods and then dashed into the pretty, timber-framed cabin set back off the path and sheltered by a copse of trees. It blended so nicely into the forested landscape that she would have otherwise missed it. Fortunately, the front door was unlocked and she darted inside out of sight. The tears wouldn't stop coming, so, with her back to the door, she just slid down to the warm, hardwood floor and cried.

It took her a few moments to realize she wasn't alone in the cabin. She didn't know who the place belonged to, but evidence of a man's clothes and boots laid a trail to what must be the bedroom. Above her head, a Stetson hat hung from a peg beside the door. In the distance, she could hear shower water running and someone singing. The distinctive sound of Ivy's music was playing on the audio sound system, and the aroma of good, hot food was permeating the air reminding her that she had missed lunch. Though she wanted to, she couldn't leave because she could still hear Payton's voice calling her name. When the shower water turned off moments later, a gloriously naked and barefoot Brian Montgomery walked into the great room, drying his hair and face while continuing to sing on key to the music. It wasn't clear who was more surprised, her or him.

"Kiley, right?" he asked, uncertain of the correct pronunciation, but he had the presence of mind to pick up the remote and shut off the music. No one, outside the family, knew that his cousin, Whitney Ivy Alexander, is the lead singer of the top musical group, Ivy, and that her teenaged triplet sisters were also members of the group.

"KiLe," she corrected.

It sounded the same to him, but that was irrelevant at the moment. "What's going on? Why are you here? Are you crying?" he asked, holding the towel bunched in front of his genitals.

Momentarily entranced, the towel left the rest of his beautiful, masterpiece of a body free for her perusal. He was truly mesmerizing. Other than a gold chain, which read **FAMILY**, encircling his neck, she had never seen a completely naked man before. Droplets of water clung to his creamy, sun-tanned skin and hard pecks, matting the baby-fine blond hairs down his torso to where they disappeared behind the towel he held shielding himself. His dark blond hair was damp and charmingly mussed.

"Did something happen to my family?" he demanded, clearly concerned.

Before she could answer, someone pounded on his front door. It was probably Payton, KiLe surmised. Still, she pleaded with Brian with her eyes, an index finger to her lips, and shook her head, signaling him not to reveal her presence. She slid aside on her bottom so that he could answer the second knock at his door.

Tying the towel around his waist, he eyed her suspiciously before opening the door.

"Oh, sorry to disturb, Brian," said Payton, his Australian accent pronounced. "I didn't know you lived here. I'm looking for KiLe Hakamora, but I see you must have been in the shower. You know who she is, right?"

"Yes, I believe she's a Georgetown undergrad student who is a housemate of my cousin, Whitney Alexander. She sings with your band, doesn't she?"

"Yes, that's her. If you see her, would you let her know I'm searching for her?" asked Payton. "It's very important that I speak with her."

"I'll do that when I see her. You're Payton Bradshere, right?"

"Yes, you're right. Okay, thanks, mate," he said as he started to turn away, but then turned back before Brian could close the door. "Look, Brian, she's upset and ran in this direction. Where does the path go beyond here?"

"It's a bridle path, so it goes in any number of directions, including the Havenhurst Country Club, golf course, and residential community a few miles away. It's a private, gated community, but we have access to the equestrian park because we board and furnish horses for Havenhurst residents. So, you can access it from our property. Other paths go off for miles into the federal and state lands surrounding the ranch. Still, if she came this way, she could have doubled back to the main house through the path by the stream and not gone further into the wooded area."

"Thanks, Brian," he said and moved off trotting back through the woods toward the main mansion.

Brian closed and, this time, locked his door, something he rarely did. He crossed his arms over his bare chest, leaned a shoulder against the door, and looked down at the up-turned, teary-eyed countenance of the pretty Japanese friend of his cousin. When her tears fountained up to overflowing, he sighed and slid to the floor beside her. Taking her into his arms, she clung to him while her tears slid down his damp, bare chest and disappeared into the terrycloth towel around his waist.

"KiLe, Payton Bradshere is searching for you. Now, I've dispensed my duty to inform you as he asked. So, you want to tell me what's going on?" Brian asked.

"I'm just stuck on stupid," KiLe lamented.

"I don't believe that for one moment. My cousin doesn't associate herself with stupid people, but right now, I'm starving. Let me pick up my clothes, put on something decent, and then you can explain why you're upset while we eat."

She didn't speak but nodded against his warm, moist, nice smelling, firm chest.

Carefully, Brian stood up to keep himself covered and helped her to her feet. Proceeding toward his bedroom, he picked up his clothes and boots en route. Dumping his dirty clothes in his laundry room, he then put on a pair of UPenn sweats, representing his alma mater, and combed his long, strong fingers of both hands through his cap of thick, damp hair. It wasn't clear what was going on between KiLe and Payton, but it didn't take a genius to see she was hurting from the experience. Before things got out of hand and a search party was sent out to look for her, he sent a text to his foreman and to his cousin, Whitney, to let them know KiLe was with him in his cabin and safe.

Whitney and KiLe both lived at Whitney's parents' home with a select number of other Georgetown University students in the northwest Embassy Row neighborhood of Washington, DC, near the school's main campus. Whitney was in her final year at Georgetown Law and KiLe was finishing her final year in the college. In the coming week, they were starting spring break.

When he re-entered the great room, he put a few logs in the fireplace, lit the kindling, and watched. He made sure the chimney flue was properly drawing before he placed the screen in front of the hearth. KiLe, he noted, was curled up in the long corner of his L-shaped sofa in his favorite spot. Her eyes were closed and she seemed calmer. He covered her with a blanket and left her there before he went to his kitchen space. Using the remote for his robotics system, the breakfast bar rolled away from the elongated U-shaped row of base kitchen cabinets, creating a generous space for him to work and maneuver. After pulling sourdough bread from his breadbox and tossing a fresh, crisp, garden salad, he put two place settings on the breakfast bar before he woke KiLe and brought her to sit across from him at the center-post work station.

"What would you like to drink?" he asked her.

"Water is fine," she said monotone as she sat watching him work. "You didn't have to turn off the music. I like the group Ivy, too, but I don't think I've heard this CD before. They're so mysterious and secretive about who they are. They don't do interviews, DVDs or world tours; just benefit concerts from time to time."

He was glad he shut off the music because he didn't want to explain how he got a copy of a CD, which wasn't even scheduled for release until the fall of the year. He didn't encourage discussion about Ivy, but, if he ignored her, he felt it might seem strange. So, he turned on his XM Radio. "I like their music too, but I also like music from the sixties and seventies. My grandparents introduced me to it and I've been hooked ever since."

Carrying on a conversation while he worked, he got a bottle of cold water from the under-the-counter beverage cooler and a bottle of red wine from the rack by the kitchen cabinet. Decanting his wine, he let it breathe. When he lifted the lid from the crockpot, the steam billowed up, spreading the pleasing aroma of the beef stew into the air.

"Because you're being so nice to me, I'll have to sing something special from that era especially for you tonight at your father's birthday party."

"I'd like that a lot," Brian said, smiling before he sat across from her.

"You have a nice, strong voice. Are you a performer?" KiLe asked.

He chuckled and handed a bowl of stew to her. "No, but I sang in high school and college."

"Mmmm, this is delicious," KiLe moaned after tasting the food. "I didn't know you could cook." She watched him ladle up the stew into his large, attractive bowl.

"Ha," he laughed, while slicing the sourdough bread and serving a piece to her on the cutting board. Reaching into the refrigerator, he retrieved a small, ceramic pot of creamy soft butter and another of goat cheese, both churned just the day before on the farm. He put them on the breakfast bar with a similarly small pot of apple butter. Both were bestsellers from the Alex-Mont Farm produce line. "I can make a decent breakfast of bacon or sausage, eggs, and toast, and even cobble together a hoagie for lunch, but a cook, I'm not. This beef stew is leftover from Wednesday night's dinner at the main house. When there are leftovers, they bag them up for me, I bring it here and put it in the freezer for days, like today, when I can't make it to the family meals."

"This is a nice place, but why do you live here instead of up at the main house with the rest of your family?"

He shrugged. "I like the quiet here in the woods. It also provides a bit of privacy when I want it. On occasions, my sibs invade and have sleepovers here on bedrolls. Still, I have my bedroom in the mansion if I want to stay there. Sometimes I do stay over with the munchkins when dad and mom have a date night a few times a week or business or events in or out of town." Because KiLe seemed to be listening and coming out of her funk, he decided to prattle on. "Since my sister, Linda, is married, living in New York City, and operating her dance studio, she and her husband come down only for the monthly birthday party and holidays. I'm the next oldest kid of my parents' posse who is still here on the ranch. My next younger brothers and sisters, the twins, Vincent is in med school, and Geneviève is an officer in the Coast Guard. Dena is in a doctoral program at MIT in Boston and the twins, Ryan and Roger, are at Florida State University on baseball scholarships. Although they're all home now for dad's birthday and the beginning of spring break, generally, I'm the one left with the rest of the thirty-one here for me to keep an eye on."

"How does it feel to have so many siblings?" asked KiLe.

"Crazy, but great," Brian said, continuing to monitor her demeanor while they ate. Since she seemed amenable and wasn't weeping, he continued to engage her in conversation. "Do you have brothers or sisters?"

"Two younger half-brothers. Toddlers really. My parents were born and still live in Japan. They divorced since I've been here in college in the states and they've remarried other people. What about your parents?"

He nodded his understanding while they continued to eat. "I lost my first father, Derrick Jackson, when I was eight years old." Brian poured a small amount of the red wine into a goblet to taste test and then poured half a glassful before he took a long swallow. "For as long as I can remember, Derrick was my doctor when I lived in an orphanage. When he and Vivian married, they adopted Linda first, then me a month later, and the rest of the crew until he died on April Fool's Day, less than a year after they married. It was also the same day Derrick Junior was born. Dad died in the hospital nursery while holding him. After his death, Mom continued to adopt dad's health-challenged patients from the orphanage until there were twelve of us, including Derrick Junior; their only biological child."

"What about your real parents?"

He frowned. "Chuck and Vivian Alexander Montgomery are my **real** parents, but I think you mean my biological parents?"

"Yes, what happened to them?"

"I have no idea. As I understand it, from my medical records and court documents, they were crack addicts and I was born addicted to the drug. The court made me a ward of the state until I was adopted. I was thirteen when Chuck and Vivian married. They asked all of us, the first twelve, whether we wanted to be adopted again and have Montgomery added to our surnames. We voted unanimously to do it. They also offered an opportunity for any of us to try to trace our biological families, but I've never been interested in finding out the details of who they are. That's true of all of my siblings. Although about a year ago, Linda's biological half-brother, Bradley Smyth, did track her down. We've all become very close to him since then. He's become another member of the posse.

"As you probably already know, Dad and Mom continue to adopt abandoned children with health challenges, particularly conjoined twins. That's why we have so many twins in our family. They also continue to have biological children and now we currently number thirty-one. However, tomorrow is another day," he said, laughing. "We never know when another little person might be added to the group dad calls 'his posse.'"

"I didn't know that. I mean, yes, I knew that your parents adopted a lot of children, including the most recent two young Iraqi boys and one toddler Iraqi girl, but I didn't know that you had another father before Dr. Montgomery."

"It just so happens that Derrick and Chuck, best friends growing up, fell in love with the same young law school student, Vivian Lynn Alexander, at the same time. Someday, if you want to know more, I'll tell you the saga of the Alexander-Jackson-Montgomery family. However, for now enough about me. Tell me what Payton did to upset you."

KiLe sighed and sat back in the high, barrel-back, barstool seat crossing her arms over her small breasts. Looking up into Brian's face, which was an interesting cross between a youthful Robert Redford and Brad Pitt, wasn't a hardship. He had a square jaw, blue eyes which tended to look almost gray or green depending on the lighting, and shaggy, dark-blond hair which waved and curled attractively framing his face. He wasn't very tall, standing at about six feet even, but, considering she stood only five-foot, three, most people seemed tall to her. However, until today, she hadn't realized how muscular he is…or well endowed. Of course, she had been to the ranch many times with Whitney for her family's events and seen him, but **WOW**, she had not known what Brian had going on.

"Come on, KiLe. Stop stalling. What's going on?" Brian encouraged.

She was hard-pressed not to tell him she found him physically attractive, but right now, it would be highly inappropriate. So, instead, she answered his question. "I was scheduled to have a job interview at the Japanese Embassy late this afternoon, so I didn't think I could perform with Changelings for your dad's birthday party tonight. That's why Stephany was tapped to take my place and sing with the band. Some emergency came up at the Embassy and the interview was postponed at the last moment. Since I found myself free after all, I drove out here to practice with the band for tonight's performance. It's not unusual for us to have three female voices perform together with the six and sometimes seven guys. When I went into one of the ballroom's side double doors at the main house, I found Payton and Stephany tongue tickling each other's tonsils…and other body parts."

"My sister, Stephany?" Brian demanded; his anger apparent, as he abruptly rose from his seat. "She's only fourteen! I'll break his neck if he touched her!"

"No, not her, not your sister Stephany. I know she's a very good vocalist, but I'm not referring to her. Calm down, Brian, I mean Stephany Thomas. Blond, blue eyes, big boobs, long legs, and stacked. She's maybe twenty-five or so."

"Oh," he said and calmed himself enough to settle back down in his seat. "So, you ran away instead of standing your ground and fighting for your man?"

"Well, yeah," she said confusion covering her face. "I mean, they were hot and heavy into each other."

"Do you really have feelings for Payton? I mean, let me be specific. Are you in love with him?"

"Well," she hedged. "I have *feelings* for him, yes. Or, at least, I did. I don't know whether we're *'in love'* exactly."

"No, I asked whether *you're* in love with *him*."

"I don't know how to answer that question, Brian. We've dated for the past two years."

"Exclusively?" he asked.

"I thought it was an exclusive relationship."

"Did you ever verify that it is or isn't?"

"Well, no, I just assumed."

"You know what they say about people who 'assume,' don't you?"

"No, what?"

"It makes an **ass** out of **u** and **me**."

"Funny, Brian. So, you've got jokes. Ha Ha," she dryly responded.

"Made you laugh, didn't it?" he asked.

She pursed her lips and gave him a hard stare.

She had a pretty, kissable mouth, Brian thought and then turned his errant thoughts away to more serious matters. "Look, kid. Intimate relationships aren't jokes. If a man is into you, he'll leave you with no doubt in your mind about his feelings. I believe in the adage: trust, but verify."

"Are you in a committed relationship?"

"No, but this isn't about me. It's about you and how you feel."

"I feel like crap."

"Okay, whatever."

"What does that mean?" KiLe indignantly asked.

"It means it is whatever it is," Brian glibly commented.

"Well, that's as clear as mud," KiLe huffed.

Brian rolled his eyes to the ceiling before looking at her again. *She's very pretty*, he thought even with red-rimmed eyes and a red nose from her histrionics. The swing of a perfusion of straight, asphalt-black hair in what he imagined some would call a modified or layered page-boy style with a little curl at the end perfectly framed her face. Her body was small, petite really, a little muscular, and she was so achingly young.

It was troubling as to how to put this next question. It shouldn't have been difficult. He'd had *"The Talk"* with his siblings when the need arose, but KiLe wasn't his sister. Still, he plunged ahead. "Has there been a change in the pattern of your sex life with Payton?"

"What do you mean?"

"I mean, have you had fewer incidents of sex?"

"We haven't had sex. I'm Japanese," she said as if that explained it all. Brian just stared.

"What?" KiLe finally asked, when Brian continued to stare at her.

"Okay, roll back the tape a moment." Brian ran his fingers through his hair, crossed his arms on the countertop, stalling, and thought before he asked. "Are you telling me that you and Payton have been involved for two years of exclusive dating but haven't been sexually active with each other?"

"Well, no, we haven't. I mean, I haven't had sex with anyone. I'm a virgin …"

"Stop!" Brian said, leaning back and holding up both hands to ward off further discussion.

"Why? What is it?"

He shook his head and swallowed the wine in his goblet before he began clearing away dishes and loading them in the dishwasher. He didn't know of any woman other than his sisters who made it out of her teen years and remained a virgin.

KiLe climbed down off the barstool and came to stand in front of him. "Brian, please tell me what you're thinking," she pleaded.

Oh, no, that wasn't going to happen, he silently vowed. *Not when his libido just torqued up a level.* He hadn't had sex in quite a while and remembering how KiLe appreciatively looked at his nude body, had his blood warming. Still, she deserved a response that didn't include offering to take her to his bed and solve her virginity issue. "Look, KiLe, in most intimate male/female relationships, sex is a foregone conclusion. You said you've dated Payton for the last two years, but you haven't incorporated sex in the equation. Payton is what, twenty-five or twenty-six? Most men in a committed relationship don't date for two years before having sex."

"Tucker Cavanaugh waited," she indignantly argued while protectively crossing her arms. "I mean, he and your cousin, Whitney, are waiting to be married before they have sex with each other."

Brian nodded, agreeing with her statement. Whitney, in her final year of law school and her fiancée, Tucker Cavanaugh, an active-duty Marine and physician completing his residency program at Georgetown Medical Center, were both still very young and bordered on genius-level IQs. They were both virgins and, indeed, waiting for their wedding this coming summer to be sexually active. "As I understand it, that's a mutual agreement between them. Tucker and Whitney put the completion of other goals and objectives ahead of engaging in premarital sex. It was their mutual decision to have an emotionally committed bond and believe they've achieved that level of maturity in their union. They've been engaged for almost two years. That's why they finally set a date for their wedding. They're each other's best friend. Do you have that type of understanding and committed relationship with Payton? Have you discussed mutual goals and objectives going forward? What's the plan?"

When she stared at him blankly, he nodded, "Enough said," and continued cleaning up.

CHAPTER 3

Brian gave her a lot to think about, and, indeed, KiLe was thinking. She was comfortably ensconced on the U-shaped, sectional sofa again, this time awake and watching the flames in the fireplace devour the logs. When Brian turned off the music, there was a barely-there hum of the dishwasher Brian started as well as a load of laundry churning in the washer. It was so quiet and rather hypnotic watching wood become ash with only the pop and crackle of the fire adding sound.

Well, there was also the tap of computer keys, but she could block that noise out. She did it all the time when she was studying.

Brian was right, though. It was quiet in the timber-frame cabin in the woods. It was a really nice cabin, too, she thought, looking up at the vaulted, wood-beamed ceiling. Fans hung from each beam, slowly and soundlessly turning, obviously keeping the air circulating, and the heat moving down the walls to the heated, hardwood floors. She recalled they were heated when she sat on them behind the front door. Strategically placed attractive lights and skylights lit the space to perfection.

She looked up from her vantage point to the tall, long picture prominently displayed above the fireplace. It was a black-and-white photograph of the Alexander family reunion last year in Goodwill, Summer County, South Carolina. There were hundreds of family members in every skin color, from ebony to ivory sitting on raised bleachers smiling broadly at the camera. Still, she could see Brian sitting between Linda and Dena and holding their little sister, Eden Ann, on his lap. The entire family seemed happy to be there. She met many of Whitney's and Brian's family members. They were a fun, cordial, and exuberant bunch.

Around the cabin, she noted a gallery of other family portraits, pictures, and fine art. A round table in an alcove between two occasional chairs seemed a perfect reading nook. The bookcases behind the chairs were filled with current best sellers, like Bella Fayre and works by some lesser-known authors. The sofa pit sat in the middle of the great room facing the fireplace. Brian was there at his desk, spaced between the now-closed up and hidden kitchen space and behind the sofa, working on his laptop. He was mere inches from her and occasionally answered a phone call from someone on the ranch or a business call. He was so quiet, she nearly forgot he was there. Turning around, she stacked her hands on the back of the sofa and braced her chin on her hands while she watched him work.

He briefly looked up at her, his pretty eyes beguiling, while his fingers floated over the keyboard.

"What?" he asked but didn't stop typing.

"You said you're not in a committed relationship."

"That's right."

"Would you wait until your wedding night to have sex with your bride-to-be?"

"Uh, that's a definite no," he said and continued tapping away, his eyes on his screen.

"Why not?"

"I've been sexually active since I was in my early teens," he said without taking his eyes from the screen. "Cold showers don't work for me, and I'm not into self-gratification or recreational sex. If I'm planning to marry someone, premarital sex is on the agenda. If I'm *dating* someone, sex is on the agenda."

"Why?"

"Why what?"

"Why does sex have to be on the agenda?"

He stopped typing, braced his strong forearms on the desk, and leaning forward, finally looked into her pretty eyes, his brows drawing together. "I'm a guy. I like sex with a woman. I like the way women feel, how they look and taste. How they make me feel, especially when I'm deep inside them."

"You said women, plural."

He nodded, leaned back, and went back to typing. "I don't mean that I date more than one woman at a time because I don't. One-night stands aren't my thing. I don't relish the idea of sharing a woman I'm interested in with some other guy, and I won't share my body with another woman when I'm in a committed relationship. I prefer exclusive, intimate affairs. Still, no two women are alike, KiLe. Women are wondrous creatures. I don't subscribe to the theory that one size fits all. Variety is the spice of life."

"Are you ever going to settle down and marry?"

"'Settle down?' Probably, but that term connotes a certain amount of stagnation to me. When I marry, I want to have a life of adventure with the woman I plan to live the rest of my life with. I want us to do things that intrigue us together. I'm not thirty yet. I have time to explore before I start looking for someone to enjoy the rest of my life with."

"Who do you date?"

"Women."

"Ha Ha! You know what I mean, Brian. Do you date women you work with?"

"No, definitely not."

"Then who?"

"Why do you want to know?"

"Men have a type, don't they?"

"I can't speak for all men. For me, she has to be female, comfortable in her own skin, and confident in her skills and abilities. I prefer bright, energetic women who have a zest for life and living it to the fullest. Not someone I'm related to and not a coworker. I rule out women who would lie, steal, or cheat. Ax murderers are off the table, too, along with anyone who uses illegal substances, drinks to excess, smokes or has a criminal record." He stopped and thought about his last statement for a moment. "Well, I might reconsider someone with a criminal record if she went to jail to protest injustice. Otherwise, all's fair."

"It's as simple as that for you?"

"Uh, yeah. I don't need to make it complicated. If a woman can carry on an interesting conversation without saying 'you know' or 'like' or 'uh, huh' often, it's a start in the right direction. As I said, bright, intelligent, confident women are a real turn on for me."

"They don't have to look like a Barbie Doll, like Stephany Thomas?"

"Nope. Line ten women up behind a screen and let me carry on a conversation for say, fifteen minutes with each of them, and I can pick out the ones I'm interested in spending time with in the order of priority."

"Sight unseen?"

"Sight unseen. Women generally come with the same equipment, a brain being the most important part of their anatomy."

"Oh, you really need to take that act on the road, Brian. You're cracking me up. Why aren't you married?"

"I told you. I'm in my mid-twenties and I haven't met a woman I want to spend the rest of my life with yet. Now, leave me alone while I finish my work."

Hands still stacked, resting her chin on them, she continued to stare at him. He noticed.

"Okay, what now?" he sighed.

"Have you ever been in love?"

"No, but I've loved a woman for a very long time."

KiLe perked up at that and raised her head looking at him with eager interest on her face. "Who is she?"

"My mom. She is the best kind of woman I've ever met. She's beautiful inside and out, smart, warm, confident, fair-minded, courageous, and can carry on a conversation for hours, which keeps me involved, interested, and challenged. And no, I don't have an Oedipus complex."

"Still, she's your ideal woman?"

"She is, yes. Mom pushes all of the right buttons for me. Her only flaw is that she can't cook. She's tried, but she admits that she's a disaster in the kitchen. Even with that small impediment, if I were lucky enough to meet someone like Vivian Lynn Alexander Jackson Montgomery, someone I can respect, love, and trust with all of her positive attributes, I could stick a fork in it and be done. I'd put a ring on it and be running to the wedding chapel with her before she could think twice. Now, I have to finish this, so stop being a brat," he said and focused on his work.

KiLe pouted but left him alone.

Hours later, Brian checked his watch and sighed. He finally finished his paperwork, needed to finish his laundry, pack for his trip, and then get dressed for the party. Family members were always expected to be early for family events. He read over his notes on his laptop and saved his work before sending out reports and shutting down. His iPhone signaled an incoming message. When he checked, he smiled and noted it was from Whitney thanking him for alerting her about KiLe. Apparently, Payton contacted her and Tucker about what happened. He was seriously concerned about her safety because, although her car was still in the parking area, he couldn't find her and it was getting dark outside. Brian sent a message back that KiLe was still with him and safely asleep on his sofa. A few seconds later, he received a thumbs-up emoji.

Quietly, he stood and stretched. He had been working for over four hours, but his accounts balanced to the penny and payroll checks would be paid out on the first day of the month for the people who worked on the three Alex-Mont Ranch properties. Thank goodness he had to do payroll only twelve times a year, instead of bi-monthly. All of the invoices were paid. The quarterly reports were sent to his parents, his uncle, Gregory Alexander, who handled his parents' financial business, and his cousin, Donald Dixon, who handled their legal matters. He was working within the operating budget he established and, even though a number of the employees received bonuses and raises, he had a nice surplus of funds at the end of the second quarter of the ranches' operation this fiscal year. He had a couple of ideas about how to handle the excess funds, but that could wait until he spoke with his parents after they returned from their mini-vacation to their island. The expenditure of funds or the launch of new projects were a part of family group discussions. His parents always included him and his sibs on decisions about the expenditure of funds. They learned not only the cost of everything but also the value of what they had. No one took their great fortune for granted.

After another check of his watch, he decided he had enough time to complete his housework, his laundry, and pack for his trip to Pennsylvania before he dressed for the party. He put action to thought and began cleaning his bathroom and bedroom and changing sheets and towels. He emptied his laundry bag, separated the rest of his clothes, starting another load and stacked the third load in preparation. He pulled a soft duffle from his walk-around closet and put his toiletry bag inside before adding a few clothes and his laptop.

"Are you going away?" asked KiLe, leaning against his bedroom door jamb while watching him work.

He hadn't heard her get off the sofa, but now that she was awake, he could clean the rest of his home. "I am, yes. I'm leaving for Monroe County, Pennsylvania, early in the morning."

"Are you taking a woman with you?" she asked as she came to sit barefoot, tailor-style on the end of his nicely-dressed, king-sized bed to watch him pack.

"Well, there's a thought," he said and grinned, "but no. I've got work to do on the ranch up there and in the area."

"How long will you be away?"

He shrugged. "At least a week, maybe two or three. It all depends. We get snow late in the season in the Poconos, so that will be a consideration of how long I stay. I like cross-country and downhill skiing, so I might take a day or two to enjoy the trip."

"The Pocono Mountains?"

"Yes. That's where Monroe County is located."

"I've never been to the Poconos. I've never even been skiing."

He stopped, crossed his arms, and stared at her. "I suppose you want me to ask you to go with me?"

"Yes, Brian. Thanks for asking. I'm on spring break and I have nothing to do next week. I'll be happy to keep you company. Since I no longer have a guy friend, I don't want to just mope around the house by myself. Everyone in the Georgetown house has made plans to go away. If you let me go with you, I promise not to get in your way."

"You'd be bored." He couldn't believe he was even considering letting her go with him.

"I won't. I promise. Please, Brian, would you let me go with you?"

He thought about it and decided to strike a bargain. "Okay, you may go to Pennsylvania with me only on the condition that you go up to the house right now and talk with Payton about your issues. Maybe you two can work it out and you'll want to spend the week with him after all. I don't want or need the drama if he finds out you were with me all afternoon and gets the wrong idea about what was going on in here while he was frantically looking for you. Considering I wasn't dressed when he came to my door, he might draw the wrong conclusion."

She chewed her bottom lip while thoughtfully looking up at him.

He knew he was in trouble when his eyes involuntarily dropped to her mouth again and stayed there for long, ponderous moments before slowly looking up into her eyes again. If he let her go with him, he could avoid her, he promised himself. He was sure of it. His family's home in Pennsylvania was even larger than the one here. He could share meals with her a few hours a day and continue to focus on his tasks. Resolved, he figured, what could go wrong?

"Okay," she said. "I'll agree to talk with Payton on the condition that you'll be my date tonight at your father's birthday party."

Okay, he didn't see *that* coming. This wasn't going to be as easy as he thought. He laid out what he expected of women he dated and she comes up with this idea? There she sat on his bed, grinning up at him, biting on that enticing lower lip tucked between her teeth. He found himself nodding in agreement instead of shaking his head no and wondered whether he had lost complete control of his senses.

KiLe hopped up, did a rump-shake dance, and put on her coat before sprinting out of the cabin. He rolled his eyes and shook his head at her glee. He hoped he hadn't just made a monumental mistake.

Later, when Brian walked into the ballroom, there was a circus show amount of activity underway. The decorations were receiving the final inspection. Food stations were being situated. The tables were beautifully dressed in his father's favorite colors. He didn't see KiLe or Payton, but the band's equipment was arranged on the elevated stage and members of Changelings were tuning their instruments.

Oh, yeah, his family loved a good party, he ruminated, smiling while doing a visual inspection of his own. He noted the Secret Service was there working with the Richardson Security Team and Claudia and her dogs, so he didn't disturb them.

The loud squeals and giggles emanated from his sister, Teresa Angelique, a toddler evading capture from their brother, Craig. It was his primary responsibility to keep an eye on the small escape artist. The little imp barreled directly toward him like a kamikaze pilot, grabbed him around his legs, and then put her arms up to be lifted. He bent and swung her up, tossing her into the air causing more squeals and giggles. *Was he destined to play knight in shining armor to all the young ladies in distress today?* he wondered.

Teresa Angelique palmed his face with her small hands, demanded *"Kiss,"* and puckered-up her pink, rosebud lips. He acceded to her demands and kissed her lips before burying his face in her little neck, causing her to laugh like a loon and squirm. She smelled of all things youthful and pure. Of sunlight and baby powder. She was not his sister by blood, but by love. He loved her and all of his siblings as if they were born to the same two people. Each time a new child was added to the family, they held an adoption ceremony, each pledging to take care of each other and the new addition. The oldest always became the god-sibling of the youngest. He never ceased to be grateful for the gift of this family.

He continued to steal kisses from Teresa Angelique as she wiggled and giggled in his arms.

"Hey, Cuz," hailed Whitney on her approach. She and he shared a kiss and then she stole kisses from Teresa Angelique, too, who clamored to get down on the floor.

When Brian put her on her feet, she ran full out into the next person she could use for her entertainment. This time it was Claudia's dogs receiving Teresa Angelique's amorous attention. Then it was the stern-faced Secret Service agent, who couldn't conceal his smile at her demand to be lifted for a kiss. Still, Craig had his eyes on her, Brian noticed, so he didn't intervene.

He turned his attention back to his cousin. "How's it going, Whitney?"

"All's good. I thank you for helping KiLe. She ended the relationship with Payton though she's still pissed with Stephany. KiLe didn't confront her. I don't know what you said to her, but she's upbeat about going to Pennsylvania with you for the week. She went home, packed a bag, and wants to stay here tonight so that she won't hold you up in the morning. I told her it was okay and assigned her to one of the bedrooms on the third floor. I posted it on your calendar and alerted security. Tucker and I just finished talking with her before we left her to get dressed. We thought we were going to have to change our plans and stick around town for her benefit or take her with us, so we thank you for saving our plans."

"You're welcome. What are you and Tucker going to do?"

"He's taking me to his home in Poland Springs, Maine, to visit with his parents and grandparents so we can spend time working on our wedding plans with them. He was born and raised there. It's the first time we've had an opportunity to go for any appreciable amount of time. Also, his high school is holding a three-day, class reunion next weekend. It will allow him to reconnect with some of his friends who he will want to invite to our wedding. We'll stay until after Sunday dinner and come back Sunday night. When will you be back from Pennsylvania?"

"I'm not sure. It will likely be two weeks at a minimum. I presume you're flying one of the jets up."

"I am, yes. Why?"

"If I can't get back here next weekend, would you fly into Pennsylvania and pick up KiLe on your way back here?"

"Sure. That's doable. We'll keep in touch during the week."

"Great," he said and shared another kiss and hug before they parted. It was a pure stroke of luck to get his cousin to pick up KiLe. Otherwise, he would have had to bring KiLe back and then turn around and return to Pennsylvania all in the same day. Whitney, an experienced pilot who is qualified and certified to fly almost any type of aircraft, including the big jumbo jets, just saved time for him. Considering her father is U.S. Air Force General Benjamin Alexander, a jet fighter pilot and astronaut who flies the space shuttle, Whitney comes by her skills in the cockpit of any aircraft naturally. She had been flying since she was eight years old. Now she is twenty-one and would soon be married this summer to Tucker during the family's Juneteenth holiday reunion in Summer County, South Carolina.

In fact, at that very moment, Whitney's father, his Uncle Benny, is on SPACEHOME, an artificial planet under construction in outer space by over a hundred workers headed up by Dr. Tate Kennedy, the world-renowned astrophysicist. Uncle Benny, Dr. Kennedy, and a crew of workmen launched seven months ago and would not be back for another month. Brian thought about how enormously proud of his family he is.

Family members and security were everywhere he roamed in the mansion. He kept abreast of what was going on through the earbud hooked around his left ear and a hair-thin face mic. He was stopped several times to talk with security and others while on his way to the kitchen to converse with the cooks. They wanted to bring on two more people as sous chefs and asked him to consider it. With the completion of the second-quarter report, he was ready to give the go-ahead for the new hires. Still, he needed to know who they had in mind. Everyone at the ranch not only went through several levels of interviews but also an extensive vetting process and background checks, including DNA, fingerprints, and retinal scans.

His mother's role as a U.S. Supreme Court Justice, although loved and respected by most, still garnered detractors who would attempt to do her harm. She is also one of the wealthiest women in the world, which made her a prime target for kidnapping. He was responsible for her safety at home while Richardson Investigations and Security was primarily responsible for all other times. There was currently no threat of which he was aware. However, he never let his guard down where his family's safety is concerned.

Controlled chaos reigned in the industrial-sized and equipped kitchen when he entered, but that wasn't unusual. The three cooks planned and served meals at least three times a day for every day of the week when the family members were in residence and the preschool was in session. They also managed to make health-conscious snacks available. He left it up to the cooks to determine their schedules, days off, and vacation times. As long as all of the shifts and tasks were covered, he didn't stick his nose in. All of the cooks lived on the property and were long-term employees of the Alex-Mont Ranch.

However, he didn't expect to see Anna Menendez-Gaza Jones working side-by-side with the cooks. She was the majordomo of his Uncle Benny's house in the Georgetown section of Washington, DC, where Whitney and KiLe lived. Anna's daughter, Angelique, the supermodel and movie actress-turned-Le Cordon Bleu certified chef, was there, too, with three of her students and two other chefs. Angelique, whom they called Aunt Angel, is the wife of his uncle Gregory Alexander. Nor did Brian expect to see the brothers, Isaac and Wesley Greenfield, the owners of Greenfield Brothers' catering, bakeries, and coffee and tea shops, putting the finishing touches on a tall, beautiful, multi-layered birthday cake. On another table, Wesley's three oldest adopted children, Cole, Marcus, and Simone, were tying pretty ribbons around a multitude of small, attractive gift boxes of cake. Considering the number of boxes which were already carefully stacked on a cloth-covered cart, they seemed to have been at it a while. The table would be rolled out and positioned by the front entrance of the ballroom as parting gifts for the guests at the end of the evening.

Four men carried in two huge ice sculptures from the walk-around freezer. One was the date of Chuck's birth and the other was a bucking bronco with a rodeo rider waving a Stetson in the air. They set the frozen art into very long, oblong pans and began to decorate the displays with greenery to mask the drain where the water would be collected and flow out into catch basins.

Anna, the Greenfields, and their spouses, close family friends, are on the guest list for tonight's event, Brian affirmed checking his sister, Linda's list. The guest list is Linda's part of the birthday party project to work out with the Secret Service and Richardson Investigations and Security. In Angelique's case, she and Chuck were in-laws. He had helped raise her since she was eight. He escorted her down the aisle when she married. Now because she was married to Vivian's brother, Gregory, it made her even more closely aligned with the family, as is her brother, Miguel, the superstar actor and fashion model. Miguel recently launched a singing career and performed with Changelings when time permitted. Home from UPenn on spring break, Miguel would be performing tonight with the group.

Brian came up behind Anna, Angelique and Miguel's mother, and hugged her while snitching a shrimp canape from the tray she was working on. She returned the hug and delivered a kiss to his cheek while swatting him firmly on his bottom, something she had cause to do many times dating back to when he was eight. Anna helped raise him and his sibs as if they all were hers. In the early days, as a young widow with two children, Anna lived in the house in Georgetown and did the cooking and cleaning for Vivian and her children before and after Derrick's death. They were as much family as the rest of those Vivian and Derrick and then Vivian and Chuck adopted.

Anna, still the majordomo of the Georgetown house, married their next-door neighbor, world-renowned concert violinist Fenster Jones. Anna boasted about raising another crop of young ones now; her own grandchildren, Angelique and Gregory Alexander's rambunctious preschool boy and baby girl.

"When are you going to toss Fenster over and run away with me to Borneo, Anna?" Brian asked, still hugging her diminutive stature.

"I'm too much woman for you, *Chico*," she joked. "You need, what they call it, uh, a starter wife?"

He laughed at the quip, her Peruvian accent pronounced. "As long as you fed me good food, I'd be a good husband to you," he teased.

"Ha!" she retorted, pursing her lips. "Go away with your fresh self," she joshed back, sending him on his way with a kiss on his cheek and a flick of her hand.

"You don't know what you're missing," he said, nipping another canape and quickly scurried away to avoid another swat to his bottom. *"Melvin?"* he called out above the din to the head cook.

"Yo!" hailed back the middle-aged, former active duty Marine, mess-hall cook.

"Talk to me. Give me names. I'm on board with the extra kitchen help."

"Good. Joshua and Teddy. I want to start them out tonight. I need the extra hands."

That surprised him. Joshua and Tedra, who they called Teddy, were a pair of sixteen-year-olds who lived on the ranch and were the children of existing, long-term ranch hands. They sometimes worked with the housekeeping crew. He had no idea they were interested in learning to cook. "Have them fill out the paperwork and put them on the payroll as of today, agreed?"

"Already as good as done. Thanks, Brian. They'll do good work for us."

"Of that, I have no doubt. They're good kids. Keep me posted on their progress. Aunt Angel expanded the cooking school in Atlantic Beach, South Carolina. If the kids are interested and work out for you, I'll give them a recommendation when they graduate high school."

"Solid," Melvin called back without breaking stride on the food preparation. They were expecting upwards of three hundred guests for cocktails, the dinner, and dance. The food would be served buffet style, with food stations at strategic locations around the ballroom and in adjacent salons with ample seating. His family could do formal, sit-down, seven-course meals with ease, but they were more the informal type; not at all rigid people. Also, though the attire would be semi-formal, the ambiance would not. His dad, still a country boy at heart, would be subjected to an old-fashioned hoe-down; a real hootenanny, cowboy style.

Now that he dispensed with that task, Brian moved on to follow up on other details. Ranch hands, both male and female, volunteered to park cars as guests arrived at the south-side *porte-cochere* entrance hall outside the ballroom. Other volunteers would perform as waitstaff carrying trays of hot or cold *hors d'oeuvres* and sparkling cider or champagne for the guests. Four open bars were on both sides of the ballroom with two bartenders, each who would serve beer, wine, and other spirits. There were also champagne fountains at various places around the ballroom.

He moved across the ballroom as the massive crystal chandeliers' lights high above were adjusted and candles on the festive-colored tablecloths covering round tables of twelve were lit. The stage was deserted, but the canned music began to play from strategically-placed speakers adding to the ambiance. Four large video monitors were lit, each displaying scenes of his dad's life from birth and subsequent events, including his years as a basketball star and featuring Chuck and Vivian as a couple with all of the children. That was the work of his brothers, the twins, Ryan and Roger. They were the technology gurus of the family and had visions of building careers in the film and video arts industries.

At the double-door entrance to the great hall, his siblings, led by his sister, Linda Montgomery-Hamilton, the world-renowned prima ballerina, with her husband, and baseball icon, Will Hamilton, were forming the receiving lines to greet guests and see to their comfort. He greeted his sibs and Linda's husband, just as the first of a line of cars drove two abreast up the long driveway from the county road and pulled under the *porte-cochere* to discharge their passengers. Then the cars were quickly and efficiently driven away to a secure parking lot where Claudia's canines were on duty.

Chauffeurs were accommodated in the pool house with food, soft drinks, and entertainment, too. There was security of the human variety at the front gate and other strategic places on the ranch. Upon arrival, pictures were taken of guests and, in the security office, facial recognition equipment was put into action. The guests would receive a copy of the photo as a memento of the event and be none the wiser that the photos were a security measure.

CHAPTER 4

KiLe slipped into her dress for the evening while purposefully ignoring Stephany Thomas, who shared the dressing room with her and Marsha Allen, another songstress. Generally, there were only two of four female vocalists who regularly sang with Changeling at any given time or event. Tonight, all four females would perform. All of the six male regular band members sang and played instruments. Apparently, Miguel Menendez-Gaza and Whitney would join the group, too.

Changelings' performance this evening would be the highlight of their multi-year collaboration because it would be in front of such a distinguished group of guests. Not only were doctors from Chuck's private hospital and Georgetown Medical expected to be in the audience, but also members of the House of Representatives, the U.S. Senate, the U.S. Supreme Court, and even the President, First Lady and all four of their adult sons. Still, for her, KiLe thought the highlight of her evening would be the chance to spend more time with Brian Montgomery.

She had just learned that the bandleader, Mike Giaconni, and his wife, Trisha, both of whom sang, were running late. They had a toddler at home who they were going to have to bring with them because their babysitter had bailed at the last moment. Extra babies were never a problem in the Alexander-Montgomery household. Apparently, Brian had seen to it that a bed was available for the baby and he would be taken care of by a licensed sitter.

Mike would have to work out on the fly who would solo or take the lead on what songs. *That shouldn't be a problem as long as I don't have to sing duets with Stephany*, thought KiLe. The band was called Changelings because they all had interchangeable skills, both with voice and musical instruments. She knew Whitney and Tucker were joining the band tonight because Chuck is Whitney's uncle. Whitney didn't sing but played guitar, while Tucker could play almost any instrument put in his hands. He had a good, strong voice, too, and would likely play drums if Mike played guitar with Whitney. Miguel would probably play guitar, though with his dark, Latino good looks and sexy voice, all he had to do was make an appearance and the women would go wild. However, until Mike and Trisha could get there, Tucker, another man with movie-idol good looks, would have to take over as bandleader. KiLe would not have to remind Tucker not to pair her for a duet with Payton or Stephany. She may have reluctantly forgiven Payton, but not Stephany.

Still, no matter the enmity between them, she would never do anything to screw up Changelings' chances for success. They were a good group and were offered a contract to record for the musical magician Trey Kennard. He had a studio in London, England, and one in New York City. She didn't mind doing studio work as long as it fit in with her free time and school schedule, but she wouldn't be able to travel with the band when they went on a world tour during the coming summer school break. Most of the band members were like her, still in college, grad school or like Tucker doing his medical training. She was resigned to either work through the summer or take on more classes. Her parents would never agree to let her sing rather than continue her collegiate career. Her father, a bioengineer and owner of a biofuel company, was traditional Japanese. Her mother was a tenured professor at the Tokyo International University of America and a high-society maven before her marriage to the upstart businessman. Both parents held post-doctorates and expected her to do the same. Singing was permitted as a hobby, just as gymnastics and playing the flute were, but her parents would never permit it as a career option, KiLe knew.

At a young age, she was exposed to a vast array of activities and excelled at gymnastics, placing during the Olympic trials, but shortly thereafter her parents steered her to academic pursuits. Even though she was almost twenty-two years old, they controlled every aspect of her life. They released the reigns slightly only when they permitted her to come to America to continue her education at the prestigious Georgetown University. They did so only because of the school's sterling reputation in international affairs, and because Benjamin and Stacy were permitting Whitney to come to America.

Benjamin and Stacy Greene Alexander, Whitney's parents, owned a brownstone in the Georgetown area adjacent to the famed Rock Creek Park. They agreed to let KiLe live in the large, multi-level house with Whitney and other advanced scholar students. KiLe's parents worked closely with the Alexanders on various councils and boards in Japan and held Whitney and her family in the highest esteem. Whitney's father, a U.S. Air Force astronaut and her mother, a Navy Admiral, garnered high social status and respect in Japan. Both were also military attachés with the American Embassy in Tokyo, liaisons with the Japanese government, and they were involved in other countries as members of the Pacific Rim at the highest echelons of each country.

Whitney became one of KiLe's mother's star pupils when she was in college at the university. As a result, they socialized in Japan and entertained them in their homes.

KiLe sincerely liked, respected, and trusted Whitney and her family, but she wished her parents trusted her to make more of her own decisions the way Whitney's parents did. KiLe was expected to toe the line without exercising any independent thought or judgment. Conversely, Whitney's parents encouraged her to push the boundaries and to think outside the box.

Of course, KiLe's parents had reputations to uphold. *"Losing face"* in Japanese society meant a death blow to one's sense of dignity or prestige in the social contexts. Her family would go to any length to *"save face"* and preserve their established positions in society. Taking action to ensure that one is not thought badly of by his or her peers was drummed into her from infancy. KiLe adhered to her parents' direction. However, of late, she noticed how Whitney achieved her family's love, trust, and respect without having to be submissive to their edicts. It was such a life-affirming experience that KiLe felt emboldened by it.

She witnessed the same interaction not only between Whitney and her parents but also between Brian's rainbow-coalition family members and their parents. With an adoptive father, Chuck, who is white, and a mother, Vivian, who is black, Brian and his siblings spanned the distance between the two extreme ethnicities. Nevertheless, KiLe noticed that there seemed to be a mutual love, respect, and trust binding the family members together.

She didn't feel the same about her own family's dynamic. Both of her parents were Japanese, so they didn't have the racial or cultural barriers to contend with or overcome in Japan. However, her mother's high-society family was extremely wealthy while her father's family initially was not. The Hakamoras achieved Japanese A-list status together long before they divorced. Still, her mother apparently carried on a long-term adulterous affair with the dean of one of the university's departments and her father married his female executive assistant. Her half-siblings were born before the ink was dry on the divorce decree and the subsequent marriage licenses. KiLe felt there was no trust, love or respect to be had in her family.

"KiLe?" Stephany said, suddenly standing beside her.

"What?" asked KiLe, the surliness evident in her voice.

"Look, kid, I really don't want to cause any issues between the band members. They've known and liked you a lot longer than me. However, unlike you, I really need this gig. I barely made it out of high school and never went to college. I'm pushing thirty hard and I don't have a family with a pot full of duckets like you do. I'm a waitress from the Ozarks with a set of pipes and a body that gets men's attention as my only assets. It was either stay home and marry my third cousin twice removed or strike out for the big city. I didn't have enough money to make it to New York City. So, I've stayed here in the Washington, DC, metropolitan area waiting for a big break. I've had a few gigs on stage in the theatres here, but this is the first real chance I've had to make it big."

"All I've heard is I, I, I, Stephany. What's your point?"

"It's about Payton, because he was the easiest one to use as my way into the band. I really wanted Tucker, but he doesn't know other women exist other than your pal Whitney. Payton, as I said, was easy for a predatory person like me. When you caught us together today, he was really scared you'd do something to hurt yourself when you ran away. Visions of Hari Kari and some shit like that were in his head. I apologize for the way you found out about us. I think you have talent, and I wouldn't want you to hurt yourself."

"I'm Japanese, but I'm not a defeated samurai warrior!" she snapped. Still, she understood Stephany's point. Hari Kari is an ancient form of ritual suicide that those whose shame was too unbearable would use to restore their honor in death. Maybe her parents might subscribe to that way to save face, but she never would.

"All I'm saying is don't trust a guy, like Payton, with anything breakable like your heart."

Lessons learned, thought KiLe, as she watched Stephany walk out of the dressing room. She and Payton already had *"The Talk,"* and he admitted he "liked" Stephany. He also said he couldn't spend any more time waiting for KiLe to trust him enough to have sex with him. So, since she wouldn't "put out," and sleep with him, he was moving on. He apologized, under penalty of death from Tucker Cavanaugh and Whitney Alexander, for the way she found out he and Stephany were sleeping with each other behind her back. Of course, he offered the classic, *"it wasn't her; it was him."* All in all, it was a very dignified, civilized experience which left her glad she hadn't "put out" the way he wanted. At least she didn't have that shameful burden to bear.

Then she realized her parents would never have approved of Payton Brasher in any event. He's an Australian who, although he's educated and holds a master's degree, wears his hair long in dreadlocks and plays and sings reggae music like a native Rastafarian. So, she dodged a bullet there, but still, he is a great kisser. Although the truth is that Payton never inspired her to go beyond kissing. However, what did she know? She kissed only one man in her life. Now she began to wonder how it would feel to kiss Brian Montgomery.

His mother looked smoking hot in her fire-engine red, shimmering, sleeveless tube sheath which hugged her curves like seal skin, Brian thought. She got shouts and whistles for her deft and dexterous dance moves from the men and women in the crowded ballroom. None was more appreciative than those offered by her husband, Chuck, who, for a man who stood nearly seven feet tall and was celebrating another birthday milestone, showed off some pretty skillful and nimble dance moves of his own.

Of course, Brian's brothers, Ryan and Roger, had to get in the mix and dance with their mother first while the others, Vincent, Andrew, Derrick

Junior, Darren, and Spencer, lined up to dance with her in succession. The same was true for their father. Linda claimed the first dance since she was the oldest daughter, followed by Geneviève, Dena, and Samantha.

Brian had to laugh when his mother spotted him and danced her way over to grab his hand. "All right, handsome son of mine, show me what you're working with," she teased, so he did until his grandmothers, Sylvia Benson Alexander and Harriet Jackson Montgomery, joined in. He was surrounded by the most important women in his life and he loved every moment of it.

His problem was that his mother and grandmothers could *dance!* Age was nothing but a number to them. So, he called in reinforcements—his brothers Craig, Preston, Reed, Micah, Ronnie, Stanley, Alexander, Nelson, Connell, Scott, and Patrick, Jr., though he is still a babe in arms.

They were rocking it old school with the long, Soul Train lanes with people lined on both sides and the middle opened to strut their stuff. Cameras were rolling front and back and showing on the video monitors high up on the walls. Mike Giaconni was emceeing the dance marathon while his band played and sang a variety of music. *It took a while to get such a large group of people down the lines, but there was a great deal of rump-shaking going on,* thought Brian. That was especially true of retired Admiral and President of the United States Clarence Gordon and his wife of forty-plus years, an active-duty General, and Army Ranger. They obviously danced together for many years because as they came through the Soul Train line, they didn't miss a step.

At one time, Brian's aunt, Whitney's mother, Stacy Greene, was then Admiral Gordon's executive officer fresh out of the naval academy in Annapolis, Maryland. She continued to work for him as she climbed the ranks of the Navy until now. As the top naval diplomat to countries along the Pacific Rim and a U.S. Navy Admiral, Stacy was also on the President's Joint Chiefs of Staff. Her husband, five-star Air Force General, jet fighter pilot, and astronaut Benjamin "Benny" Alexander, was also the top Air Force diplomat to the Pacific Rim countries and on the President's Joint Chiefs of Staff. Benjamin, who he, his sibs and cousins called "Benny and the jets," was one of Vivian's three brothers and Whitney's father. Benny was the one to teach her and other family members to fly. One of the President and First Lady's sons is under Benny's command in Hawaii.

Brian felt as close to his Uncle Benny and Aunt Stacy as he did to his parents. Benny and Stacy introduced the President to the Alexander family. Not coincidently, when a spot opened up on the U.S. Supreme Court, Vivian Alexander Jackson Montgomery's name was submitted by President Gordon to the U.S. Senate for confirmation. The only opposition came from elements who claimed that she would have to spend less time in the bedroom should she be confirmed. The acrimony during the #Me-Too era was so intense that those senators were impeached or defeated during election cycles. Others argued that because she is one of the wealthiest women in the world and had an international law practice as a fledgling attorney, she would have an inordinate amount of conflicts of interest.

Vivian, while a law school student at Georgetown, was in an advanced scholars group mentored by former Senator from California, Gustafson Fehey. Now the Dean of the law school, Fehey was lifelong friends with President Gordon and continued to mentor Vivian and her pals. Vivian, upon graduation from law school and ranked in the upper one percent of her class, worked on the Senate's Ethics Committee; a committee then-Senator Fehey used to chair.

She and her other law school pals, in the advanced scholars program, formed Alexander, Carter, Chandler, Charles, Lightfoot and Towson, PA, one of the most prestigious young legal practices in the country winning upwards of ninety percent of their trials and negotiations, many of which were argued before the U.S. Supreme Court and The International Court of Justice, otherwise known as the World Court in the Hague. Vivian was selected in her fifth year of private practice to be on the U.S. Court of Appeals, one of thirteen such appellate courts in the country. She wrote textbooks, articles for law journals, and lectured at Georgetown and other prestigious law schools domestically and abroad. That his mom was confirmed as the youngest Justice of the high court, with her connections, credentials, and background, was a foregone conclusion. Brian and his sibs were enormously proud of their parents.

Standing away from the spotlight gave Brian a chance to observe KiLe on the raised platform wearing a short, black, glittery, postage-stamp-sized dress. It was similar to the dresses worn by the other female vocalists, including his cousin, Whitney. The men wore black-and-white combination costumes, reminiscent of the Gatsby era. Either white jackets and black, loose-fitting slacks or the reverse; black jackets and white slacks, were striking. Sparkling red suspenders held up their slacks, but they were shirtless with a black or white bow tie around their necks. The women mimicked the white bow ties to complete the black costumes they wore.

KiLe looks too sexy by half, thought Brian, even though she was small in stature. She could also belt out songs to raise the roof. He actually hadn't heard her sing before and found her extremely talented. Coupled with her energetic dance moves with bare legs and six-inch heels while singing the Chaka Kahn classic, "Tell Me Something Good," she had his blood draining from his head straight to his groin. Her attractively muscled body still showed remnants of her days as a gymnast. *Maybe it isn't such a good idea to let her come to Pennsylvania with me*, he thought, but he had always been a man of his word. So, he would stop thinking of her as his favorite flavor of ice cream and wanting to lick her from the bottom up.

"What's on your mind, brother mine?" asked his sister, Dena.

"You really don't want to know the answer to *that* question," Brian said wryly.

"Since you've been standing here in the shadows scoping out KiLe Hakamora like she's on your dessert menu, it wouldn't be hard to guess." She laughed at his stunned expression.

"You really scare me sometimes," and shook his head at her accuracy.

"Well, at least I like KiLe. The last woman you dated, Eleanora, was a real space cadet. I'm truly glad you dumped her."

He was, too. He enjoyed women with brains, like Eleanora, a scientist, but she lived in the cosmic universe outside of time and space. When she started talking about their extra-terrestrial connection, he was ready to find the Millennium Falcon and jump into hyperspace to get away from her. The sex was good, but visions of the bar scene from **Star Wars** invaded his dreams for weeks after he ended their intergalactic connection. His sister wasn't going to let him live that one down. Yet, he didn't mind his siblings' intrusions in his life, because fair exchange was no robbery. "So, where is your flavor of the moment?"

"If you mean Drew Hamilton, he's not my 'flavor of the moment.' He's my flavor of the year who is in the game room with Craig, Vincent, and Geneviève shooting pool."

Brian laughed, but it seemed his sister's relationship with Drew was heating up. He would have to pay closer attention. "At least I like him better than the Russian."

"He was German and that was over a year ago. Ya gotta keep up, brother mine."

"Hasn't Drew learned yet not to shoot pool with our siblings? He hasn't been able to beat any of them in the two years since you started bringing him home with you."

"Hope springs," Dena laughed. "Come on out of the shadows and dance with me."

He shrugged and took her to the dance floor. "You know you can't out dance me," he confidently said.

"Hey, Drew isn't the only one with a life quest. Someday you will get old, Brian, and I'll still be younger than you." She laughed, executing a clever move which he easily matched.

KiLe watched Brian as he danced with his sister Dena. They were laughing, obviously trying to out-dance each other and having a lot of fun. Then, their sister, Stephany, joined the dance-off. Watching them enjoy each other made her smile. **Whoa!** She didn't know Brian could move like that. When he sexily swiveled his hips, her jaw literally dropped open. She had known him since she came to America and Whitney introduced her to her family. That had been nearly four years ago now. This was not the first time she met or interacted with Brian in a social setting, but she was so into Payton at the time, she didn't pay a lot of attention to other men. Now, she was more than a little interested in learning things about Brian Montgomery.

To her way of thinking, he seemed open, easy-going, and honest. She liked those traits about him, and the fact that he looked like he just stepped off the cover of a high-fashion, men's magazine, was no hardship either. He wore his designer ensemble with a careless sophistication most men couldn't achieve on a bet. Yet, she'd seen him in working ranch clothes that showed off his raw masculinity to perfection. Actually, she had noticed his jeans had stress patches in interesting places.

He was pleasing to the eye regardless of what he wore and even more so when she got lucky and caught him in the buff. He had healthy, hard-looking, toned muscles which didn't come from working out in a gym. The back of him looked as good as the front. His hands were a working man's strong hands with callouses on his palms, yet his nails were clean and well-manicured. He obviously took good care of his body but didn't seem to be overly aware of the impact his good looks had on women.

The band was coming up on a twenty-minute break. After a potty run, she planned to make her way over to Brian and chat him up. Right now, however, the band torqued it up while Mike introduced the members of Changelings.

"Ladies and gentlemen, KiLe! Her name may be short, but not her sound! Let's hear it!"

She took the microphone from Mike, closed her eyes, and belted out an impossibly high and strong note on her vocal register. The crowd went wild with shouts, whistles, and clapping while she sang one stanza of the song and did her signature female versions and interpretations of Luther Vandross' vocal vibrations. Then she bowed and handed the mic back to Mike.

"Oh, yes, ladies and gentlemen, she's got more for you after the break. Next, we have Chet Powell . . ." he said continuing with the band members' introductions until he ended with his wife, Trisha, and himself. Mike brought the band to a crescendo and then all stopped. Silence reigned until the crowd again erupted in adoration. Their recently cut club-music CD was cued up. The spotlights lowered to darkness and they began to leave the stage amid continuous applause.

KiLe hurried to the restroom, hoping it wasn't too crowded. Fortunately, the one in the dressing area was empty. She quickly took care of her needs, washed and dried her hands, and headed back to the ballroom. She grabbed a bottle of water on her way. While guzzling it down, she was brought up short when she spotted Stephany Thomas gazing adoringly up at Brian Montgomery.

CHAPTER 5

Okay, this is getting a bit beyond a friendly conversation, thought Brian, as Stephany of the bottle-blond hair, blue eyes, and the stacked figure continued to interrogate him. Apparently, someone had given her the four-one-one on him and she was merely confirming that he is, indeed, the eligible, multi-millionaire featured with others in this month's issue of *Stallion* magazine.

A family friend and his mother's law firm partner, Bill Chandler, is also the owner and publisher of the magazine. Brian lost a poker game to the man he and his sibs call "Uncle Bill" and, as his wager was appearing in the magazine or Bill having to spend a week mucking out the horse barn, he was paying dearly for that loss. Since he merely modeled three outfits in Bill's line of high-fashion *haute couture* men's clothes, the magazine used only his first name. Of course, his horse, Lucky, and his Labs were also in each photo and made better models, Brian believed, than he did. He wasn't sure how women found him in a magazine geared mainly for men, but several had. He knew some of his pals from college had seen the article and were ragging him about being "the playboy cowboy." He expected no less from the college rat pack, a group of guys with whom he played collegiate varsity NCAA lacrosse for four years at UPenn. He hoped to return the favor and have Bill talk his pals into posing for upcoming issues of *Stallion* magazine. However, for the moment, he had to extricate himself from Stephany's clutches . . . and, as if someone said abracadabra, there was KiLe, his date for the evening. He was grateful he agreed to KiLe's terms after all.

"Uh, please pardon me, Stephany. I see my date and I want to spend some time with her." He didn't wait for a response, but skirted Stephany and headed straight for KiLe who had a wary expression on her face. "Hi, babe," he said, taking her into his arms, kissing her quickly, and then guiding her into a dance on a slow number.

KiLe immediately got the gist of the situation when Stephany stared daggers at them, crossed her arms, and pouted. It made KiLe's day, so she looped her arms up around Brian's neck, her six-inch high heels bringing her five-three height up closer so that when she went to her toes, her head was just under his chin. She grinned up at him. "I think you should kiss me again. This time because Payton is watching."

"Cut it out, Imp." He grinned at her, but having her in his arms like this was increasing his heart rate. She was a good dancer and easily followed his lead; her body enticingly molded against his.

"Well, Stephany is beautiful. You could do worse. In fact, I'll help you out and tell her you're on the market and looking for someone exactly like her to warm your bed," KiLe cheekily grinned.

"I'll turn you over my knee and warm your bottom if you do," he threatened and snorted, but he didn't miss the mischievous glint in her eyes.

"Okay, if you don't kiss me . . . and I mean a ***real*** grown-up kiss, ***Stephony***," she said purposefully mispronouncing her name, "will mysteriously have access to your private cell phone number."

"Why you little minx!" he said, feigning censure. "I thought we were pals, but you would sic her on me, your one true friend?"

"Stop stalling, Brian, and kiss me," she teased. So, he did, and her toes involuntarily curled in her high-heeled shoes.

Brian wasn't sure whether the earth tilted off its axes, but something was definitely out of whack when he kissed KiLe Hakamora. She was so sweet, he deepened the kiss chasing the rush of something electric, like a jolt of lightning through his bloodstream.

KiLe wasn't ready when Brian pulled his mouth away from hers, but even she knew shock and awe were in her eyes. They stood still, arms looped around each other and regarding each other for ponderous moments.

"Well," they both said in unison and couldn't find the words to describe what that kiss did to them. It was definitely unprecedented for both.

A hand took hold of hers and dragged KiLe toward the stage platform as if she were an errant child. Still, she turned her head and watched Brian as she was spirited away. He was looking at her with surprise evident on his face, too.

Whitney turned her back to the audience as the band began to reassemble and blocked KiLe's view of Brian. "Here's thing one, KiLe. Brian is my cousin and I love him like he's my womb mate. So, thing two is if you're only playing with Brian's emotions in retribution for how Payton treated you, he's no boy toy. So, you'll have me to deal with."

KiLe looked up at her friend Whitney. "Payton who?" she said sincerely. "Believe me when I tell you, Whitney, when Brian kissed me, before you snatched me away from him," she reverently touched her lips, "I literally saw stars."

It took a moment, but Whitney finally laughed when she recognized the shocked expression on KiLe's face and shook her head. "I know the feeling well. It's exactly how I felt the first time Tucker kissed me and I've had variations of the same sensations ever since."

"Whitney, I like him…Brian, I mean . . . a lot. It may have started out as a joke, but I promise this is not a reaction to my break-up with Payton."

"I believe you, KiLe, but take it slowly until you get your feet planted solidly on the ground again. I meant what I said. Brian is one of the good guys and I wouldn't want to see either of you hurt.

As KiLe looked at Brian in the audience, she wondered whether she would ever feel like her feet were planted on Terra firma again. Right now, after his brain-numbing kiss, she felt as if she were walking on clouds.

By two o'clock in the morning, the last cars full of guests were pulling away from the ballroom entrance hall. The President's helicopter, Marine One, the large Sikorsky VH-3D Sea King, lifted off only minutes earlier with the presidential entourage on board and could still be seen in the clear, cool night sky heading toward the city. A contingent of the Secret Service was packing up their gear in preparation for departure after a debriefing with Richardson's agents. Brian's volunteer helpers were breaking down the breakfast buffet which was served at midnight, the decorations were dismantled, and the tablecloths were bundled into large, rolling laundry baskets with the cloth napkins. The band was packing up their equipment and taking it through the side ballroom entrance to their van. Brian helped as the tables and chairs were stacked on rolling carts to be placed in storage until the next occasion. In less than twenty minutes, the ballroom's Brazilian cherry hardwood floors were being swept by people wielding wide, soft, white mops, so he got out of the way and went to check the kitchen.

He could smell the industrial-strength cleanser used to guard against salmonella and other bacteria before he was inside the door. The teens, Joshua and Teddy, were wet mopping and steam cleaning the surfaces and tile floors while Melvin sat on a stool and handled his paperwork. He would always be the last to leave his kitchen on any given day.

"Hey, Brian," Joshua hailed. "Careful, the floor is wet."

"Thanks, Joshua. I'll be outta your way in a moment. Melvin, do you need me to sign off on anything before I leave?"

"No, man. You've already signed off on the budget I submitted. I'll text you if I need anything we haven't already discussed."

"Solid. I'll see you in a few weeks." They shared a fist bump and turned to leave.

"Brian?" Teddy called out, halting him. She came forward and gave him a big hug. "Thanks for letting us work here. We want to go to culinary school when we graduate. If the offer to give us recommendations to attend the South Carolina school is a possibility, we'd appreciate it."

"Do as Melvin tells you and you'll have my support and Angelique's too. I've already spoken with her about your interest in furthering your education at her school."

"Thanks." She squeezed him again before going back to her steam mop.

He left the kitchen pleased that the two teenagers had a clue what they wanted to do with their lives. Ever since he came to live on the ranch as a child, he knew this was the life he wanted to live. His parents and grandparents were his support system then and now. However, they insisted that he attend college before making a final decision about what he wanted to do as a first career option. He was glad they forced the issue because he learned so much from the experience. He had always been a conscientious student because his parents would accept nothing less. However, it was actually his idea to attend UPenn's Wharton School of Business to obtain his master's degree and, again, his family gave him their full support.

When he walked back into the ballroom to the sound and sight of the heavy buffers crisscrossing the floor, he noticed Miguel talking with Whitney, Tucker, and KiLe. He passed on his belief, that his undergrad and graduate degrees were highly beneficial, to Miguel Menendez-Gaza, who was now following in his footsteps at UPenn.

"Brotherman," Miguel hailed as he and Brian exchanged a firm handclasp and brotherly one-arm hug.

"What's up with ya?" Brian rejoindered.

"Just finished my midterms before I came home. Looks like I'm gonna make Phi Beta Kappa just like you did." His grin was wide on his youthful handsome face.

"Yo, man, that's great!" Brian said as the group, at large, gave Miguel their congrats. He was truly happy for Miguel. However, his attention strayed unerringly to KiLe, as he remembered the magical kiss they shared earlier in the evening. Now he wondered whether it was real or a figment of his imagination. He needed time to think about it, so he mentioned to her he would call to wake her up in a few hours and left the ballroom to get some sleep, too.

Still, sleep eluded him and he ended up taking a nap for a few hours. That would have to suffice until tonight. He unloaded the final stack of sheets and towels in his dryer, packed the rest of his clothes, and checked the cabin for cleanliness before going to his truck. He drove down to the fishery barn to retrieve dry ice-filled coolers with fat, whole trout, salmon, and shrimp packed inside and secured the coolers in his truck bed. Checking the heated dog houses secured in the back of his truck, he noticed their water bottles were nearly empty. He kept a supply of water in his truck for himself and his dogs. He replaced them with fresh ones. While he went about performing menial tasks, like checking his tires, the oil in his truck, etc., he vowed he'd make an early night of it in Pennsylvania so he wouldn't spend too much time alone with KiLe.

Since the fox wasn't caged in his truck bed, he figured the animal hadn't been caught yet. He whistled for Starsky and Hutch, who bounded up into the back of his midnight-black, extended-cab truck. When they were secure, he pulled to the front of the mansion. KiLe came out and quickly descended the long, wide, but shallow Pennsylvania bluestone steps. Before he could get out of the truck to open the door for her, she was climbing up the running board, launching her duffel into the back seat, and seating herself inside.

"Oh, it's really chilly out here," KiLe said.

"Turn on your seat warmer. It shouldn't take long for the truck to heat up."

She grinned at him and he realized his statement could have been received as a double entendre.

"Oh, no you don't. You know exactly what I meant, brat."

"My bottom is warming up already," she cheekily said as she fastened her seatbelt. "You probably won't have to spank me."

Brian shook his head, grinning, and put the truck in gear. He was glad she was keeping it light as they chatted for the next few hours. He found her to be an engaging conversationalist as they discussed a wide range of topics. Eventually, KiLe drifted off to sleep while Brian entertained himself listening to an audiobook romantic mystery written by his cousin, Adelaide Jackson. As he approached the small town of Hazelton, Pennsylvania, his gas light came on. They were close enough to keep going to the ranch, but the dogs needed to stretch their legs. He pulled off the Interstate at the next exit. The parking lot of a small, open-all-night convenience store and gas station was deserted except for a car idling at the side of the building.

Brian thought it strange that a car would be running, but unoccupied. So, he kept an eye on the car while he inserted his debit card into the gas pump, keyed in his security code, and began filling his tank. When he looked toward the store, through the front windows and doors, he saw a clerk with his hands raised in the air and a man at the register with two others grabbing stock from the shelves before pushing the racks to the floor. Quickly, Brian pulled his phone from his pocket and dialed 911 before darting to the idling car and letting the air out of the two back tires. Back at his truck, he pulled a length of rope, his rifle from the truck cab, and quickly loaded it before waking KiLe.

"What?" she asked groggily and confused by Brian's instructions to get down on the floor and not to come out until he gave her the green light. Then he disappeared from her view.

She didn't waste time on inane questions but did as instructed. After a while, when a gunshot sounded, she snapped alert.

The three men bounded out of the store and were met with two snarling labs that had them skidding to a stop. One of the men started to aim his gun at the dogs, when Brian standing behind and to the blind side of them cocked his rifle and calmly said, "If you shoot my dogs, you'll be making a life-ending decision. Toss the gun away, get on your knees praying my dogs aren't too hungry and lay face down kissing the concrete."

Although he could hear the scream of sirens in the distance, Brian took time to hogtie the criminals' hands and feet behind their backs as if he were roping a steer in record time for prize money at a rodeo. When finished, he left his dogs to guard the criminals and went inside to see what could be done for the store clerk. The middle-aged man was sitting on the floor holding his hand to his bloody shoulder wound. Brian tore off the man's shirt sleeve and examined the wound. It was a through-and-through, so he packed both the front and back with ice packs he found in the refrigeration case of the store and bound the wound with the long sleeve.

"Brian!" a familiar voice rang out. *"Are you all right in there?"*

"I'm good, Uncle Seth," he called back and heard him enter the store. "I didn't do a thorough search of those guys out there, but the place in here is clear. Your deputies can come in," he said to his grandfather's brother, Seth Montgomery, the Monroe County Sheriff. Brian had identified himself to the police dispatcher when he made the 911 call and asked that his granduncle be notified. "Call for an ambulance. Gunshot wound to the shoulder. He's lost a lot of blood, so he's likely to be shocky soon."

"Got it," Seth Montgomery, a tall, strapping man with sharp, piercing blue eyes, handsome face, and a shock of healthy-looking, attractive, pewter-grey hair, said standing over Brian while he called for the ambulance. "Boy, you sure know how to make an entrance," he remarked when Brian stood. He had watched as Brian worked on the store clerk's wound. "Your daddy taught you well. Now go release your dogs so my deputies can stop pissin' their pants and get within ten feet of them robbers."

Brian snorted a laugh and whistled for his dogs, who immediately came bounding into the open door. They plopped their butts down at his feet, looking up at him, their tongues lolling with their tails rapidly brushing the floor. He knelt and gave the dogs a brisk rub sending them into doggy euphoria. When he looked up from them, the robbers were being carted away by the deputies and KiLe stood in the open door with concern clearly on her face. Before he could come to her, she ran to him and launched herself into his arms, her arms banded tightly around his neck.

"I was so scared you were hurt when I heard the gun go off."

Whoa! It's all right, KiLe. I'm fine," he soothingly said as he carried her with his hands under her bottom out of the door. Her legs were locked around his waist like a vice and he could feel her trembling. The ambulance, with its lights flashing, pulled to a stop before the medics rushed inside the store. He didn't pay attention to the flashes of light going off in his face as he went to his truck and put KiLe inside. He whistled his dogs inside the truck, retrieved his rifle, and then climbed in, putting KiLe on his lap. He just sat holding her for ponderous moments until her tremors began to subside.

"Don't do that again, okay?" Looking up into his handsome face, she knuckled away her tears.

He smiled and kissed her forehead, but she palmed his face and spoke with a serious expression on her pretty face with fresh tears on her cheeks. "I mean it, Brian Montgomery. Don't you risk your life like that again."

When he would have laughed, she kissed him and everything drained from his conscious thoughts. He never sensed the series of lights from the camera shots which were being taken of him and KiLe by the reporter standing directly in front of his truck.

CHAPTER 6

It was full light when Brian and KiLe said good day to his Granduncle Seth and made their way to the front of the sheriff's office in Stroudsburg, Pennsylvania. They had given their statements to the detectives, the county attorney, and signed documents attesting to the facts. Apparently, a local gang, of which these three were purported to be members, was suspected of committing armed robberies all around the Monroe County area and in the adjacent counties. Although Brian could attest to what occurred only to his certain knowledge, the local law enforcement officials were appreciative of his efforts. If a plea deal wasn't struck with the three criminals to turn state's evidence on other gang members, he would be notified when a trial date was set.

"Hold up, Mr. Montgomery," hailed one of the deputies. "You and your friend might want to go out a different exit. The press and news media are lying in wait for you to come out."

"Oh, joy," groaned Brian, aggrieved. He shook his head. "I don't have a choice. My dogs are in the truck and I'm parked out front."

"Okay. Let me have your keys and I'll see what I can do to clear a path for you."

Brian handed over his keys and ten minutes later, the deputy came walking into the office from a different direction.

"Your truck is in the impound garage where the reporters can't see it. Follow me and I'll open the back door of the garage. You can drive away without anyone seeing you leave."

He noticed that the deputy was paying a great deal of attention to KiLe. For some reason, that bothered him. "Thanks, deputy?"

"Turner, David Turner. You're welcome, Mr. Montgomery. Ms. Hakamora." His smile was over broad when he looked at KiLe and he held her hand a beat or two longer than necessary.

"Mr. Montgomery is my dad and granddad. Please call me, Brian, David." He offered his hand.

They shook, then Brian and KiLe followed the deputy out to the garage.

"Here's a card if you need to get in touch." He offered a card to both of them, but his sentiment appeared to be directed at KiLe.

Less than twenty minutes later, Brian pulled to the tall gate, which barred entrance to the Monroe County Alexander-Montgomery estate. He keyed in the access code and the gates opened and then closed once they were inside. As far as the eye could see, the fields were covered with snow at least a foot deep, but someone had cleared and treated the black-top driveway up to the mansion.

KiLe sat forward in her seat when they came around a bend, clearing a clump of trees to reveal a mansion four stories tall with snow-peaked spires, turrets, and long, wide balconies cascading down the sides in a pyramid style to the main level. There were what looked to her like ornamental trees growing on each level, with other potted plants and pretty outdoor furniture covered with the recent snowfall. "This is your home?" KiLe asked, her voice awed.

"It is, yes. It's an old resort that was abandoned and overgrown long before I was even born. The previous owners died and the land and building went into receivership. Initially, my dads, both Derrick and Chuck, bought it from the state with the idea of remodeling and reopening the resort. Derrick bought into a ski resort in Vail, Colorado, and planned to have the two locations linked with other resort properties he planned to purchase. Before he could make good on his plan, he died and mom inherited Derrick's interest in the property."

Brian pulled the truck to a stop in the circular drive and let the dogs out to run while he and KiLe stood looking up at the mansion. "Mom was angry with Chuck because he never told her Derrick had a severe heart condition, hypertrophic cardiomyopathy. So, for five years after Derrick died, Mom wouldn't even speak to Chuck. We lost Granddad Grover Jackson, Derrick's father, and Grandma Esther Hardyston Montgomery, Chuck's mother, during that time. It was hard on me and my sibs because we loved Chuck as much as we did Derrick. We had to sneak around behind Mom's back to see him. Then on Derrick Junior's fifth birthday, April first, he let it slip to Mom that Chuck bought a pony for him and he was going to get it at a party on the ranch while Mom was away on business in Chicago. We thought we were in for a serious tongue lashing from Mom. However, the next day, she brought all twelve of us to the ranch and buried the animosity between herself and Chuck. Shortly after that, Chuck and Mom announced that they were in love and planning to be married during the Juneteenth holiday family reunion that same year.

"When they came back from their honeymoon, we all moved to the ranch. Chuck and Mom renovated this place and made it our home and ranch instead of a resort. Then they built the ranch in Goodwill, Summer County, South Carolina. Now we spend as much time as we can between all three places with Dad's and Mom's families and on an island in Bimini Derrick owned for many years before he and mom married. My parents went to that island for a mini-birthday vacation this morning.

"We've made some good memories here." He looked up and around at the renovated resort, which was now a home. "Come on. I'll show you around. Althea Hardyston, Grandma Esther's sister, is the house majordomo. She's probably waiting breakfast for us and I'm starving."

They left the truck in the driveway, hefting their duffels, and entered what must have been, to KiLe's way of thinking as she turned in a circle, the resort's grand lobby with its intricately designed marble floors, walls, and round, sturdy pillars holding up twenty-foot-high coffered ceilings.

Brian knew the house was daunting to anyone seeing it for the first time, but his stomach was growling. "Come on, kid. Ya gotta keep up," he teased, slinging an arm around her shoulders as he headed them through the long, wide halls toward the back of the mansion. When they reached the dining hall, there was an unobstructed, panoramic view of the snow-covered Pocono Mountain range through floor-to-ceiling windows and doors. A table was set for three and Danny Montgomery, one of Seth's four grandsons, sat reading a newspaper and having coffee.

"Well, hell, look what the cat finally dragged in." Danny gave Brian a manly hug and then pushed him aside to regard KiLe from the bottom up. "Well, hello, my lovely," he reached for KiLe. "Granddad said she's a looker, but damn, that is a gross understatement."

"KiLe Hakamora, this is my cousin, Daniel Montgomery. We call him Danny. He's one of Granduncle Seth's grandsons.

"The best of his grandsons," boasted Danny.

"Don't believe anything this man says. Hell, if I line up all of his exes in a row, you can see the flowchart of his mental illness," warned a tall, sturdy-looking woman who entered the room carrying a tray of piping hot food. She put down the tray and fiercely hugged Brian. "This one isn't much better," she teased. "Your dogs came in through the doggy door. I left them in the mudroom and fed them," she said to Brian and then turned and said, "Hi, I'm Althea Hardyston. I'm the grand aunt-in-law to these two bucks," she shook KiLe's hand. "You can call me Aunt Althea. Everyone does. Grand aunt-in-law is too much of a mouthful. You must be KiLe Hakamora. Seth just called a moment ago to say you were on your way. I'm surprised to see you because Brian usually doesn't bring anyone with him when he comes up to work the ranch."

"I blackmailed him," KiLe confided and had both Althea and Danny barking a laugh.

"Serves him right. Now, sit, sit, sit and eat before this food gets cold," Althea insisted animatedly and added another place setting to the table.

"Where may I freshen up, Honorable Aunt Althea?"

"Honorable? Well, I like the sound of that. Come with me." Althea led the way to a well-laid-out restroom with six stalls and six spigots over a long, stone trough to wash her hands.

There was nothing about this converted resort that wasn't appealing, KiLe thought as she took care of her needs and returned to the awesome salon where the three sat talking over coffee.

"Did you bring up the fish and shrimp I asked you for?"

"I did, yes, Aunt Althea. I even cleaned and boned them for you. They're in coolers in my truck. I'll bring them in after breakfast. I'll trade you for a haircut."

Althea released the band and ran her fingers through Brian's hair. "Yeah, you could use a trim, but I won't take off too much. You and your dad look good with long hair. I don't know how, but your hair grows so fast."

Both Brian and Danny spotted KiLe and stood until she was seated.

Althea led the grace. "Thank you, Heavenly Father, for looking after the Montgomery babies and fools and keeping one of them from getting shot up this morning. Amen."

"I was careful, Aunt Althea. Didn't Grand Uncle Seth tell you that?"

"He said you were brave, not careful. You're like your daddies, Derrick and Chuck. Fools rush in where angels fear to tread."

"I felt the same way, Honorable Aunt Althea." KiLe noticed as Brian began to serve her plate before passing it to her. He also served Danny and his grandaunt's plate, too, she noticed. "He was brave and foolish. He could have just called the police and driven away, but instead, he stayed and apprehended the criminals."

"They were a bad crew, those boys. I hear tell they're with a gang over in Wilkes-Barre, Seth said. It's believed they've been terrorizing the local store owners around these parts for months. County folks all around the area will be glad to see the back of those three and hope the rest get arrested soon, too. It's a shame all of them couldn't be locked up today," Althea declared and continued. "Still, I'm proud it was one of our own who took the three of them down, but they're a mean, vindictive bunch. So, you watch your six, Brian."

"I will, Aunt Althea." He continued to eat his breakfast. He wasn't particularly worried about repercussions, but he knew his parents would be. He checked his watch. By now, his parents were on the way to the island and wouldn't check in until later tonight or in the morning. With any luck, no one would disturb their vacation. His grandparents, Bernard and Sylvia Benson Alexander and Stephen and Harriet Jackson Montgomery, were handling things at the ranch in Maryland while his parents were away. He knew the recently wed Stephen and Harriet would have already received calls from their offspring and other family members who live in Monroe County. So, he would have to call and reassure them that he was all right.

"How was the party?" asked Danny.

"Fantastic. Dad and Mom had a good time and a lot of their friends showed up, including the President and First Lady. KiLe is one of the band members who performed for the party and she's got a voice like you wouldn't believe," boasted Brian. He went on to tell them about the highlights. "Ryan and Roger will have something up on the family's secure intranet page sometime today. They videoed the entire event and they're home for spring break with Dena, Geneviève, and Vincent."

"Sorry I had to miss it," said Danny.

"*Ha!*" laughed Althea. "Our Danny Boy has a dilemma among three women he's been dating off and on. Couldn't figure out how to take one to the party in Maryland without the other two finding out."

"Oh, no, Danny. Say it ain't so," Brian teased his cousin.

With chagrin mapped on his handsome face, he said with wonder evident in his voice, "Man, I don't know how I get myself into these things. Maybe, if I spent more time in Maryland or South Carolina, this wouldn't happen to me."

"It only means you'd find a way to be in more trouble than you are here," Althea suggested. "You should be more selective, like Brian. He dates only one woman at a time," she said for KiLe's benefit.

"Oh, he's not my date," KiLe quickly interjected.

"Really," Danny said, his interest apparent in his wide, beguiling smile and the gleam in his pretty blue eyes.

"That's not what you said last night," Brian reminded her. "Let's go, KiLe, before I have to hurt Danny. I'm putting you in the room next to mine to keep an eye on you." He rose from the breakfast table. "Thanks for the good grub, Aunt Althea." He kissed her temple and then turned to Danny. "I served, so you can help by cleaning up and then get the fish and shrimp out of my truck. I'll be back down shortly and we can go over the accounts before we head out."

"Works for me. I'll be seeing you, KiLe." Danny smiled.

Brian snorted a laugh and led KiLe away. They picked up their duffels and headed for the back stairs, which led to the upper floors.

As they walked up the wide, spiraling marble steps, KiLe couldn't help but look up the four stories to a high skylight that bathed the circular staircase in bright sunlight. On the second-floor landing, Brian held open the heavy door for her.

"To the left," he directed and she moved that way. Approximately, midway along the thickly carpeted hallway, Brian stopped and opened a double door ushering her inside.

"*WOW!*" KiLe exclaimed when she stepped inside the suite. To her right was a sofa in a sitting area complete with a desk, coffee table, and wall-mounted flat-screen above a gas fireplace. A wall to her left partially bisected the room where a king-sized bed could be seen with a dresser against the opposite wall, small round table with two chairs and another wall mounted flat screen above the dresser. Wide barn doors provided closures for the bedroom space and a sumptuous four-piece bathroom. A small kitchenette spanned the wall by the entrance to the suite. Bridging both ends of the suite were wall-to-wall, ceiling-to-floor glass bi-fold doors that provided unencumbered access to a terrace where furniture was attractively arranged with potted plants and trees. *The view was phenomenal,* thought KiLe.

She stood looking into the vastness of the mountain range, which seemed to go on unspoiled forever. "This is incredible, Brian," she reverently said.

"It is pretty spectacular. If you're up early enough, you can see the sunrise on the snow-capped mountains to the east and the sunset to the west. It's difficult to see in the daylight, but at night you can sometimes see the lights from the homes of our family members who live here year-round."

She sighed, hugged Brian around his waist, and laid her head against his firm chest. "Thank you, Brian, for bringing me with you. Even though you scared me to death this morning, this makes up for all of it."

He laughed and put his arms around her shoulders for a quick squeeze before letting her go. He couldn't do more than that for fear he would take it too far. He was entirely too close to a bed and had the desire to see the vistas from a horizontal position with KiLe nestled naked in his arms. He thanked providence that he had business to tend to and needed to get started.

Opening the door midway the sitting area of the suite, he entered the suite next door to hers. He unpacked his things and stowed his duffle in the closet before checking the list of things on his iPad he needed to see to.

"This is where you stay when you come here?" asked KiLe standing in the doorway between the suites. "No cabin in the woods to use as a hideaway?"

He grinned. "It is," he said without looking at her. She was entirely too distracting, so he kept his eyes on his iPad. Using the remote, he turned on the flat screen and superimposed his schedule on the larger monitor checking his details and adding a few to the list.

"What's that?" KiLe asked, coming into Brian's living area and sitting on the end of the sofa.

"Montgomery land. It's a tree farm. A couple thousand acres." Well, it was much more than that, but what the hell. The details weren't important at this juncture of their relationship. He had learned the hard way to be circumspect about his wealth. He didn't think it was particularly necessary where KiLe was concerned. Still, it was his usual practice at the beginning of any relationship.

"You own all of that?" she incredulously asked.

"No, well, yes, in that it's the Montgomery family logging and milling consortium. Our branch of the family is equal partners. As tree farms go, it's not that large. Liam Montgomery is a master carpenter. He designs and builds timber-framed structures," he said while changing his bomber jacket. "He built my cabin when I graduated from grad school. Now, go back into your room so I can change my clothes. You're free to roam the house which has plenty to see and do. There's an indoor pool, exercise gym, sauna, and a game room on the lower level or a music studio if you want to practice. There is also a library and video lounge to watch movies."

"What are you going to do?"

"Danny and I have to meet for a bit, and then we're heading out to check on the farm animals and to the base camp job site to tag trees."

"May I go with you?"

"We'll be outdoors most of the day, KiLe. It's going to be very cold out there on the upper elevations of the mountain ranges. Did you bring heavy weather gear?"

"No, not really, but my shearling coat is pretty warm," she hopefully said.

He doubted it was warm enough, but if she wanted to go with him, he could surely get her outfitted. "What size are you?"

"Six."

"Okay, that means you're about the size of my twin sisters, Laurel and Laura. I think we can find something to fit you. Come with me." He headed out of his suite's double doors into the long hall and then up another flight of steps to the third level of the house.

KiLe looked into the open bedroom doors of the suites they passed. Some had two double beds and others could accommodate four people in bunk beds. Each seemed to have a gas fireplace and beautifully decorated motifs. Though she couldn't see it, she imagined each room also had a kitchenette. Finally, they turned into one of the rooms with two double beds and a sweet setup for the twin preteens. She confirmed, yes, it came with a kitchenette.

Several snowsuits were hanging in the closet among other clothes, shoes, and boots. Brian picked the bright red one over the blue or the black ones. In the snow, a red snowsuit wouldn't be mistaken for some animal, he told her. Deer hunting season was still in effect. In the built-in drawers, Brian pulled a synthetic bodysuit and accessories to pile on layers. From the shoe tree, he picked up a pair of ski boots and heavy socks out of a basket on the shelf.

"All of this?" KiLe asked as Brian continued to hand the clothes and a pair of boots to her.

"We'll get the rest of the things you'll need from the mudroom. For now, I'll step outside while you try on these things."

KiLe looked up at him as he stepped outside the walk-around closet. She undressed and then piece by piece began to layer on the clothes. Surprisingly, everything fit, including the boots. Gathering her clothes and boots, she stepped out into the bedroom suite where Brian paced while talking on his phone. When he spotted her, he disconnected the call.

Brian took the bundle of clothes from KiLe and regarded her attire. "Are you too warm in this?"

"Not yet."

"Good. Let's go back to my suite so that I can change my clothes."

CHAPTER 7

An hour later, after he and Danny finished their meeting in the home office, they entered the kitchen where Althea capped the last thermos of hot coffee and packed bottles of cold water while she and KiLe conversed. "You picked out some great fish, lobsters, and shrimp, Brian. Thank you."

"You're welcome, Aunt Althea. Maybe we can have baked fish for dinner tonight?" he cajoled.

"That's what I said, too," commented Danny. "Of course, I'm coming to dinner to get better acquainted with KiLe since she's not your lady friend."

"Maybe I'd better amend that statement while I'm here," KiLe joked. "I just dumped a two-year relationship with another guy yesterday. I can handle only one guy who is a serial dater in the same week."

Althea laughed. "That-a-girl," she said, smiling. "Brian, I thought I'd have some company while you were out and about today, but it looks like you're taking KiLe out with you?"

"She'll get tired of hanging out with us. When she does, I'll send her back to you," Brian said and laughed as KiLe pouted.

"You're leaving your dogs, right?"

"I am, yes. The snow is too deep for the dogs where we're going. Plus, if Liam is working with one of his falcons, I don't want my dogs on its lunch menu. In any event, we'll be back before dark." He headed into the large mudroom where a long row of skis was racked. He took down a pair for KiLe and then he and Danny selected some for themselves. "You're going to need these," he said, passing ski poles to KiLe. Then he selected goggles, ear muffs, a ski mask, ski cap, scarf, and insulated gloves dressing her in the heavy weather gear for what he knew to expect at this and higher elevations in the mountains.

"I thought we were going in your truck. You know I don't know how to ski, right?" asked KiLe.

Brian nodded while he and Danny prepared themselves to brave the cold. They all carried backpacks and ushered KiLe out of the back door. When outside, they tied lassos around their waists before fitting KiLe's snow boots onto the skis. Once they had on their skis, they handed the lassos to her and then they were off across the fields pulling KiLe along.

She watched their motion in coordination with their ski poles. Soon she got the rhythm of their strides so she could move with them instead of just being pulled along behind. It was hard on her arm, leg, and thigh muscles, but it kept her warmer to cross-country ski with them.

The sun was bright against the unsullied white snow and the air stingingly brisk as the wind kicked up snow, swirling as if it was a twister. KiLe was thankful for the ski mask and sunshades. It was very cold, but somehow exhilarating being out with the smell of clean, fresh pine air in the bright sunshine. Occasionally, they would hit a downhill space and it was a good thing she held on to the ropes or she would have gone flying off the side of a cliff.

They saw spring gobblers, wild turkeys, elk, deer, rabbits, mountain goats, pheasants, quail, and squirrels on their way. Brian and Danny stopped long enough for her to snap pictures with her iPhone before moving on. They pointed to the different trees in their apple orchards, explaining what they were and the birds and geese flying overhead. It was a true education she would never have imagined.

They had been on their skis for over an hour when KiLe noticed bright red barns grouped against the unrelenting white snow with livestock in various corrals. Men, women, and dogs were working together to usher the livestock through shoots single file and into different barns. The cows wore bright yellow ear tags with numbers on them and other data. Each cow's tag was being checked off of an electronic list before the shoot was opened and the steer ushered to the next stall.

Hands went up, acknowledging Brian's and Danny's arrival. Curious stares greeted KiLe as they skied to a stop. Brian and Danny helped her first before they took off their skis. She took off the ski mask to shake the snow off of it and fluff out her hair.

"How's it going?" Brian asked a tall, lanky, young guy who was sitting on a fence consulting an iPad.

"Better than with you, cousin. I had to wrangle only a few hundred steers this morning, but I hear you took down a whole passel of bad guys with your bare hands before dawn," Pierce Montgomery, Danny's brother, said laughing.

"Yeah, yeah, yeah," Brian ragged. "This is . . ."

"KiLe Hakamora," Pierce supplied and smiled at her while climbing down off the fence. "'*Pretty as a picture,*' Aunt Althea said and she ain't never lied. I think we should have a spring wedding, don't you, KiLe?"

She laughed at him and moved closer to Brian, putting her right arm under his left one. "One Montgomery at a time is more than enough for me," she teased.

Pierce regretfully shook his head. "I could have made you a star."

"For the night," teased his brother, Danny. "Our Pierce is a one-night-stand kind of guy."

"Oh, he of the merry-go-round dating dares to speak?" Pierce laughingly questioned.

KiLe looked on as the drop-dead handsome brothers joked with each other. They could almost pass for twins with the beautiful blue eyes and thick eyelashes, which would make any woman envious. Yet she was not tempted to do anything other than be content to stand next to Brian.

"Your horses from Tina Justice and Nick Collins arrived yesterday. I've kept them quarantined until the Doc had time to check them. They're a beautiful herd of wild horses and should really enhance your bloodline."

"Right on time. I was down in Argentina for ten days with Tina and Nico selecting the ones I wanted and arranging for transportation and delivery. Has the doctor found anything so far?" Brian asked Pierce.

"Nothing with your herd or mine, but it's early days yet. He finished with your buffalo last week, but he just started with the cattle. You have eighteen new buffalo calves, but we think we have as many as ten, maybe more steers missing. I may have to have Kadijah take the helo up and do a grid search until we find them.

"I know you're behind schedule," Pierce continued, "so if you want to head over to the base camp, I've got a couple of two-up touring snowmobile models on my truck I'm testing."

"Thanks, Pierce. That'll work. I need to get over there, so I'll have to see to the horses later in the week after the Doc has checked them."

"Sure enough. I'll help you unload the mobiles. Danny can take over here and I'll go with you." He handed the iPad to Danny, who climbed up on the fence and resumed checking off the cattle as they came through the shoot.

"Who is Kadijah?" asked KiLe of Brian once he maneuvered the snowmobile down the ramp from Pierce's truck.

"Kadijah Jackson Montgomery. She's Martin Montgomery's wife and Derrick Jackson's younger sister."

"She's a pilot?"

"She is, yes. She has a commuter air service and she handles search and rescue for the Sheriff's Office in Monroe County. She also works with the fire department and the hospital."

"Search and rescue?"

"Yes. You see, the Pocono Mountains are the largest tourist attraction in the state of Pennsylvania. People sometimes get lost in the hills and mountains and we have to participate in search parties. Some get careless and start forest fires. She can fly over an area and dump water or chemicals to douse a forest fire before it gets out of control." He helped to unload the other snowmobile. "Over a billion people have visited the area on tours and vacations. That's why the dads were thinking of reopening Point of View as a year-round resort."

"Point of View?"

Brian laughed. "The name is Mom's idea. She calls it Point of View North."

"Then your ranch in Summer County, South Carolina, must be Point of View South?"

"Actually, she calls it Another Point of View. The legal name for the Maryland ranch is the Alexander-Jackson-Montgomery Consortium, but we do business as Alex-Mont Ranch. Chuck instituted the name after Derrick's death and never changed it after he and Mom married."

"The Jacksons are still an integral part of your family," she guessed.

"They are, yes. When we come here, it's to spend time with both the Montgomerys and the Jacksons. It's easy since there have been three marriages between the two families. Almost everyone in both families still lives in Monroe County."

"Three marriages?"

"Yes. In addition to Martin and Kadijah, there's Stephen Montgomery, my grandfather, Chuck's father, and Harriet Jackson, my grandmother, Derrick's mother. They haven't been married that long. Then there's Bob and Sheila Jackson Montgomery, my uncle and aunt. They were the first to marry when the dads were still in their preteens. They've been married for many years."

"You're very close to them, aren't you?"

"Yes, I am. Just like with my immediate family, I forget that I'm not connected by blood. The Montgomerys and the Jacksons don't make the distinction either. "Okay, now, less talk, KiLe. I've got work to do, remember. Take off your backpack and put on this helmet. You have to hold tightly onto me," Brian instructed as he straddled the snowmobile and put the backpacks into the saddlebags. "If I know Pierce, he's built these buggies to move like the wind."

Pierce grinned and started his engine with a roar. Brian followed suit and off they went at break-neck speeds across the fields.

"Yes!" KiLe squealed as they raced the wind. *This is such an exhilarating feeling being out in the bright sun,* she thought as they passed by homes, which looked as if they should be on a Currier and Ives holiday card.

It was a good thing Brian put her ski mask back on her because even with the helmet's shield down over her face and the mobile's windshield, the icy gusts of wind found a way to chill her cheeks. However, her arms were around Brian's waist and tightly holding to the front of his belt. She could feel the warmth of his stomach through her insulated gloves and his taut stomach muscles. A thrill hummed in her blood from the fun of speeding along, but more so from the feel of holding onto Brian.

Sitting between KiLe's open thighs was not a good thing for him to think about or for his libido. He was definitely feeling the need to mate rise in his blood hard and strong. Her hands holding his belt were only inches from his rising manhood. Yet, he had to remain focused on the path they were making through the snowpack, something which was hard to do. To ensure KiLe's safety, he mentally dismissed the vice-like grip her thighs had against his and pushed faster to reach their destination.

It took only fifteen minutes to reach the logging road where the pristine snow had been turned into slush. Though the windshield was a barrier against blowback from Pierce's snowmobile on their faces, it didn't protect against the muck collecting on their feet and legs. He would have to have KiLe taken back to the ranch house to change out of what were likely damp clothes now.

They rounded a bend in the road, which hugged the side of the steep hill. *They were riding perilously close to the edge and there was no railing to keep them from falling*, thought KiLe, but the changing views of the valley as they climbed were breath-stealing. Up ahead, over Brian's shoulder, she could see a clearing where massive equipment was loading impossibly long, thick logs onto a truck and trailer. Even at a distance, the sound of buzz saws was horrendous. People were shouting *"timber!"* as huge trees were felled and then stripped of their branches before being measured and loaded on different trucks. To KiLe's eyes, the huge equipment looked like an invasion from ***Star Wars'*** mechanicals.

Just as they parked, a loud whistle sounded and all of the noise and commotion stopped. Those in the camp hailed Pierce's and Brian's arrival as they all began to move toward a tented area. Others arrived in ATVs of all types, as well as in rugged-looking snowmobiles and trucks. Inside the tent were backpacks hanging on hooks around the perimeter and battery-operated coffee urns with condiments spread out on a table. People piled in filling thermos mugs with hot, aromatic coffee or making hot tea or cocoa and began to take seats at tables or in chairs with trays on their laps. The tent's flaps kept the wind gusts down, KiLe noticed, as she stamped her feet to get feeling back into them. Others took their lunches outside and sat on any available flat surface to eat and talk.

Brian and Pierce were hailed by nearly everyone around the campsite and raucous chatter and laughter ensued. They introduced KiLe to those who stopped to talk, but the conversations ran the gamut about things outside of her purview. Although both Brian and Pierce kept her in the conversation, for the most part, she just listened to the lively discussions.

During the discourse, she learned there was some type of bowling competition coming up during the week. Brian was being cajoled into taking part on the Montgomery-Jackson team against others slated to participate. Since it was a mixed-league tournament, she was also invited to join in.

"I've never even held a bowling ball," KiLe admitted. "You can't possibly want me to join you."

"You've got to start somewhere," said Pierce.

Just then, a scream ripped through the air overhead and people left the tent and looked skyward.

"Is that Liam's bird?" asked Brian of Pierce.

"Probably. He's over on the ridge working her. Let's go see," suggested Pierce leading the way to their snowmobiles and mounting up again.

"Come on, KiLe, this may be interesting for you to see," said Brian.

Ten minutes later, they came to a ridge where another scenic valley spread out for miles below them. Three people stood on the outcropping of a hillside with their eyes skyward. A large bird with an impossibly wide wingspan was circling and then, with lightning speed, it swooped down and skimmed over a body of water that meandered twisting and turning through the valley floor. When it zoomed up again, in its claws, the bird carried away a fish wiggling and twisting in its grip as it gained altitude.

As they drew closer and got off the ski mobiles, they joined three other people on the hillside. One of the people, a woman, turned to look in their direction and broadly smiled at Brian.

"Hello, Brian," the woman warmly greeted, her eyes shining and her lips sporting a sexy grin.

"Keep your eyes on your bird," a man, who looked so much like Pierce they had to be related, cautioned stridently.

The woman immediately snapped to attention and then raised her heavily gloved left arm. Like a shot, the bird bulleted toward them but landed on the woman's arm with its wings spread wide and the large fish still in its grip.

KiLe thought it was the most frighteningly awesome thing she had ever seen. The woman took the fish and handed it off to the third man who was talking on a cell phone.

"She's a real beauty, Gayle, and you're learning to work her," Brian commented. Then turning to KiLe, Brian offered, "Mr. Gaylord Hightower, Gayle, this is a family friend, KiLe Hakamora. She's a student at Georgetown University. Mr. Hightower owns Hightower Resort Hotels in the area and his daughter, Gayle, is his entertainment director."

Mr. Hightower nodded but didn't leave his phone conversation. Gayle looked her over from the bottom up and also nodded before turning to regard the bird on her arm.

"Nice to meet you." KiLe offered her hand, but Brian pulled her back, forcing her to lower her arm and stepping partially in front of her. At that moment, the bird spread its wide wings as if to attack or take flight, but Gayle successfully held it in place.

"Careful, KiLe," Brian cautioned. "This is a Peregrine Falcon. It's a bird of prey and very dangerous. Liam Montgomery, this is KiLe Hakamora, one of Whitney's housemates."

"I heard you came up with Brian. Welcome." Liam nodded but kept a watchful eye on Gayle and the bird she held. "He's correct about the bird. She was born in captivity, but she's been taught to hunt. Improperly handled, she could rip through your arm."

"Liam Montgomery is another one of my brothers," offered Pierce. "He's one of a very few people who train birds in the United States."

"This is Star Fire. We're training Gayle to work with her," said Liam.

"Liam breeds birds of prey as a hobby because of the dwindling wild populations. Due to the toxins used in farming and industry waste, systematic persecution as undesirable predators, habitat loss, and the resulting limited availability of popular species for falconry, particularly ones like this, are becoming more rare," Pierce added.

"I've never been this close to a Falcon other than in a zoo. They're much larger up close than I thought. How long have you been working with her?" KiLe asked.

"Sixteen months. Soon I'll be able to take her home, right, Liam?"

"If you continue to make steady progress with her, Gayle, you should be able to take her home in six more months," Liam commented. "The keeping and training of any raptor are strictly and tightly regulated by U.S. state and federal laws. Anyone in the U.S.A. who is interested in flying raptors must seek out a state and federally licensed falconer, like me, to sponsor him or her through an apprenticeship period lasting two years at a minimum, often considerably longer." Liam briefly looked toward KiLe and Brian. "This is not news to Gayle. I've explained this to her before." Continuing Gayle's lesson, "You have to give her your full attention, Gayle, or she'll lose respect for your direction and refuse to come to you when you signal her."

Gayle gave Liam a sardonic look, all but rolling her eyes at him. *Clearly, she isn't a woman who takes no for an answer or likes taking instructions,* thought KiLe. As she watched and listened to the discussion about the bird and falconry in general, she began to notice that there seemed to be an undercurrent going on between Liam, Gayle, and Brian. Gayle was certainly an attractive woman with pretty green eyes and naturally dark red hair, which she wore short and nicely framing her face.

"I want to work her one more time today," announced Gayle.

"No. That's enough for today. The logging will start again shortly. Star Fire will be distracted by the noise and not want to cooperate. We'll take her out again tomorrow or the day after as our schedules allow. For now, lift her and pass her to me."

"For Pete's sake, Liam. Let's send her up again," Gayle argued.

"You know the drill, Gayle. I make the rules. Now, pass her over." He stepped in front of Gayle and raised his equally heavily gloved arms so that the big bird stepped from one arm to the next with practiced ease. Liam fed the bird a treat for following the signals correctly then put a hood over the Falcon's head to shield its view.

Liam took the fish from Mr. Hightower and immediately walked away toward a truck with a large cage in the back. Gayle looked after him, consternation written all over her face.

"We need to get back," said Pierce.

"Agreed." Brian offered his goodbyes. However, Gayle got his attention, halting him and walking closer into his personal space. After a few moments of discussion, Brian turned and called out, "Pierce, would you take KiLe back to the base camp? I'll catch up shortly."

"Sure thing." Offering a supporting hand to her, Pierce ushered KiLe to his snowmobile.

"Okay, what's this about, Gayle? You know this thing between you and Liam shouldn't include me."

"You still have feelings for me, don't you, Brian?"

"Friendship feelings, Gayle. What we had in college was an eon ago. We're not kids anymore and we don't play games, especially not with my cousin."

"Why can't we see each other, Brian? Are you with someone else? The Chinese girl, for example?"

"No, I'm not, and KiLe Hakamora is Japanese. As for me, I'm not on the market for a renewal of our previous affair."

"I think you purposefully deny your natural reaction to me."

"You're an exceptionally beautiful woman, Gayle, and you know it. We had a good time for a while, but now that's over and done. You showed me that you want Liam and you know Liam has feelings for you. I'm not going to stand in the way. Besides, your father likes Liam a great deal more than he ever liked the idea of me with you."

"I can handle my father."

"Perhaps, but *I'm* not going to be handled. So, let's call off this confusion you're creating or we won't even have a basis for a friendship," he succinctly said.

"Gayle," called out her father. "Let's get back to the office. We've got meetings this afternoon."

She continued to stare into Brian's unrelenting eyes before she turned away and followed her father to his chauffeured car. Brian watched her go and then waited for Liam to approach.

"You're crazy as hell for wanting to build something with Gayle, Liam." Brian remorsefully shook his head.

"Yeah, I know, but I've almost got her tamed. She's afraid of what's between us and doesn't know how to react when I don't bend to her demands. She's running in all directions, trying to figure out how to avoid her feelings for me."

"Well, please keep her crazy ass away from me." Brian gave his cousin a one-arm handclasp embrace. "I don't need or want the drama."

"Yeah, it looks like you've got your hands full. KiLe is a real babe." He laughed. "She's a little on the young side, isn't she?"

Brian shrugged. "She's older than she looks. She might look fifteen with her petite body, but she's legal and twenty-two, in her last year at Georgetown undergrad. From what she told me on the way up here this morning, her parents want her to get a master's degree in science and a doctorate in a record amount of time. She seems a little ambivalent about what she wants to do for a career."

"Whitney said she has a powerful voice," Liam commented.

"She does," Brian nodded in agreement, "and she has great stage presence."

Liam's brows lifted in question. "Are you interested?"

"I don't know yet. We haven't spent that much time together."

"It's been a while for you. After seeing you in *Stallion* magazine, the women in town have been asking about you."

"*Oh joy,*" he lamented. "Maybe seeing me with KiLe will stem their interests."

Liam snorted a laugh and threw an arm over Brian's shoulder. "Fat chance."

"Yeah, you may be right. Look, since I'm here, I'm going to take a walk up to say hey."

Liam squeezed his shoulder. "You want me to come with?"

"Nah, I'm good. I won't be long."

Liam nodded, "I'll see you at the base camp shortly," and with long-legged strides walked toward his truck.

Brian turned and walked up the terraced incline to where Derrick's and Grover's gravesites were located. "Hey, Dad, Granddad," he began and spent time talking to them, bringing them up to date on current events. Not surprisingly, his conversation included quite a bit about KiLe Hakamora.

CHAPTER 8

KiLe sat by the tent, waiting for Brian to return. Her backpack was in the saddlebag on his snowmobile with her lunch inside. She got a cup of coffee, but it was so strong it had her nerves jumping. She thought that she would probably be awake all night. However, the important thing is it was hot.

Finally, she looked up when she heard the snowmobile coming. Lunch was almost over, but Pierce and some of the workers shared bits of their lunches with her. *They ate what looked like seven-course meals*, she thought. It was good food, but they ate more than she could eat in three sittings. By the time Brian came to the tent, she was pretty full.

"Sorry. I forgot I had your backpack," Brian placed the item on the table in front of her.

"Not a problem," she said but wondered what delayed him for so long. She admitted to herself she was curious about Gayle Hightower of the pretty green eyes and "come hither" smile.

"Did Liam take the bird home?" asked Pierce of Brian.

"He was headed in that direction with the bird and the fish. He said he'd be here," Brian said as he opened his backpack and took out his lunch. The thick beef and barley soup was still hot when he poured it into the cup, so he started with that before he opened the hoagie.

"Are you going to cut for the Hawthorn's cabin?" one of the loggers asked Brian.

"We are," Brian nodded. "I got the plans back from JaiHonnah Baylor last week."

"Let me see what it looks like," one of the women asked.

Brian introduced KiLe to one of the crew bosses before he handed his iPad across the table.

"This is a big one." The woman looked up at Brian.

KiLe thought the woman's voice had a foghorn quality to it as she talked while flipping through the electronic pages.

Brian nodded. "I'm taking down the oaks over on Sandy Ridge."

"Good location, Brian. That area needs thinning out. We also need a fire break through that area," commented Pierce.

"I noticed. That's all old-growth timber and I want to take it down before some disease infects it. I'm also going to deconstruct that old timber-framed barn on our spread. It must have been erected in the seventeen hundreds."

"Yeah. You don't need it with the new horse barns and arenas you've built. Are you going to reuse it for the Hawthorn project?"

"I am, yes. I'm thinking about using the bones to construct my place up by the mountain lake. No use in letting the barn wood go to waste." Brian spooned up another mouthful of the thick soup.

"Man, those are some big logs. I don't know how the hell you're going to get them up on the mountain by your lake," someone commented.

"I'll likely have to fly them in. I'll talk with my sister, Eve. She's with the Coast Guard and can fly aerial cranes, which are used to lift heavy or awkward loads. The helicopters carry loads connected to long cables or slings to place heavy equipment when other methods are not available."

The guy nodded, agreeing that may be the only way to get the logs up the mountain.

As Brian talked and ate, KiLe noticed how good the beef and barley soup smelled. So, she opened her thermos and began eating, too, surprised that she was a little hungry again so soon. It was delicious and went well with the ham and cheese hoagie she found in the backpack with a fat dill pickle and a bag of chips. She couldn't eat the whole thing, so she put half of the hoagie in front of Brian while he continued to talk with others seated at the table about the various timber frame projects they had on the schedule.

Brian fascinated her and he wasn't even trying, thought KiLe. She liked how he was clear and concise about his plans and could converse on a wide range of topics. He was a leader and knew how to give direction and get buy-in from the men and women who worked for the Montgomery family without being overbearing. He, obviously, was not opposed to rolling up his shirtsleeves and working side-by-side with those in the Montgomerys' employ. He seemed to garner a great deal of respect for that alone.

KiLe particularly liked the quick grin and perpetual smile, which was a default expression of the Montgomery men. Even when Liam joined them, there were smiles, fist bumps, and high fives heralding his arrival. He took a backpack from his shoulder and began unloading it.

Twenty minutes later, a whistle sounded ending the lunch break. Debris from the meal was tossed in a big metal barrel riddled with holes which looked like gunshots. The debris was set afire with kindling from the felled tree branches. Buzz saws were started and more trees fell shaking the ground amid the loud noises.

While Brian conducted an impromptu meeting with his cousins, KiLe got up and stood by the open door of the tent while the conversations continued behind her. She was watching the men and women at work cleaning up the fallen debris from the trees and loading it into a chipper while another group of people followed planting what looked like new seedlings in a precise row, guided by the string tied tightly from one post to another.

"Bored?" Brian asked, standing closely behind her so that he could speak directly into her ear.

"Not hardly. Are those people over there planting new trees?" KiLe pointed while looking up at Brian over her left shoulder.

"They are, yes. We're planting Christmas trees and trees for landscapers in this section this year. When we sell the trees, we include the root ball too. We're taking down only what we need to complete projects and fill orders for lumber, but we practice reforestation to keep the soil from becoming a mudslide during rainy weather or after a heavy winter snowfall melts. We have mountain lakes in the upper elevations, and, when the snow-pack melts, we could get flash flooding. In another three-to-five years, these trees will have grown substantially.

"When I was a little kid, this area was being harvested. It's been harvested twice more since then." He put his hand on her shoulder, but when she turned her head to look up at him, something electric rocketed through his system as she gazed intently at him and particularly at his mouth. "I have to go over to the Sandy Ridge area. Do you want to go with me or stay here at the base camp?"

KiLe nodded. "I'll go with you." She was thrilled as he kept his hand on her as he guided her out. He headed for a truck with the *Montgomery Logging and Mill, established in 1690* logo on the door panel. The keys were already in it when they climbed in and deposited their backpacks in the back seat. They drove up a winding road with sharp switchbacks, steadily climbing higher to a point where they were completely closed in by the tall trees. The road became more like a goat path, but it seemed as if they were in a secret garden; the woodland area so beautiful it created a cathedral-like canopy affect overhead, nearly blocking out the sky.

She looked out of the windows, her head on a swivel to try to capture everything around them as Brian made a path through the trees. When they came to a clearing, other workers were already there, spreading out in every direction tagging trees with an **X** using bright orange spray paint.

"I suggest you stay in the truck. The snowpack up here is a little deeper than it is at the base camp and it would be difficult for you to maneuver when you're pint-sized. Also, although there's snow on the ground, this area does have snakes who may not appreciate you stepping on them."

She gave him a horrified look. "You can't go out there knowing you could be bitten, Brian."

There was that quick-silver grin of his which said *every little thing would be all right*. "Of course, I can," he said and got out of the truck. He pulled several cans of spray paint from the truck bed and struck out in the knee-deep snow.

When Brian returned sometime later, he laughed. KiLe sat on the roof of the truck tailor-style fighting off the cold. "What are you doing up there, kid?"

"Watching for snakes, of course. For all I know, you could have parked on top of a nest of them and they'd find some way to get into the truck. This way, I can see them before they could get to me." She huffed out a frustrated breath. "Stop laughing, Brian. It's not funny! I'm afraid of snakes."

"I hate to tell you this now, kid, but snakes can climb trees and hang from branches. However, they're more afraid of humans than we should be of them. Come on and let me help you climb down from there before a snake drops on your head. We've done all we can do today in this section. We're losing the light and from the look of those clouds, we're going to get more snow in a few hours."

KiLe looked up. It was difficult to see the sky through the trees, but she assured herself that there were no snakes above the truck. Still, she scrambled over to where Brian waited. He plucked her off the roof as if she weighed nothing and brought her into his arms. She wrapped her arms tightly around Brian's neck and her legs securely around his waist before she pulled a mean face at him. "You have to stop putting your life at risk, Brian!"

Even through the layers of clothing, her position in his arms had sparks firing his internal engine. He really needed to have sex soon with someone or he wouldn't survive the week with KiLe, he knew. Maybe Joelle, the school teacher, or Haylie, the new account manager at the bank, or maybe Susan, who owns an antique shop in Stroudsburg. These women were on his radar, but he had not made time to cultivate more than introductions, a few drinks, dinners and a friendly relationship with any of them. He had lunch with them all during periods when he came here before. He also had every intention of making time to narrow down his choice to date one of them exclusively during the time he would be here in the area this time. Now, KiLe's presence put a hold on that aspect of his plans.

Still, because KiLe's eyes and mouth were the only parts of her face visible through the ski mask she wore, his eyes dropped from hers to her cherry-colored lips. Every one of the women went out of his head. One moment he was looking at her mouth and in the next second, they were joined in the delicious tastes of each other. He slanted his mouth over hers and she opened to him while tightening her hold around his neck.

A lifetime seemed to pass as Brian leaned KiLe back against the truck. He kept telling himself he would stop kissing her in a few more seconds. Still, it took one of his men yelling, *"Get a room!"* as they were piling into their vehicles to leave the job site, before it penetrated the maelstrom in which Brian found himself. Finally, with a great deal of effort, he was able to pull his mouth away from KiLe's sweet lips.

"KiLe," he breathed, pressing his forehead to hers and closing his eyes. He was shaken with the need to mate with her and the feeling of something more. "We can't do this."

"Why not? Are you involved with Gayle? Is that what took you so long to come back to the base camp?"

"Gayle?" he questioned, frowning at her as her inquiry finally resonated. He pulled back and looked into her eyes. "No, not anymore. We broke off our relationship. We're no longer involved."

"I thought you said you weren't in a committed relationship."

His brows beetled. "That's true. I haven't been in a relationship for nearly a year."

"Then, if you and Gayle broke it off last year, are you trying to rekindle your relationship with her?"

'Whoa! Wait! That's a *hell no*. Gayle Hightower and I had a *'relationship'* back in college at UPenn, but it wasn't an exclusive one. We were more like 'friends with occasional benefits.' The flame burned brightly between us when we made time to be together until I brought her home, here to go skiing and she met Liam. She's been slowly twisting in the wind, trying to figure out how to get him to bend to her will ever since then.

"You see," he continued, "she's a bright and engaging woman, but a bit of a dominatrix in the business arena. That's a red flag for me. She thinks she can handle her intimate relationships the same way. The problem is, Liam is more aggressive in business and in his personal affairs than she. They're like two wrestlers circling each other for years, trying to figure out how to take each other down and pin one another to the mat. She believes that by becoming interested in something he enjoys, namely falconry, she'll ingratiate herself with him to the point where he can't resist her. I'm betting Liam will be patient and let her surrender to him of her own accord within the next year. They'll be married and having babies in less than two. We've all got money in the pot on when it will happen."

"Liam seems like such a patient, mild-mannered man."

"Ha!" Brian scoffed. "He gets everything done without raising his voice or anyone's ire, that's true. However, it's a façade. Still, he's a very smart man and one of the most revered businessmen in the area. Liam also has

a pedigree that reaches back to the Mayflower. That's why Mr. Hightower prefers Liam over me. He considers me a mutt because I have no history before I was eight years old when I was adopted. He tolerates me because of who my parents are.

"Gayle is a daddy's girl who has always gotten her way and whatever she wanted. She came after me in college until she met Liam. Then their relationship became this paradox: What happens when an unstoppable force meets an immovable object?"

KiLe frowned. "If she wants Liam, why was she giving you those sultry looks?"

Brian laughed. "Because she's trying to find Liam's trigger point to rattle him. She doesn't really want me. Rather, she wants to make Liam jealous. That's all. However, we're both on to her game plan and we're not playing according to the way she has it scripted." He looked at KiLe askance. "Why are you asking?"

"You're not dense, Brian," she huffed and sighed.

"No, I'm not, but you, literally, just ended a two-year relationship yesterday with Payton Bradshere."

"I know, but I never felt with him the way you make me feel when you kiss me. I like kissing you a lot more than I ever did when I kissed Payton."

"That's not a big leg up, KiLe. Considering you've kissed only two men in your adult life, you may want to sample a few more for comparison," he said wryly and mentally winced at the thought of her being in another man's arms.

"All right, then line up Danny, Pierce, and Liam and as many more men as you can find and I'll kiss each one. We'll see whether they make my heart race, my breasts peak, and my toes curl the way you make me feel when I kiss you."

He looked skeptically at her. "Uh, that's a definite no. I'm not lining up men for you to kiss. Now, get in the truck so we can get out of here before it starts to snow and we end up being snowed in on this mountain. I don't relish the idea of sleeping in the truck because we can't get safely down the roads." Even though as heated up as he felt from her words, his body temperature alone would probably keep them warm in the truck if he were buried balls deep inside her all night.

Brian arranged to drive them home in one of the Montgomery Mills' pickup trucks rather than take the snowmobile and skis. The sky was going grey, causing the light to fade earlier than normal. As a result, Brian turned on the headlights to see in the diminishing daylight. Dotting the paths they drove, KiLe could see house lights in the distance through clumps of trees and smoke rising from chimneys. Except for the presence of road signs, it really didn't appear there were roads under the surface of the snow. Indeed, when they approached the mansion, it wasn't through the front gate. Somehow, they ended up on a lower level of the mansion where a garage door opened and Brian pulled the truck inside.

When he turned off the engine, they could hear his dogs barking. They took off their headgear, got out of the truck, and climbed the steps, KiLe slower than Brian, to a door which led into a large mudroom. The dogs sat looking up at Brian, vibrating energy with their tails frantically wagging.

"You've got a good pair there," Althea commented from the kitchen about Brian's dogs.

"Have they been out for a run lately?"

"No, they haven't and I waited to feed them."

Brian looked down when he heard KiLe giggle. She was on her knees, playing with his dogs as they licked her face and tried to climb all over her. He let her play with them for a while longer while he took off his heavy outerwear. Then he opened the mudroom door to the garage and ordered the dogs out. They clamored down the steps bumping into one another in their rush and through the garage to the outside.

He reached down, offering KiLe a hand up and noticed how stiffly she moved. "Do you swim?" he asked her.

"Some, yes."

"Did you bring swimwear with you?"

"No, I didn't think it would be warm enough to swim here."

"Okay, do you think you can find your way to Laurel and Laura's room?"

KiLe nodded. "I think so, yes."

"Good. Go find a swimsuit and a cover-up in their closet to wear, then take the elevator down to **G1**, and meet me in the pool. There are signs which will point the way. We'll have a swim before dinner."

She nodded and Brian watched her trudge out of the breakfast room toward the elevators down the wide hallway. He continued to watch her until she disappeared from sight and shook his head. *Whatever was he going to do about KiLe Hakamora?* he wondered. Her toes weren't the only ones curling when they kissed. He was already at half-mast when he had her up against the truck in the woods. When he looked up, Althea was smiling at him.

"Curiouser and curiouser," she sagely said.

"What?" he asked.

"You know *'what,'* Brian Alford Jackson Montgomery. You've got feelings for that young woman and don't try to deny it. As many times as you've come up here to work and when you come to have fun with your family, not once have you brought a woman with you. The last time you did was when you came here with members of your lacrosse team, their girlfriends, and Gayle Hightower to ski during spring break while you were still in college."

"The only time you call me by all of my names, I know I must be in trouble. However, this time, I haven't done anything yet to get me in hot water. Speaking of which, I'm going to swim. Has the pool been heated?"

"Of course, it has. I took a swim just before I started making dinner, but don't think that just because you're as handsome as sin, I'll let you get away with diverting the conversation away from your behavior," she mildly scolded. "Now, I'll let your dogs in and feed them. Off with you and mind that you don't start thinking with your other head."

The woman must be a mind reader like his sister, Dena, thought Brian as he went up the steps to his suite. He had been thinking about KiLe Hakamora with the wrong part of his anatomy. However, the kisses he and KiLe shared were real enough that his feelings for her were going beyond the thought of just having sex with her. He was beginning to care about her. All other things being equal, there were no caution flags flying yet when he thought of her. She was pushing all of the right buttons for him; bright, articulate, nakedly honest, and an above-average conversationalist. Although she isn't quite comfortable in her own skin yet, she seems to know the limits of her skills and abilities.

As he pulled on a pair of swim trunks, he thought they would have time alone together to get better acquainted. He could put the sex aside to determine whether they even *"liked"* each other on a more personal level before he introduced sex into the discussion. However, it was for damn sure he wasn't a eunuch. He would not resist making love to her for two long years. He slipped his feet into his flip-flops while threading his arms into the shirt he used as a cover-up. He needed to get a few laps in to expend his excess energy before she joined him in the pool.

KiLe felt excited to be spending time with Brian. She knew she was distracting him from his work, but he didn't complain about it overmuch. He just did whatever came next on his schedule to make up for the time he lost in the sheriff's office early that morning. Then taking her cross-country skiing slowed him and Danny down in getting to the farm to see about his livestock. Then having to use the snowmobiles to try and make up time. Still, he didn't have enough time to finish tagging the trees he needed in the forest and would have to start all over again early the next morning.

She yawned and stretched while dressing for the pool. It was a good thing she found bathing suits in his sisters' closet with the tags still attached. Then, too, it was a little disheartening she could wear Brian's little sisters' clothes. Huffing out a breath, she checked her appearance in the full-length mirror and saw what she always saw. She was petite and barely weighed in at a hundred pounds. Her muscle tone was still good from her days as a gymnast, but she wasn't as curvy as she would like to be and certainly not as tall. She huffed out another frustrated breath and went to join Brian in the pool.

Brian stroked the length of the pool again and flipped to do the backstroke on his return trip. He had a nice little rhythm to his strokes, just as his dad had taught him all those years ago. He thought about it now.

Chuck Montgomery hadn't made a big deal out of the fact he couldn't swim at thirteen years old. He sat in the pool with him and talked him through the steps, just the two of them. It took a couple of months, but he conquered his fears of the water and eventually qualified as a lifeguard by age seventeen. The look on his parents' faces was pure pride when he received his certification.

He learned over the years that no matter the challenges, Chuck and Vivian Alexander Montgomery were solidly in his corner. They proved so, even more, when they gifted him, at age twenty-one, with a staggering amount of money. Because of their generosity, he never took more than one dollar a year as his salary for the work he performed or the career he created for himself. The majority of his expenses were taken care of as a member of the Alexander-Montgomery family. For the rest, he lived comfortably off the interest of the money in his personal bank accounts and investment dividends. Thanks to his academic background in business and his Uncle Gregory's guidance, he more than doubled the gift his parents gave to him by his twenty-sixth birthday. His parents trusted him to handle his business and he made it his primary objective to never disappoint them or himself.

He really is a good swimmer, thought KiLe as she sat down in one of the warm, bubbling spas adjacent to the large, eight-lane swimming pool and watched Brian cut cleanly and smoothly through the water. His body was beautiful, with broad shoulders, muscular arms, thighs, and legs. His waist was narrow leading to well-proportioned hips and a firm butt. In addition to the pronounced six-pack, he wasn't carrying an ounce of fat, just bone and muscle. She didn't notice until now that he had a five-o'clock shadow, which added to his ruggedly handsome appeal. His hair was a dark blond and a little longer than was fashionable on some men, but on Brian, it made him looked like a rock star.

Many of the Montgomery family members were musically talented. She had heard them play instruments and sing before and wondered why she hadn't noticed Brian during those jam sessions. Funny that so many things about Brian escaped her notice, but he loomed large in her thoughts now.

Brian noticed KiLe sitting in one of the build-in hot tub spas which spilled into the pool and cut across the lanes to reach her. "Don't you want to swim?"

"I'm not that good at it and this pool is pretty deep."

"Are you afraid to be in deep water?"

"I am."

"You really need to move and keep your muscles limber."

"Why?"

"You did a lot of new things today, like cross-country skiing. If you don't work out, you're going to be pretty stiff tomorrow."

"Won't sitting in this spa help?"

"It will, yes, but it's better if you exercise in this warm water."

She looked skeptically at the large pool. She could see the lane lines at the bottom of the pool on this end and the numbers indicating the depth, but not at the other.

He sensed her hesitation and held out his hand to her. "Come on, kid. I'm right here. I won't let anything happen to you."

After a long moment of consideration, she moved toward Brian. "Do you have water wings?"

"We do, yes, but we won't need them, okay? They're like training wheels on a bike. Eventually, you have to take them off."

She trusted him to keep her safe. So, holding on tightly to him, she slid into the water. She felt something on his arm and ran her fingers over it. "What's this?" she asked turning his arm so that she could see more closely. "Someone branded you?" she asked with shock in her voice.

He looked at his arm. "A part of my misspent youth."

"This looks like the emblem for Phi Beta Kappa. It's one of the oldest societies."

"It is, yes," he said but didn't admit he was also chapter president for two years of the five years he spent between college and grad school. He just got on with her swimming lesson. "Okay, that's good. Now relax and let's see what we're working with. Let's swim across the lanes for now. We don't have to go into the deeper end just yet."

"Okay, but you'll be right beside me, right?"

"I'll stick to you like glue." He watched her dog-paddle her way across the pool while he side stroked next to her. "You're doing fine."

They moved up and back several times before he began teaching her how to lengthen her strokes. She was game, but still apprehensive, so he didn't introduce the idea of swimming to the deeper end of the pool. Instead, as she mastered one task, he began to teach her another and slowly moved into deeper water. Before long, an hour passed, and she was getting tired. They climbed out of the pool and grabbed towels to dry off and terrycloth robes from a closet to wear.

"I'm heading for the sauna. Dinner should be ready shortly. You might want to dry your hair and slip into something comfortable before we eat."

"May I join you in the sauna?"

"Uh, sure, but let me put the curtain up. I usually don't wear clothes when I'm in there."

"Oh," was all she could manage to say at the thought of seeing Brian nude again. "Do we really have to have a screen?"

Brian laughed. "I don't have a problem with it, but I don't imagine you've been completely naked in front of a man before."

"You're right, I haven't, but I'm not afraid to let you see me without clothes."

Funny, he had never had a problem with nudity in front of a woman or seeing naked women before without wanting to have sex with them. However, KiLe might be the exception.

This was truly going to be a challenge to keep his hands off KiLe in a hot sauna when they were both naked. He turned on the sauna, set the thermostat and timer, before entering the room. Pulling a curtain that bisected the space, he was giving privacy to both sides of the chamber. It was paneled in decay-resistant, thick Cedar, and rich in color with natural oils. All of the walls and benches were Kiln dried by Liam at the Montgomery Mills.

He opened the door to find KiLe waiting. "Okay, you can come in now, KiLe. I've set the curtain so that you will have complete privacy."

"Thanks, Brian. I haven't been in a sauna since I came to America. This one is really nice and spacious."

"You're welcome. Make yourself comfortable. I'm going to lower the lights. The temperature is regulated automatically and the timer is set for thirty minutes. If it gets too warm for you, there's a bucket of cool water by the bench."

"I'll be fine," she said and went quiet for a few moments.

Brian could hear her disrobe as he did the same and stretched out on his back on a bench. He closed his eyes, stacked his hands behind his head, and relaxed.

"Brian?"

"Yes," he answered without opening his eyes or moving a muscle.

"You remember when you said you would tell me about the Alexander-Jackson-Montgomery saga someday?"

"Yes, I remember, but I'm not going to tell you now. Neither one of us has had a lot of sleep. We had to hit the ground running this morning. We have all week to talk. It's time to relax and shut off your mind."

"Okay, but don't forget you said you would tell me."

"I won't forget. Now rest."

"Okay."

Brian let the sweat bring out the impurities in his skin and then turned over to lay on his stomach. He was having difficulty with the fact that KiLe lay a short distance away completely nude. He could see her in his mind's eye as she was in his sister's swimwear and tried desperately to think of her as he would one of his sisters. That worked only for a short period before his need to mate caused his blood to warm. He consciously shut down and tuned out the world until the buzzer sounded.

Taking a towel from a rack, he dried his face and slipped back into his robe before he called out to KiLe. When she didn't answer, he peeked around the curtain and found her sound asleep and lightly snoring.

CHAPTER 9

When KiLe woke, it was broad daylight or as much daylight as she could see through the curtain of fluffy white snow falling on the terrace, furniture, and plants outside her floor-to-ceiling movable glass wall. Even though she couldn't see the vistas, the snow was beautiful and pristine.

Then it dawned on her. She had been in the sauna with Brian as the last thing she remembered. Now she was in the bedroom suite next to his and wearing her Georgetown University sleep shirt. She couldn't remember anything between the time she was in the sauna and now, but she was definitely hungry.

She showered and dried her hair before she dressed and knocked on the adjoining door, which led into Brian's suite. When she heard nothing, she opened the door and went inside. The bed was made, but Brian wasn't in the suite. Finding her way down the back stairs, she went into the breakfast room and found Althea having coffee and reading a magazine.

"Well, top of the morning ta ya," Althea jokingly said. "What can I get for you to eat?"

"Thanks, Honorable Aunt Althea. I'll wait for Brian before I eat."

"*Ha!*" she barked a laugh. "Brian's been gone since oh-dark-thirty this morning. I don't expect he'll be back much before dark tonight. He had one of Pierce's trucks, so he had to pick him up on the way to the base camp."

"In the snow?" KiLe asked, surprised.

"Sure. A little bit of snow don't usually stop anything up here in the mountains. We're lucky if we get three to four good months without snow falling on this elevation. We're way above sea level here."

"I didn't know. In that case, whatever is easiest is fine with me. I'm not a picky eater and I don't have food allergies."

"Okay, would you like breakfast or lunch?"

KiLe's brows drew together in confusion. "What time is it?"

"Oh, it's about ten-thirty, I'd say."

KiLe's eyes popped wide in disbelief, causing Althea to laugh.

"Settle down and have a cup of coffee, tea or cocoa. There are several types by the Keurig and condiments, too, on the beverage bar. I'll bring something for you in a few moments." So saying, Althea left the breakfast salon.

KiLe did as suggested and brewed a nice hot cup of black coffee. She settled at the table where Althea was reading. When she sat down, she noticed what looked like Brian's picture in the magazine. Even upside down, she recognized him. She picked it up and turned back to the beginning of the article, which was about the new fall men's clothing line by famous, high-fashion designers. Brian was featured in three photos wearing different ensembles. He was drop-dead gorgeous in each shot even among some of the more famous male models she recognized. He had real charisma and sex appeal.

"Have you seen that before?" Althea came back in with a tray of piping hot pancakes with a rasher of bacon and a selection of hot fruit toppings and syrups.

"No, uh, no, I haven't," but her eyes were on the large brunch variety laid out before her. "Wow," she said on a reverent breath and breathed in the food's aroma.

Althea laughed at her antics and settled with a fresh cup of coffee to keep her company while she ate.

"Brian never mentioned that he's a male model."

"Actually, he isn't. Not professionally anyway. He was forced to pose because he lost a poker game with the magazine's owner, Bill Chandler."

"Um," KiLe had to cover her mouth and chew. The food was just that good. "I know Bill. He lives in Whitney's parents' Georgetown brownstone in Washington, DC, with us. Even though six students are living there, three women and three men, Bill kind of looks out for us when he's in town. He's a sports and entertainment attorney with clients all over the world. He also produces movies, owns and operates two magazines, has a line of men's wear, and models when the mood strikes him or when it's for a worthy cause.

"What I didn't know is that he got Brian to pose for him."

"It wasn't easy. That's for sure. Brian isn't the type of man who craves the limelight."

"He's apparently a *bona fide* gentleman, too. He must have put me to bed last night."

"He carried you up to your suite and called me to dress you for bed. Once you were tucked in for the night, he came down here and had dinner with Danny and me. We talked with his parents, grandparents, and siblings to assure them that he is all right after his ordeal with the robbers. Then we played cards for a while and watched television before everyone went to bed."

"I slept through all of that."

"Brian said you had very little sleep the day you arrived and he dragged you all over creation all day yesterday. He figured you really needed the rest."

"He's right. I was more tired than I realized. He's really good about things like that, isn't he? I mean, he pays attention and he's very intuitive. He knew I had never skied before and took the time to make sure I didn't wake up this morning feeling like the Wreck of the Hesperus."

"He does, yes," Althea agreed. "He's always been a responsible person, especially when it comes to looking out for the welfare of his family and the people he works with and manages. He's a good boss."

Understanding dawned. "You work for Brian?" KiLe asked.

"I do, yes, but he makes it feel like I work **with** him. I was in the war and, when I retired and came home, I didn't have a clue or a plan about what I was going to do with myself. Brian used to come here a lot when he was in college and grad school. Sometimes he'd bring his pals with him, but not always. He would come see me at this little house I used to live in with my parents and my sister. All were gone then and I was alone. Everyone seemed to be under the impression that after being in the Army, I wanted to be left alone. The next thing I know, my nephew, Chuck, came by and he and my other nieces and nephews moved me out of that sad little place and into this mansion. Sometimes Vivian and Chuck let close friends come here to use it. The Chief Justice of the Supreme Court and his family love it here. They're frequent visitors. Now, some member of the family is in or out of this house all the time. Chuck made me the property manager and I've enjoyed every moment of it. I know it was Brian who instigated it. He won't admit it, but he won't lie to me and tell me he didn't have a hand in convincing his father to hire me here. So, I know exactly what you mean when you say he pays attention. He's just like his daddy. I love him and all of my sister's family as if they were my very own."

"What was he like as a kid?" KiLe was warming to the subject of Brian Montgomery.

"Shorter," Althea laughed.

KiLe laughed, too, and they continued to chat, getting better acquainted.

"So, you never married?" KiLe asked later in the conversation.

Althea shrugged. "Stephen Montgomery and I were high school sweethearts. After graduation, he wanted to get married while he was in trade school to become a mechanic. However, I wanted to see a bit of the world before I settled down. So, I enlisted in the Army. When I came home for a visit four years later, Stephen had married my younger sister, Esther. They already had three stair-step children, Bob, Errol, Frederick, and John was on the way. I couldn't even be mad because I was the one who chose to leave and not agree to a committed relationship. So, I left again and didn't return until I got word that my sister had died suddenly of an aneurysm. She and Stephen had a good life together, raising their four children to be upstanding citizens. I didn't know them and although Esther told them about me, they had never met me until the funeral.

"It took years for us to develop any type of close relationship and, with Stephen's help, we're closer now. Then Stephen announced he was in love again. This time with Harriet Jackson. She, her husband, and seven children moved here from Philadelphia while I was away in the war. You see, Chuck and his brothers used to go into Philadelphia to work as carpenters, electricians, plumbers, masons, and to perform other construction work on inner-city projects. They lived at the job site in their mobile homes. Chuck is the youngest boy. When he was out of school for the summer, his brothers took him with them to fetch and carry and to clean up the construction sites every day. However, when Chuck should have been working, he used to go watch the kids play basketball on an outdoor court near where he and his brothers were working and living. He was only nine years old at the time, but big and strong for his age. He didn't know how to play the game, but one day this kid threw the ball to Chuck and asked him if he wanted to learn to play. The kid was twelve-year-old Derrick Jelon Jackson. Even at a very young age, Derrick was as good as Wilt Chamberlain and Kobe Bryant who were also from Philadelphia.

"Derrick worked with Chuck every day on the basketball court and taught Chuck how to become an expert player. As a result, Derrick and Chuck became the best of friends. They were like a salt-and-pepper Frick and Frack. After a while, you didn't see one without the other. When summer ended, Stephen and Esther invited Derrick to visit them and Chuck at the farm on the weekends. Eventually, the families became very close. So close that my nephew, Bob, married the Jackson's oldest girl, Sheila. That led to Stephen and Esther's decision to sell Montgomery acreage to the Jackson family.

"When Grover Jackson, a former Marine and Mississippi farmer, retired from the Philadelphia Post Office, he, his wife Harriet, and their children built a farmhouse here and moved in. They were the only people of color in the community. It took a while, but they did very well farming their land and fitting into the community. Harriet opened a new beauty salon and spa offering services, including facials, manicures, and pedicures, in addition to cutting and styling hair, which the other salons didn't offer. I was a barber in the service and Harriet hired me on.

"In the interim, nationally, Chuck and Derrick became two of the top basketball players in high school, college, and in the pros. They were the Gale Sayers and Brian Piccolo of the NBA; closer than brothers."

"Until they fell in love with the same young woman," KiLe surmised. "Vivian Alexander."

"True, but that didn't end their friendship."

"Because, like Brian Piccolo, Derrick and Chuck knew Derrick had a serious heart condition," KiLe reasoned.

"He did, yes. Derrick had to leave professional basketball when he was at the top of his game. Chuck shortly followed because a man who is almost seven feet tall couldn't keep playing at least eighty games a season and not have irreparable knee injury and pain. After they retired from professional sports, they went to medical school and became doctors. Derrick was a pediatrician and pediatric surgeon. He developed some type of webbing system, hardware, and software, which revolutionized pediatric medicine. Chuck became the Chief of Emergency Services at Georgetown Medical Center in Washington, DC. They were both multimillionaires as athletes, but Derrick's invention shot him into the billionaires' club. Not that it mattered to either one of them what material things they had. They continued to think of themselves as two country boys temporarily away from the farm." Althea smiled at the memory.

"Were they so close that Chuck sacrificed his love for Vivian because Derrick loved her too?"

"That's exactly what happened. Brian's not the only one who listens and reads between the lines. You're very intuitive, too, KiLe."

"I'm an incurable romantic. Theirs is such an incredible love story. The three of them must have had a forever kind of love to be that close."

"They did and still do. You can see it in the children they continue to adopt and the ones which are natural-born to them. They have this boundless kind of love that affects any and everyone who knows them. Chuck and Vivian are each other's best friend and an unbreakable unit. Brian, when he commits to a woman, will have 'a forever kind of love' to share, too."

KiLe got the point. It was a veiled instruction not to mistreat her grandnephew, Brian. Much like the warning Whitney issued a few days earlier. They were a close-knit family and very protective of one another. She nodded in understanding to Althea before the older woman rose to clear away the brunch dishes.

"Is there anything I can do to help?"

"Not unless you want to bathe Brian's dogs. They've been out playing in the snow and mud and now they're filthy," Althea laughed.

KiLe's brows drew together. "I've never washed an animal. What do I have to do?"

"Come with me. I'll show you."

KiLe followed Althea into the mudroom and then through another door where a shower stall with a low wall and glass door were located.

"This is where Brian usually washes his dogs," Althea instructed. "When it was a hotel, this was a kennel where guests could board their pets while they stayed here."

"Well, I guess this couldn't be very difficult." KiLe sighed as she looked down into Starsky's and Hutch's soulful brown eyes. They sat impatiently at her feet, wagging their tails.

"I suggest you change into something you don't mind getting wet. Dogs tend to shake the water off their bodies without a care about who could get soaked," Althea suggested.

KiLe changed into the same swimsuit she wore the night before and soon after began washing the frisky, muddy dogs. An hour and a half later, Althea couldn't contain her laughter. She took a lot of pictures because KiLe looked as if she was the one out playing in the snow and mud, but the dogs were clean and dry. Their midnight black fur was glossy and soft to the touch. KiLe brushed and dried them with a hairdryer. The dogs looked as if they adored her every touch.

"Okay, boys, you stay clean. Now I have to go take another shower," she directed.

"You did a good job, KiLe, but now I'm afraid to let them out because they'll just go play in the mud again."

"Maybe, I can take them for a walk out the front door. There isn't any mud that I saw out there."

"You may have a good thought there," Althea agreed.

"Okay, at least it's stopped snowing. I'll go get cleaned up, change clothes, and take them for a walk."

"Sounds like a plan. I'll get dinner started while you're out."

CHAPTER 10

"We better call it a day," said Pierce. "We've got sleet and icy conditions on the roads in the upper elevations. If this keeps up, the crews will have to walk down the mountain."

"Agreed," said Brian. "We've done as much as we can today. Let's call it a wrap and hope we have better weather conditions tomorrow." He went to the horn and gave it several blasts signaling the end of the workday.

"You going to make it to the bowling alley tonight?" asked Liam of Brian.

"If it's not that bad at the lower elevations, I'll be there."

"Be sure to bring my future ex-wife when you come, Brian," called Danny.

Brian snorted a laugh. "Why don't you come to the house and invite her yourself?"

"And have you kick my ass six ways to Sunday? Not on a bet, pal." Danny laughed.

"Yeah, you got that right," added Liam.

"Our Danny Boy is going to have at least two of his current three female friends in attendance at the bowling alley tonight. Get your tickets early for the show. You bring the popcorn, Brian," teased Pierce.

Whereupon Danny flipped his brother the bird, good-naturedly, of course, before they climbed into their trucks with the other departing crew members and left the base camp.

Brian pulled into one of the garages at Point of View thirty minutes later. Fortunately, at this elevation, the temperature seemed to be hovering just above the freezing point, so the roads were passable. Still, he hefted a couple of fifty-pound bags of sand and placed them in the flatbed of his truck. He didn't want to get stuck on the road if the temperature dropped and turned the melting snow to ice.

Then it hit him. He hadn't heard his dogs when he pulled in. That was strange. Usually, they sent up a racket when they heard him enter the garage, so he took the stairs two at a time. When he entered the mudroom, the dogs were nowhere in sight.

"I'm home, Aunt Althea," Brian called out. He was chilled to the bone. The inside heat enveloped him like a warm blanket **causing a tingling and prickling sensation all over the body** the moment he stepped inside.

"You're early. Something wrong?" Althea came forward, wiping her hands on a towel.

"No, just icy conditions, freezing rain, and sleet. It's about five, maybe ten degrees colder up there than it is at this elevation, so we called it a day." Brian hugged her and kissed her on her temple.

"Good thinking. I should have dinner ready in about an hour. You have time for a swim if you want."

"Maybe I will. Where are my dogs? I didn't see them out back."

"KiLe took them out front for a walk. Remind me to show you some pictures when you come down for dinner. For now, come on while we have time and let me cut your hair."

Twenty minutes later, Althea handed a mirror to him. "You know I don't need that." He passed the mirror back to her. Running his fingers through his hair, he knew it was just as he liked it. She was a very good barber and sometimes worked at Harriet Jackson Montgomery's salon. He got the broom and swept up the hair and put it in the trash, before hugging her.

"KiLe should have been back in here by now. Maybe you should go see about her."

"Okay." He headed toward the front of the mansion. When he reached the front, he noticed KiLe in the distance shaking her finger at his dogs as if scolding them and then she pointed to the house as if to direct them to go in that direction, but they just lay on the wet blacktop and rolled over exposing their bellies for a rub. This, apparently, exasperated KiLe because she continued to scold them while they continued to play and beg to have their bellies rubbed.

It was comical, so he stood back out of sight and watched the show. He would have stayed longer, but it was cold outside and she wasn't making headway with getting his dogs to follow her instructions. So, he whistled and Starsky and Hutch took off racing toward him as if shot from a cannon. Momentarily KiLe stood with her fists on her hips shaking her head before she walked toward him.

Something about that face of hers and that body just did it for him. He could see she was cross and fussing, but as she drew closer, he just pulled her in and covered her mutinous mouth with his. After a moment's surprise and hesitation, she melted into his embrace and the world for him spun off its axis again.

When he pulled free of her lips, she looked up at him, her eyes shining and a grin edging her kewpie-doll mouth. "Well, hello, sailor. Do you come here often?"

He put his forehead against hers and closed his eyes. "What in the world am I going to do about you, KiLe Hakamora?" he rhetorically asked.

Still, she answered. "Shut up and kiss me again?"

So, he did, for long moments of bliss just enjoying the feel of his mouth on her and running his tongue against hers. It took time to realize that his cell phone was buzzing and vibrating in his pocket. In a fog, he broke off the kiss, looked down into KiLe's eyes as she steadily looked up into his, and reached for his phone. "Montgomery," he answered.

"Brian, it's Pierce. I stopped by the barns on my way home. We're definitely missing some livestock. If the weather is good tomorrow, I've asked Kadijah to take me up to search for them."

"How many do you think?"

"Six to twelve. Doc finished the exams and the injections. At least six are missing."

"Okay, there's not much we can do on the ground, so I'll help coordinate from the barns with a recount."

"Solid. I know this screws up our schedules. It just seems like we can't catch a break. If it's not the weather, it's the stock."

"We'll figure it out, Pierce."

"Yeah, but at what cost?"

"It's done for today. We can't go back and do anything about it now. We can do only what comes next."

"Yeah, you're right. I'll see you later at the bowling alley?"

"I'll be there," he said and disconnected.

"What's wrong, Brian? You look worried."

"We're missing at least six cows. I have to change my plans for tomorrow and work with a recount of the livestock."

"What do you think happened to them?"

"I don't want to speculate. We'll figure it out tomorrow. Come on. Let's go in. I need to shower and change before dinner." With that, he opened the front door and whistled his dogs inside. He usually didn't bring his dogs in through the front door, but he had his concerns about what might be going on. He didn't want his dogs outside for the rest of the night unless he was with them.

"Do you want me to hold your soap?" KiLe teased.

"Cut it out, Imp," he scolded, but he liked the idea a little too much for his comfort.

Brian thought he would bust his gut laughing. The pictures and video Althea showed to him of KiLe washing his dogs were hilarious. There was more soap foam on her than on the dogs. She was covered in mud splatter from head to toe, as was every surface in the kennel bath. It was a good thing he had to hose down only the tile.

"...and then, after all the work I did, those two went right out and rolled in the mud and snow again," she fussed.

That explained why she was scolding Starsky and Hutch in the middle of the driveway, Brian thought, but could not stop laughing.

"Then they start running around like crazed animals and jumping into the snowbanks getting wet. Although their coats are black, the snow was so deep, I couldn't even see them until they jumped up and started running into more snow again. They were like Jacks-in-the-box. Suddenly, they would just jump up out of nowhere and scare me half to death. Your dogs are crazy," she huffed.

"They're still puppies and prone to play. They did the same thing when I raked leaves into piles around the cabin. They run from one pile to another completely covering themselves and creating havoc. If I didn't see them jump into the piles of leaves, I wouldn't have known they were under there."

"Still, all that work was for nothing," she stewed.

"It's the thought that counts." Though sincerely meant, he took one more look at the pictures and burst out laughing again. She looked at the pictures with him and laughed, too. Still, the idea stuck with him that, although she had never done it before, she actually washed his dogs. No woman he ever dated would have done that. He was already getting in deep before she did that. Now, he could only acknowledge his feelings for her were spiraling out of his control.

The Roll-a-Rama was what passed for high entertainment in the community on a Monday night. Although the parking lot was crowded, most of the cars and trucks belonged to Montgomery employees and their families. If they tried to have this roll-off on a Friday or Saturday night, it would never happen. Bowling leagues took up most of the lanes on the weekends and many nights during the week.

They were early enough, so Brian found a relatively dry parking space right up front where someone was leaving. He got out of the truck and skirted the bumper to open the front and back doors of his truck for his aunt and KiLe to step down to the running board and then the ground. He made sure there was no ice in their path. Then he gathered his and his aunt's bowling bags and hefted them to the front door. They joined others who were arriving and waved to a group he knew as they were leaving.

Once inside, the noise level was horrendous. Bowling balls cracked against ten pins and duckpins in rapid succession. Bells and whistles went off on the pinball machines and electronic games lined up against the back wall across from the bowling lanes. Almost all of the twenty or so pool and air-hockey tables were occupied with games underway. Table tennis matches were mob scenes. Over that chaos, orders for food rang out via the sound system and patrons came on the double to pick up their pizzas, hot Buffalo wings, hamburgers, spare ribs, French fries, tater-tots, blooming onions, onion rings, hot dogs and any manner of other artery-clogging finger foods. Hostesses hefted ten to twenty bottles of beer and cups of cold sodas on wide trays while teens, working for pocket change, bussed tables, swept or vacuumed carpeted floors along the expansive interior.

Noise reverberated off the relatively low ceilings when children, on an adrenalin rush of candy and sweet sodas, ran helter-skelter playing raucous games, screaming at the top of their voices, and bobbing and weaving between people headed to some other location in the madness. Lights brightly flashed when anyone made a strike making it hard to explain that KiLe needed to get bowling shoes in order to be permitted to play.

She had never been in a bowling alley, pool hall or old-fashioned pinball machine arena before. There was also a room where a Bingo game was underway and another room where the people were playing cards or board games like chess, checkers or backgammon. Her eyes were wide trying to capture it all, so Brian had to use hand signals to guide her through the process.

They successfully got a pair of new bowling shoes for her in the equipment shop. Brian bought a new pair for her rather than have her rent a pair that had been worn by too many other sweaty feet to count. Then came the selection of a bowling ball. She liked the jade green agate one for its pretty color without regard for its weight or size.

"It is believed in Chinese tradition that green jade symbolized the five virtues of humanity, which are courage, modesty, justice, compassion, and wisdom. Therefore, having this piece of stone will also imbue its wearer with these gifts," KiLe stated proudly.

"However, you're not Chinese. You're Japanese as you staunchly remind everyone," said Brian, which earned him an elbow to his solar plexus from KiLe. He didn't argue the fine points with her any further. Instead, he simply purchased the jade green ball she wanted and had her small hands fitted for the boring machine to calculate the three holes for her thumb and fingers to fit comfortably. He kept his mouth firmly closed as she selected a pink bowling bag to hold all of her brand-new gear.

Once she was properly outfitted, Brian guided KiLe down the long, wide promenade past row after row of bowling lanes until he found where his name and hers were listed on the overhead lit scoreboard. Liam was already there and bending his arm with a cold beer in his hand. Brian sat at a round table to take off his boots and put on his bowling shoes. The table sat ten and was behind the step-down pit area which led to the lanes. KiLe followed suit, changing out her street shoes. Althea came up to the table after rolling a few practice balls and passed a key to him. He took his boots, KiLe's and their coats to the locker and put everything inside pocketing the key while Althea took KiLe into the pit at the scorekeeper's table to show her how the game is played.

"Mr. Montgomery? Brian Montgomery?"

"Yes?"

"I'd like to interview—."

"I don't give interviews."

"This is about—"

"No comment."

"But—."

"No comment."

Getting the attention of the waitress for their area, Brian ignored the reporter and ordered food and drink to be delivered after everyone arrived. When he looked up, Danny was approaching with a helpless expression on his face and escorting two women, one of whom Brian knew because he had taken her out for coffee, a couple of dinners and drinks the last time he was in town.

Oh, joy, he silently lamented. Now he knew the reason for his cousin's pained expression.

"Yo, cousin, you remember Mary Louise and her friend, Haylie Leverette, don't you?"

"Of course. How are you, Mary Louise, Haylie?" he asked and watched as Danny rolled his eyes to the ceiling behind the women's backs in an obvious show of distress.

"Fine, Brian," said Mary Louise. "We heard you were in town again. Everyone is talking about how you and your dogs apprehended all those guys after a big shootout in a gas station over in Hazelton."

"Uh, it wasn't a shoot-out, really, and it was only three guys. Just one shot was fired, but I'm glad it wasn't worse."

"People are calling you a hero, Brian," said Haylie, admiration in her voice and speaking for the first time. "It was my brother-in-law's third cousin's husband who was shot. He was working a part-time job he needed to pay for braces for his middle son's teeth. He said you saved his arm and his life."

"I didn't do that much. I'm just glad he's all right," he said and noticed Danny leading Mary Louise away. He appeared to be deserting the field or trying to find a secluded corner. He, apparently, needed to talk his way out of a sticky situation with Mary Louise because his other girlfriend Marla Baines was closely observing the situation.

Brian made a mental note to follow up on the guy who was shot and his son's need for costly dental work. Haylie's voice brought him out of his musings about the wounded store clerk.

"He was interviewed in the newspaper and by the local cable television company in Stroudsburg. Did you see it?"

"Uh, no, I missed it," he said and absently scratched the back of his head embarrassed. "I've, uh, been a little busy since I hit town yesterday."

She stepped up into his personal space. "Is that why you haven't called me? You were too busy? I thought we started something, Brian."

"I'm sorry for it, Haylie, but it's the truth. I've been behind schedule since I arrived Sunday morning and that little dust up at the gas station just delayed things more."

"So, the rumors are not true that you brought some oriental, high school girl with you this trip?"

That put his back up, but his face remained unreadable. "The rumors are mistaken. KiLe Hakamora is a Japanese national. She's in her last year of college at Georgetown University, not high school, and she's well over the age of consent. She just ended a two-year relationship with someone who was important to her and needed a break. She also happens to be an incredible songstress and a housemate of my cousin, Whitney Alexander. You remember Whitney, don't you, Haylie? KiLe is a close friend of hers… and mine."

That seemed to set Haylie back on her heels a step or two, he thought. It also dropped her off his list of women with whom he considered taking their relationship to another level. Backbiting women were appreciated only when they were between the sheets, not when they were willing to castigate someone they didn't even know for no good reason.

"If you'll excuse me, please, Haylie, I need to get some practice in before we start the tournament. It was good to see you. Take care of yourself." He didn't wait for her response or offer more before he turned away and walked down into the pit where his grand aunt and KiLe sat discussing how the scoring worked.

He took one bowling ball from his bag and put it in a polishing cloth bag to roll it around before setting it on the return rails. He did the same with the second ball and then pulled on his leather wrist and hand brace. He could feel Haylie's eyes on him, but he didn't look up in her direction to acknowledge her. He also spotted the reporter on a cellphone clearly upset and animatedly arguing with someone on the other end of the call. When he picked up the first ball, aimed, and then hurled it down the hardwood lane toward the pins, he turned his back before it struck because he knew it would be a strike the second it left his fingers. The second ball was the same as were the third and fourth even after he changed lanes. Either he was in a zone or he needed to burn off a mad or two. Whatever it was, it was working.

"*Whoa!* Man, you were zoning tonight," boasted Danny two hours later as he handed over Brian's share of the winning pot of money. "Scoring two-seventy is sweet," he said and then looked around to ensure no one else was listening. "Sorry about earlier. I didn't tell Mary Louise you were going to be bowling tonight. I didn't even tell her *I* was bowling tonight because I had a date with Marla. Mary Louise heard you were in town and checked around with others on the job site who knew you were going to be here. Then, of course, she gets on the phone to Haylie. They picked up my sister, Molly, and were lying in wait when I got here with Marla. You can imagine how that went over." He rolled his eyes, frustrated.

"No big thing, but I wonder how that newspaper guy knew I would be here?"

"No clue, but some of the guys mentioned that he and some other reporters have been nosing around trying to get info on you."

"I don't understand why. The robbery isn't a big deal, even in Monroe County."

"You know how it is, Brian. Anytime there's a Montgomery's name in print or on screen, especially about one of Chuck-the-basketball-icon's kids, it brings out the sneaks, peeks, and snoopers. They start coming out of the woodwork with claims too numerous to count."

"Yeah, I do know. I hope that's the last I'll hear of this 'hero' foolishness."

"Not when all you kept saying is 'no comment' to every question he asked you. Trust and believe there will be more inquiries."

"I'll be glad when this whole thing is over…"

"What 'whole thing'?" Molly Montgomery, the younger sister of Liam, Pierce, Danny, and Anderson asked. She plopped down, straddled Brian's lap, looped her arms around his neck, and tried to kiss him on the mouth.

"Nothing," he said. He tried to lift her to her feet and extricate himself from her grasp. "Up with you, kid," he said just as he spotted KiLe returning from the restroom with Althea.

"Oh, so now I'm not good enough for a kissing cousin either?" she lambasted him. "You just dumped poor Haylie, who was sure you'd put a ring on it before Christmas and have you wedded and bedded by spring next year. Now you won't kiss me?"

"It has nothing to do with her and it wasn't that deep between Haylie…" he began before she tightened her grip, swooped in, and ravished his mouth. He pried her arms away, breaking her hold on him and stood forcing her off his lap.

"Stop it, Molly," Danny harshly scolded.

She menacingly turned toward Danny. "You can't tell me what to do! You're not my father…or are you?"

"That's enough, Molly," Brian demanded in censure.

"Same goes for you, Brian, whoever the hell you think you are. You're not my father, but you think you're better than me. Yet, you bring your chink here, parading her around like she's not a slut. Hell, just like me, you're not even a real Montgomery!"

"Stop that this minute, young lady!" thundered Althea, the tone of her voice drawing attention from people in close proximity.

"Fuck you and the horse you rode in on, bitch."

The slap was loud, swift, and stunning. Molly stood stock still and mute, shock covering her face as she palmed her red cheek.

Althea grabbed Molly's wrist, pulling it away from her face, but holding on tightly to her. "Understand me, little girl. I am your grand aunt and I love you dearly, but if you ever speak to me or anyone of mine with that nasty tone and filthy mouth of yours again, I'll slap the taste out of your mouth and tan your hide. Do you hear me?"

Molly nodded as tears flowed down her face.

"Good! Now apologize!"

"I'm sorry," she blubbered.

"That will do for now. Go wash your face and blow your nose," Althea ordered.

Molly fled into the restroom, her cries loud in her wake.

"Have you got her?" Althea asked Danny.

"Yes, Ma'am," Danny answered. "I'm sorry, Aunt Althea. She didn't really mean what she said to you. I'll make sure she gets home."

"Good. Now, come on, Brian. I'm ready to go," Althea said and marched with military precision toward the exit just as Liam and Pierce came back into the building and headed to the table.

"What's wrong?" Althea asked, noticing the anger displayed on her grandnephews' faces.

"Someone slashed our tires and the gas caps are off," Liam announced.

Others who were still getting over the shock of Molly's behavior and Althea's swift punishment turned and headed for the exit, Brian included.

CHAPTER 11

"I guess I got here at about six-thirty," Danny reported to Sheriff's Deputy David Turner while officers interviewed other victims. "That's about right, isn't it, Brian?"

"I think so. Grandaunt Althea, KiLe, and I arrived, at least, thirty minutes before you, so that sounds about right. I really wasn't paying attention to the time. I was busy getting KiLe outfitted so that she could bowl with us. I can check the time of the receipt for KiLe's outfit." He dug it out of his wallet and handed it to the deputy. "Grandaunt Althea may have a better idea of the time since she picked up the lane assignments and got a locker for our coats and boots."

"Can you think of any reason someone would pour sugar into your gas tanks and slash only the tires of the Montgomerys' trucks and people associated with you?" Deputy Turner asked.

Danny and Brian looked at one another. Danny shrugged. "I can't think of anyone unless it's retaliation for what Brian did to apprehend members of the gang from Wilkes-Barre."

"Has anything else happened?" the deputy asked.

"Not that I'm aware of at the moment," Brian offered. "Still, it had to be someone who knows us and knows the people who work with us. You're right. It was only our vehicles which were vandalized."

"Well," Danny hedged, reluctant to bring it up. "Haylie is pretty steamed with you. I think she would know all of the Montgomery family and our employees' vehicles on sight."

"Maybe, but so do Mary Louise and Marla," said Brian. "They're not singing your praises right now, Danny, but I don't see any of them as the type to go around vandalizing cars and trucks. They know every family here tonight and I'm sure they wouldn't want to leave these families, and especially not the children, stranded on a cold night like this. For these people, their vehicles are critical to their livelihoods. I don't believe Mary Louise or Marla would do this to people they grew up with all of their lives."

"Yeah, you're right. Still, don't forget about that newspaper guy. He was spitting nails when you wouldn't speak with him."

"A member of the media tried to interview you, Brian?" Deputy Turner asked.

"Without success," Brian nodded.

"If he didn't do it, maybe he saw something. What is his name?" the deputy asked.

"I have no clue. I'm sure he said his name and the name of his news organization, but the noise level in here is pretty high. I didn't try to hear him, but he's not someone I've seen before. If Grandaunt Althea, Liam, Pierce, and Danny didn't recognize him, he's not from around here."

"Still, I'll see whether his face is captured on the security cameras in here or whether anyone else recognized him." The deputy folded close the little book he used to record his notes. "That's all for now. I'll follow up with you when or if we find out more.

"I believe Sheriff Montgomery arranged for the county school buses to take all of you home."

"He did, yes, Deputy Turner." Brian shook the man's hand.

The deputy pulled them in closer and furtively looked around before he whispered. "I understand that your sister, Molly, got a little rowdy, Danny, and that Ms. Hardyston took her down a peg or two. Do you think there's any connection between that and what happened here tonight?"

Danny shook his head, frustrated. "It's a family matter, but we learned what happened just after the dustup between Molly and Grandaunt Althea. Molly hasn't left our sight since Liam and Pierce came in to tell us what happened. She came with Mary Louise and Haylie. They arrived after Brian, but before I got here."

"I know this is sensitive information. I won't inquire unless the facts lead us toward that direction."

"Thanks for your discretion, Deputy," said Brian in parting. "We'll just chalk it up to the Ides of March, like this freakish weather we've been having." He and Danny turned and walked back toward the table where a different deputy finished interviewing KiLe and Althea.

KiLe positioned herself so she could see Brian while he and Danny were being interviewed by the same deputy who helped them at the sheriff's office the day before. She and Althea sat at a table with a sullen Molly and answered questions from a different sheriff's deputy. KiLe was still reeling from the vicious argument between Molly Montgomery and Althea. She was introduced to many of Brian's family members who were warm, welcoming people, but had yet to be introduced to the young woman who caused the embarrassing commotion. The lip-lock Molly laid on Brian was indelibly etched in her mind. *They were cousins, right?* KiLe tried to assure herself. She had come to understand that the Montgomerys are a tightly-knit family with close, loyal friends and employees, but not backwoods people who intermarried among family members.

A number of Brian's uncles and cousins were there with their families or significant others. Of the ones she met, the married ones seemed to have married people from other places outside Monroe County. They were all such a very handsome group of men, who the women, young and old alike, gravitated toward. She witnessed the number of women who made it their mission to catch the eye of at least one of the Montgomery men, particularly those trying to snag Brian's attention. Even Seth Montgomery, Brian's granduncle, was eye candy, she noted as she watched Brian speaking quietly with him.

"That's good of you, Brian," said Seth. "The store clerk will be okay. The bullet did damage a nerve, though. He could use the help you're offering. I'll take care of it for you."

"Thanks, Uncle Seth. However, I'd appreciate it if you didn't mention to him where the money is coming from."

"Mum's the word. Don't worry. I'll find out what dentist or dental clinic the family uses and let you know. It shouldn't be that hard. There aren't that many in the county."

"Thanks," Brian said as he and Seth parted.

KiLe was impressed with the way Brian handled himself and recognized that she was being overly sensitive because of her recent experience with Payton Bradshere. He was handsome too and a band member who developed a following of groupies. Not as many as Tucker Cavanaugh, but enough to be noticeable. Still, Payton relished the attention women paid to him, unlike Tucker, who found every excuse to avoid the women who came onto him. He was recently subjected to a female stalker, who was obsessed with him and nearly got him killed. KiLe understood that with men, like Tucker, once they fell in love, no other woman had a chance of gaining their attention.

As she watched Brian approach the table with Danny, she was placing him in that category with Tucker and on that same type of pedestal, too. As with Tucker, there was no doubt about Brian's rugged sex appeal and understated charisma, so that when he cast his gaze on her and held it, she went uncharacteristically damp in her nether regions and her breasts peaked and pebbled. He had a confidence in his stride that didn't approach arrogance. Rather, it was purposeful, as if he knew who he was and was okay with what he saw in the mirror each day. She was more than pleased with what she saw, too.

Other teams were beginning their games. So, since the bowlers from earlier were stuck waiting for alternative transportation, all of the tables were crowded.

Brian pulled a chair from another table and straddled it backward directly behind where KiLe sat. She turned sideways in her seat and looked into his eyes. He didn't generally do PDAs, but he leaned forward, kissed her, and caressed her face. "How are you holding up, kid?"

She nodded. "No complaints."

"May I get something for you from the food concession?"

"I'll go with you and see if anything catches my attention." She rose from her seat.

"I'm making a food run. Anyone game?" Brian asked those assembled at a group of tables.

There were no takers, so with his hand resting on the back of KiLe's neck, he guided her toward the closest food concession stand. He knew everyone had their eyes on him, but it didn't matter. He had felt like kissing KiLe, so he had.

"A couple of bottles of water, please," Brian told the clerk and then turned to her. "What would you like, KiLe?"

"Another one of your kisses, but I'll settle for a bottle of water for now," she said and grinned up at him. In her peripheral vision, she could see Molly and others watching them.

Brian leaned down and kissed her again, then grinned at her. "Do you still want the water?"

"Uh, no. Your kiss filled me right up."

He dug money out of his back pocket and paid for the water; his strong arm muscles bulging with the slight movement. She could still smell the scent of his recent shower on his skin overlaid with healthy sweat. He still smelled good; his aftershave a clean, fresh outdoors scent. *Adventurer*, she believed. It was a fragrance one of his mother's companies manufactured. As they started back toward the table, Brian uncapped one bottle of water and drained it in one long pull before tossing it into a recycle bin. The second bottle he drank more slowly.

"I apologize for the long delay. I hope you're not too tired. We should be on our way shortly."

"I'm fine, Brian. I must say that I know you must be angry about what happened, but you're handling it well."

He nodded. "I am very angry about the inconvenience this is causing our employees, but anger accomplishes nothing. I'll be all right when I know whoever did this is arrested. So, let's not dwell on something we have no control over. Instead, tell me, did you have a good time?"

"Even though I knocked down only seven pins in two hours, yes I had fun tonight."

Brian laughed. "I'll admit you have a very unique delivery. I haven't seen anyone stand and roll the ball two-handed down the lane." He laughed, but her bottom up in the air as she bent forward to push the ball down the middle of the lane gave him a serious hard-on causing his jeans to tighten and his nearly perfect game to falter a bit.

She pouted for effect. "Why didn't you tell me that an eighteen-pound ball was hard to roll with one hand and in a straight line? It was totally embarrassing to try to sling the ball forward the way you do and have it end up go flying backward and rolling behind me instead. It caused everyone to scatter to get out of the way every time it was my turn to bowl. I had a better chance of knocking the people down than I did trying to knock down the pins!"

Brian burst out laughing. "Hey, you were determined to have the green jade. I tried to steer you toward the lighter-weight balls, but nothing you must do but have the pretty green one," he teased, still laughing. "Maybe we'll find time to go bowling again before you leave. This time we'll bowl the duck-pin lanes."

"Your ball weighed eighteen pounds, but you didn't have any trouble. You knocked down two-hundred-seventy pins after three games. Althea said a perfect score is three hundred pins. She even knocked down an average of two-hundred pins! Everyone else did an average of two-hundred pins or more."

"We've had more practice than you have."

"I'll say. Have you ever considered becoming a professional bowler?"

He laughed. "No, why would you ask that?"

"Well, you have your name inscribed on your bowling bag and balls. I thought you did that because you considered becoming a professional."

"Uh, no. I did that to keep down the confusion. It's not unusual for someone to mistakenly pick up someone else's equipment."

"Oh, so you come here often?"

"If I'm in the area, yes. The Montgomery Consortium supports this Monday family night event for our employees and their families. It gives us a chance to get together in a relaxed atmosphere and socialize. People can come out, bring their families, and eat junk food to their heart's content at our expense. It's not mandatory and some of our people don't come every week. It's a school night, so a bunch of teens make pocket money babysitting so the parents can have a date night or the parents bring their children and teens with them for a family night out."

"I have to admit it is good fun, but the noise takes getting used to."

"It can get pretty radical, particularly when my sibs come up for the summer or other school breaks. There's so much for all age groups to do here."

"It's quieted down considerably even though there are people still bowling on the lanes."

"This is the nine-o'clock league bowling now. They're just warming up. They'll bowl until eleven or so and then there's a midnight league who bowl until closing at about two in the morning."

"So, anyone who lives around here would pretty much know the schedule, right?"

"If you're referring to the vandalism, yes, that's the current thinking. We start bowling at seven, so most people are here before seven or they can be scratched from tournament play. The next group would most likely start arriving around eight-forty-five for a nine-o'clock start time. That leaves one to two hours when our vehicles were vandalized. We know the *'when'* it happened, but we don't know the *'who'* or *'why'* yet."

"Yo, Brian," Pierce hailed. "Let's go. The buses are here."

"Okay." He walked toward the table to put on his coat, hat, and gloves and gathered the bowling equipment for KiLe, Althea, and himself.

"I've got this," said Danny, who picked up Althea's equipment along with his own. "I'm going to have to stay over at your place tonight. I don't have a landing pad and the trees are too close to land near my place. Kadijah agreed to pick me up there at first light."

"Solid. I'll ask Grandaunt Althea to lend her truck to me so that I can get over to the barns in the morning."

"Yeah, but you're going to be short-staffed until Granduncle Stephen can get his tow trucks here in the morning to clear the parking lot of our vehicles."

"I know, but I'll work with whoever can make it in. The same thing will be true of the mill and logging teams. We'll be shorthanded. I need to speed up the process and hire additional hands for the Maryland operation and for here."

Danny nodded his agreement as they moved to the front entrance to the Roll-a-Rama.

Liam and Pierce were directing families to the different buses according to the routes the buses were going to run to take them to their homes. Liam signaled Brian and Danny to one of the last idling buses in the long row.

Fortunately, the bus drivers regularly ran these routes delivering children and teens between their homes and schools. By the time they climbed aboard and were seated, the front buses were already pulling away from the parking lot. There were only a handful of people aboard the last bus in addition to the Montgomerys. Most had sleepy children cuddled in their laps.

Before their bus pulled away, Liam and Pierce climbed aboard and were seated. Over an hour later, the last of the families were delivered and the bus was headed for Point of View. As they approached, Althea, sitting at the front of the bus, pulled out her smartphone, dialed a sequence of numbers, and the security gates opened. Ground lights came on making it appear as if it were an airport runway landing zone. When the bus pulled around the circular drive, exterior lights also came on bathing the mansion in a beautiful glow and providing interior lighting.

"Thanks, Ned," each one called out to the bus driver as they disembarked and headed for the front door.

"Sure thing. Sorry for your troubles," Ned answered.

"Thanks." Brian slowed, the last to leave. "Here's a little something for your troubles, Ned." He passed a wad of bills, his share of the tournament winnings to the older man."

"That's not necessary, Brian."

"I know, but be a pal and take it anyway. Buy something pretty for Sophie and tell her I'm still partial to her blue-ribbon-winning sweet potato pies."

He left the bus carrying his and KiLe's bowling equipment before the older man could protest. Brian knew Ned's wife, Sophie, was battling cancer. He had left his wife at home alone to come pick them up when Seth called. It was a small thing for him, but he knew it was monumental for Ned. He was a farmer and drove the school bus for the extra pocket money he needed for a household with only one income. He also knew Sophie would send over several sweet potato pies before the week was out.

When he entered the kitchen, Liam, Pierce, and Danny were raiding the refrigerator.

"What do you mean you can't cook?" Danny questioned KiLe. "You can't ski. You can't bowl and now you tell me you don't cook?"

He remorsefully shook his head. "I don't know, KiLe, the plans for our spring wedding are in serious jeopardy. We may have to settle for a long honeymoon and call it even."

"Given what I've observed of your potential wives-of-the-moment, I think I'll take a pass on your offer," KiLe rejoindered.

Those in the room erupted in laughter.

"Way ta go, KiLe," joked Althea. "With that, I'll say goodnight. Brian, I didn't let your dogs out, but I fed them before we left tonight." She shared a hug with each of her grandnephews before heading to her suite.

"I'll see to it," Brian said and immediately went to let his dogs out, but he would wait and watch while they tended to their business in the dog run he built.

"I'm beat, so I'm going to make an early night of it," said Liam, and with a beer and a hoagie in hand, he also left to turn in.

"Right behind you," said Pierce, similarly prepared with a night snack leaving Danny and KiLe alone in the kitchen.

As soon as his brothers and Brian were out of earshot, Danny sat at a table across from KiLe. "I apologize to you for my sister's behavior tonight. She's always had a thing for Brian and he's done nothing to encourage it other than to treat her like a kid sister. Molly wants it otherwise, but she's been going through an emotionally bad place lately. Ordinarily, she'd cut off her left arm not to offend Brian. Usually, she wouldn't spout off like that to anyone. Especially not to Grandaunt Althea and I know she's not a racist."

"Don't fret about it, Danny. Chink is an English-language ethnic slur, usually referring to a person of Chinese ethnicity. I'm Japanese," she joked, "but it's not the first time someone has called me such an extremely offensive term. It's been used against people of East Asian appearance, but I don't usually get my back up about other people's hang-ups and insecurities. Now **slut** is a whole new one for me." She smiled at Danny causing him to relax and smile back at her.

"Brian really picked a winner with you, KiLe Hakamora, even if you can't bowl, cook, or ski," he joked. He stood, kissed her temple, gathered his snack, and headed off to bed.

When Brian returned with his dogs, he was surprised to find KiLe still sitting in the kitchen alone. "Is everything all right?" He leaned his forearms down on the table across from where she sat.

"Yes. I was just sitting here thinking about how much fun we've had since we arrived," she teased with tongue planted firmly in cheek.

Brian snorted a laugh. "Yeah, you really brought the good luck with you, kid. Are you sure you're not Irish? I mean, St. Patrick's Day was observed a week or two ago. Although it's a legal holiday in some places, it is nonetheless widely recognized and celebrated throughout the United States."

"I've heard of this holiday, even in Japan. Saint Patrick's Day or the Feast of Saint Patrick is a cultural and religious celebration held on the seventeenth of March, the traditional death date of Saint Patrick, the foremost patron saint of Ireland, right?

"The lady is correct."

"Frankly, I prefer to celebrate Spring Break. For most of us students in the U.S. and Canada, Spring Break can occur from February eighteenth to April fifteenth. The two peak weeks are the weeks of March eleventh to March eighteenth and March eighteenth to March twenty-fifth. I find it very lucky, indeed, to be spending my spring break here with you, your family, and friends regardless of the trials and tribulations."

"Even getting mud slimed by my dogs?" he joked.

"Especially for getting mud slimed by your dogs." She gazed into his eyes.

He stood and walked around the table, leaned down, palmed her face, and kissed her mouth with a steady carnality. "I'm the lucky one," he whispered against her sweet lips. "Come on. It's late. It's time you were in bed."

She raised one eyebrow at that, causing him to laugh. "Cut it out, Imp."

CHAPTER 12

While Brian showered, he puzzled over the events of the evening. Having their tires slashed and sugar poured into the gas tanks seemed like a rather childish prank to him. When people noticed their tires were slashed and that their gas tanks were open, they would be less inclined to start their engines, which would defeat the purpose of putting the sugar in the tank. The smart move would have been to close the gas cap so as not to alert the vehicle's owner that something more was amiss other than the slashed tires. That was an indication to him the perpetrators weren't the sharpest knives in the drawer.

After the tires were replaced, the next time the engine was started, the theory is that the sugar would circulate through the system and cause damage immobilizing the vehicle. It sounds great if someone has a grudge against the Montgomerys. The problem with this theory is that it simply isn't true. As it turns out, sugar doesn't dissolve in gasoline. Pouring sand into the gas tank would have about the same effect as pouring in sugar. The sand or sugar might clog up the filter, and that could disable the car, but it's not a sure thing. Which, again, leads him to the conclusion that this is a juvenile prank, but the question is still, why.

He shut off the shower and grabbed a towel to dry himself before slipping into a pair of boxers. Generally, he didn't sleep in anything, but with the door unlocked between the suites and KiLe sleeping next door; it was his only nod to convention. In the kitchenette, he grabbed a bottle of wine and poured a glass to drink while he read his e-mail, went over his paperwork, and filed the insurance claim on behalf of the company. Before sitting on the sofa, he lit the gas fireplace and turned on the flat screen with the sound off. March Madness was in full swing. The basketball game on one of the sport's channels was either a repeat of a game played earlier or the live feed of a late west-coast game. He'd bet American money that his parents were snuggled up on the island watching the game, too. They both scored gold medals in Olympic Games and were still round-ball fanatics.

He hoped the events of the evening weren't disrupting their time together. It was so rare, with their tight schedules, that they could make time to get away for a solid week of rest and relaxation. Still, he wouldn't be surprised if a few months from now, his parents announced they were to expect a new addition to their family. Hell, even if his dad didn't get his mom pregnant again, they might just return from their vacation with another orphaned baby or two in need of medical care. That was their MO, and he couldn't be happier because of it.

Tonight, Molly accused him of not being a real Montgomery, but she was wrong. He had been a Jackson and then a Montgomery for nearly twenty years of his life. The name was second nature to him and most times he never thought of himself in any other terms. That was especially true when he was here among the bedrock Montgomery clan and at home in Maryland with his parents and sibs. None of them looked alike, except for those who were twins, but still, they thought and behaved as a unit. *One for all and all for one* was their motto. That is a bond which would never be forsaken, regardless of the scurrilous accusations hurled against him.

Thirty minutes later, he was still cracking up at the e-mail he received from his UPenn pals, former lacrosse teammates, and the ones he received from his sibs. Then he went to his spam-blocked file to clear it out. He found an e-mail in quarantine with the name **"Brian Alford,"** his legal name before he became a Jackson or a Montgomery, and found that to be curious. Because his internet provider was his Uncle Kenneth Alexander's CompuCorrect Global Company, he knew better than to open the e-mail. Instead, he sent a note to his uncle questioning the message. Not surprisingly, moments later, his phone rang. His uncle's company provided all of the hardware and software used by all family members for personal and business uses. His Uncle Kenneth, an engineer and inventor, manufactured among other things, hardware and software security systems, which were virtually hack-proof.

KiLe sat up in bed, trying to read after having spoken with her father and then her mother. Since her undergraduate studies would be coming to a close in a few more months, her parents were of the opinion she should return to Japan to be introduced into Japanese society. In fact, they had chosen a date for her "coming out" party and had lined up a number of Japanese men they considered to be suitable for her to consider becoming engaged to. These men were, of course, rising stars in the societal, corporate and/or political arena in Japan. According to her parents and grandparents, she would make an appropriate helpmate for any one of them as they rose in their respective careers.

Her parents also believed she should continue her studies at Cambridge or Oxford in England for her masters and doctorate as they had done. After all, she lived in America for four years. It was time she gained experience living in England before she returned home to marry and procreate the appropriate number of offspring. Once she had her degree from Georgetown University and her transcript forwarded, plans were in the works to have her admitted to one school or the other in England.

KiLe put the book aside, raised her legs, looped her arms around them, and braced her chin on her knees. She was getting nowhere with trying to get ahead of her class schedule for next week. Her parents' edicts were interfering with her ability to think clearly and rationally, but, of course, that was the problem she was experiencing. These were **her** parents' edicts, not her life choices to consider. It wasn't her responsibility to think clearly or rationally. She was simply required to do as instructed without question.

It wouldn't matter to her parents that she didn't want to go to England. She didn't want to have a "coming-of-age" gala. Since long before her grandparents were born, the age of majority in Japan has been twenty years old; persons under twenty are not permitted to smoke or drink. Not that she wanted to smoke, but the idea that her behavior was so strictly regulated grated on her nerves. Especially since she liked the taste of certain wines. Until recently, the young people were not permitted to vote. She was just in Japan for the coming-of-age ceremony, known as *seijin shiki* held on the second Monday of January. At the ceremony, all of the men and women participating were brought to a government building and had to listen to many speakers, similar to a graduation ceremony. At the conclusion of the ceremony, government officials gave speeches, and small presents were handed out to the new adults.

She didn't want to be paraded before a bunch of men at a gala hosted by her parents or to be told to marry some proper Japanese man she didn't even know. Acting as his hood ornament or arm candy and walking two steps behind him with her head bowed wasn't a good look for her. She would end up as nothing more than an educated Geisha, a traditional Japanese female who acts as a hostess and whose skills include performing various arts…particularly in the bedroom. She could play the flute which fit the requirement to be classically trained in music. As an accomplished and still practicing gymnast, she was healthy and fit. She was given dance lessons as a child until she left for America, so that fit into Geisha requirements. She was adept at playing tile games, particularly Mahjong and Sudoku, another requirement to be a proper wife. She only had to be instructed on how to hold a conversation to entertain her husband and his male friends at his direction. *What a mortifying thought that is!* she ruminated. When she Googled the men her parents mentioned, none of them was to her liking. Even worse, in each instance, the men her parents and grandparents wanted to choose for her were all at least ten years her senior. Two of the seven were even twenty years older than her.

Obedience to her parents' direction went without question all of her life. Defiance would mean the immediate and irrevocable withdrawal of their support and possibly being considered *persona non grata*, unacceptable or unwelcome in their lives. She didn't want that; she loved her parents and respected them. Yet, what they expected of her was counter to what she wanted for herself.

She looked at the time. It was too late to call Whitney and talk over her feelings the way she did when they were at the Georgetown house. Whitney's calm, considered conversations always helped clear away the fog of the steps and stages of growing up. They had known each other since they were six years old when General and Admiral Alexander moved to Japan to take over the military's diplomatic duties at the American Embassy in Tokyo. They enrolled Whitney in the same prestigious school where KiLe attended all of her life.

Admiral Alexander, Whitney's mother, spoke fluent Japanese and within no time, Whitney could speak it as well. Then Whitney helped KiLe to improve her ability to speak American English. As a result, they became fast friends. When Whitney's parents gave birth to triplet girls, Shannon Rose, Sharon Sylvia, and Sierra Helen, KiLe loved to spend time in Whitney's home with her family. Whitney's uncles, aunts, and cousins often came to Japan for visits; her grandparents too. Each time she was around her friend's family, she noticed how Whitney was encouraged to express her opinion on a wide variety of subjects; nothing was forbidden. Then Whitney's parents gave birth to triplet boys, Bernard Thomas, Benson Alvin, and Bradford Andre, and their home was an even more joyous place to visit. She and Whitney would take the little ones for long walks and to the park to play. Those were pleasant memories, KiLe remembered. Now Whitney's sisters were teenagers and her brothers soon would be.

It was clear to KiLe, from a very early age, that Whitney was an extraordinary individual. She could fly a plane at the age of eight and advanced through her high school and college courses far ahead of other students. She tested out of several years in high school and college.

KiLe's parents were astounded by Whitney's skills and abilities and encouraged her to learn from Whitney. Yet, Whitney cautioned her *"to always dance to the beat of her own heart and never to walk in anyone else's shadow."* KiLe learned to step out into the light, with Whitney's encouragement, when she wanted to sing in a school holiday extravaganza two years ago. She had never done anything on her own like that before and was surprised that, when she auditioned for the part against hundreds of others who were also trying out to participate in the extravaganza, she got selected. She was even given several solos in the two-hour-long Georgetown University show.

Whitney came to the audition to offer moral support, but wouldn't be convinced to try out, too. An extraordinary guitarist, KiLe thought of Whitney's skill, as well as the vocal ability she heard when Whitney thought no one was around. Whitney's voice was exceptional and reminded KiLe of the songstress Whitney Houston, but nothing would induce Whitney to sing at the tryouts.

Still, Whitney was there for her and had been since they met as children. The tryouts were where she met Payton and Whitney met Tucker

Cavanaugh. Payton and Tucker auditioned with their band, Changelings, and were also selected to participate in the holiday extravaganza. It was clear from the very beginning that Whitney and Tucker would have a forever kind of love between them and she was right. Whitney and Tucker would marry in June. They fit so naturally together and she believed she and Payton had the same type of unity. However, it was not to be. Again, Whitney's counsel, *"never to walk in anyone else's shadow,"* resonated.

KiLe learned so much from Whitney Alexander that she should be able now to stand up on her own two feet and to finally stand up to her parents and say what it is she wanted, not what she didn't want. She would ask for their support toward reaching her personal goals. She could do it in a way that wasn't disrespectful. Maybe convince them it was a better option for her to continue to complete her education in America; rather than in England. She would have to find good, strong points to support a discussion with them.

If she were to nail down the summer job with the Japanese Embassy in Washington, DC, it would go a long way toward convincing her parents she should stay in the United States. They wouldn't want her to quit her job. They would see her position as a step toward support for her career. That's what she would do! *Eureka!* She would call the Embassy on Monday and let them know she was eager to reschedule the interview they postponed.

She was so thrilled to have made a grown-up decision completely on her own that she wanted to tell someone. Scrambling out of bed, she went to the door adjoining Brian's suite and listened. He was definitely still awake. She could hear him talking, though she couldn't hear who he was talking with or what was being said. He wasn't talking with Pierce, Liam, or Danny. Still, it didn't seem as if he were speaking with his grandaunt or another woman, so she knocked and heard him say "Come" before she cracked open the door and peeked in.

He waved her in as he said, "Thanks, Uncle Kenneth. I'll wait to hear from you. Love you, too," and disconnected the call. "Are you all right, KiLe? It's late. I thought you would be asleep by now."

"Are you busy?"

"No, not really. I'm just clearing out my e-mail box. What's up?"

She came in, sat tailor style on the sofa, and faced Brian. He had his feet up on a hassock and his laptop was still open on his lap. A glass of red wine sat on an end table to his right and the fireplace was lit. He seemed comfortable and relaxed. Since he didn't shut down his laptop, she figured he still had more to do, so she needed to make this quick. "I've made a decision and just had to tell someone. I'd usually tell Whitney, but it's a little late to call her in Maine."

"Okay, so you want to pick me, your own true pal, as your second choice? This is how you treat me after I let you wash my dogs, taught you to ski cross country, and to bowl? I'll try not to be offended," he joked.

She made a mean face at him and sobered. "I've decided to convince my parents to let me stay here to complete my masters and doctorate," she said brightly and triumphantly.

His eyebrows raised in apparent confusion. "Okay, but I thought it was what you planned to do anyway. Did something happen to change your mind?"

"I spoke with my parents tonight and they've decided I should come home and audition for a Geisha position. They and my grandparents have selected seven men for me to choose from to become engaged to and marry. They have also decided that I should complete my education at Oxford or Cambridge in the UK before I marry their choice as my intended."

There was a definite pain centered somewhere in the vicinity of his heart when there hadn't been one there ever before, Brian thought. He absently rubbed the spot but received no relief for his effort. He recognized that his discomfort was caused by the thoughts of KiLe permanently leaving the United States, becoming engaged to someone, and leaving his life. He was hard-pressed to ask, but he believed life as he knew it rested on her answers to his questions. "Okay, why would you have to convince them of something you want to do? Aren't they supportive of your decisions about how to conduct your life choices?"

"They're Japanese. I'm not expected to make choices about my life. I'm expected to do as I'm told and bow to their superior wisdom and life experiences."

Brian sat and just stared, unable to form a cohesive thought.

"Brian," she whined, "why are you just sitting there staring at me?"

"Okay, how old are you?" he asked, his eyebrows raised in question and clarification.

"Twenty-two."

"Twenty-two and your parents dictate how you are to live your life?" The skepticism was evident in his voice.

"Yes, as I said, they're Japanese."

That meant absolutely nothing to him whatsoever. "What happens when you disagree with them?"

"Oh, no, I've never done that. I'm not permitted to disagree with my parents or grandparents. You're thinking about how you were raised here in America, where your parents encouraged you toward independent thinking. That's not how it happens in Japanese society."

"You would allow your parents to choose your life mate for you?" he asked sardonically.

"Brian," she whined again, "you don't understand. I must do as I'm directed or my parents would never agree to see me again."

"Unbelievable," he said, staring at her astounded. "Of course, your parents would see you, KiLe. They love you, don't they?"

"They raised me, but they're stern, disciplined people who are not prone to displays of affection. This is how my parents were raised. My grandparents are the same way, but even more stringent than my parents. They selected my father and mother to marry when they were preteens. Their marriage worked until a few years ago, but I don't think they ever loved each other. They divorced and each married other people."

He shook his head and shrugged. This was something outside of his understanding, but he would listen to her. It was all he could offer at the moment.

Fifteen minutes later, she asked. "What do you think?"

"Okay, say, for example, your plan to impress them by working at the Japanese Embassy doesn't materialize, what's Plan B?"

She blankly looked at him. "It has to work, Brian. I don't know what else to do to convince them." Tears misted her eyes.

"Okay, okay." To soothe her, he pulled KiLe into his left side and wrapped his arms around her. "Don't fret. Where there's a will, there's a way."

She laughed through her tears. "So says Confucius, except the philosophy of Confucius is Chinese, not Japanese."

"No, the idiom means there's more than one way to skin a cat."

"From the cat's perspective, they all suck. That's disgusting. I can't imagine skinning a cat. They're such soft, cuddly animals with such trusting eyes. I don't understand where you Americans get these strange sayings."

For ponderous moments he just looked into her beguiling eyes on her upturned face. Then he burst out laughing and shaking his head. "You are so literal," but really he found her charming and delightful.

"Made you laugh, though, didn't I?" she grinned, teasing him as he had teased her.

That's when he realized she was yanking his chain and popped her on her bottom. However, she only continued to grin up at him.

"When I came in, something was bothering you. Care to share?"

He shook his head. He didn't know what was going on with the e-mail address to **"Brian Alford,"** but his uncle assured him that they would get to the bottom of it. That was enough for him. No member of his family ever let him down.

"So, if you won't tell me what's bothering you, would you tell me why Molly is so upset?"

He sighed heavily. "She recently discovered the man she believed was her father couldn't be because he died three years before her birth."

"Oh," she drew out the word. "She's Liam, Pierce, and Danny's half-sister?"

"There's another brother, Anderson, who we call Andy. You haven't met him, but you're essentially right."

"Essentially? Does that mean that I'm half right, one quarter or three-quarters right?"

"It means there's another explanation for the relationship between them."

"They don't have the same mother?"

"Yes, Arabella Cascioferro Montgomery is the mother of the four sons and one daughter."

"Then she has a different father. That's why she was so focused on parentage. She's not a Montgomery?"

"She has a different father, yes, but she's a Montgomery."

"I don't understand. She accused her brother of being her father. That can't possibly be true. It's a disgusting thought, but Danny couldn't have been more than a boy himself when she was born."

"Danny is not her father."

"You're not going to tell me who it is, are you?"

"Suffice it to say, to the extent that she was rude to you, trust that her behavior has nothing to do with you."

She nodded her understanding, reached across him for his glass of wine, took a sip, and snuggled closer into Brian's embrace. "This is good wine."

"My Uncle Gregory is a connoisseur and buys old wine cellars. Winemaking is a hobby of his, too. Whenever I go to his home in New York City, I raid his wine cellar." He returned to scrolling through his junk mail, deleting spam. Occasionally, he would stop to read something and elevate it to his suspense file before continuing. KiLe was comfortable in his arm, being quiet while he continued to work. When she finished his glass of wine, he filled it again and took a long swallow before passing the goblet to her.

It felt so natural and he smelled so good she drifted and didn't realize when she fell asleep.

What was he going to do about KiLe Hakamora? Brian continued to wonder. In just a few days, she was working out to be someone he could see in his life going forward in the near term. For a young woman, she was inquisitive, funny, bright, articulate, talented, and sexy without even trying. She took on new challenges fearlessly and could laugh at herself without being offended when she was teased. She didn't pick up someone else's emotional baggage. Instead, she let racial slurs roll like water off a duck's back. Her only character flaw, if he could call it that, was that she was challenged in the self-esteem department vis-à-vis her parents. He preferred aggressive women who could stand on their own two feet and not need him to be responsible for making decisions for them. A certain amount of interdependency was expected on both sides in a relationship, but the pendulum swung both ways. He wasn't convinced KiLe could provide that type of support…yet.

When he carried her back to her bed, he looked at her beautiful face as he tucked her in under the covers. She moaned pleasurably and stretched, but didn't awaken. He had seen her naked in the sauna, covered her, and carried her up to her suite before calling Althea to dress her for bed. He wanted to slip into bed beside her that night and hold her until morning but knew exactly where his desire would lead. Instead, he made sure she was covered, turned out the light, and went back to his own bed to suffer in silence.

CHAPTER 13

When KiLe woke, it was to hear a helicopter flying low overhead. She scrambled out of the warm bed and over to the window. There, hovering over the back lawn, was a bright red helicopter sending a blizzard of snow flying in all directions. The markings on the tail of the copter read *AEA Commuter Service*. KiLe knew the logo *AEA* referred to Adventurer Executive Airlines, a company owned by Whitney's aunt, Brian's mother, Vivian Alexander Montgomery.

When KiLe came to America for the first-time years ago, Whitney and her father piloted an *AEA* private jet from Tokyo first to San Diego for two weeks and then to an airfield near Brian's family's ranch. She remembered how it was the first time she saw Brian. He was on a beautiful horse with other ranch hands, guiding a herd of horses into a corral. He was at a distance, but he took off his Stetson and waved to his newly arrived family members. Later that afternoon, she was introduced to him, but then, too, she was introduced to so many family members that her mind boggled. However, because of their selflessness and willingness to share what they had with abandoned or orphaned health-challenged babies and children, Chuck and Vivian Alexander Montgomery stuck out in her memory.

It also fascinated her that a woman owned an executive airline and ground transportation service. With Whitney's help, KiLe interviewed Vivian Alexander Jackson Montgomery, a woman who rarely consented to interviews. She wrote a paper on the company for one of her classes and received a top grade for her effort. It was even published in *The Hoya*, the twice-weekly newspaper of record for Georgetown University.

She continued to watch the helicopter hover until it cleared the snow from a landing pad and eventually set down. When a woman stepped out of the aircraft, KiLe was surprised. The only other female flyers she knew were Whitney and her triplet younger sisters, Shannon, Sharon, and Sierra

Alexander. Then she recognized Brian's grandfather, Stephen Montgomery as he got out of the other side of the helicopter. *He looked like the actor Sam Elliott in his younger days*, she thought as she watched him head toward the mansion. *The man never seemed to age. The woman must be his daughter-in-law Kadijah Montgomery*, she realized.

KiLe rushed through her morning preparations for the day and headed for the kitchen. They were assembled there, the Montgomerys, enjoying each other while having coffee and hot muffins.

"Well, there's my pretty girl," greeted Stephen when KiLe entered the kitchen.

She went easily into his arms for a kiss on the temple and a squeeze.

"I don't know whether you've met my daughter-in-law, Kadijah," said Stephen making introductions. "She's my son, Martin's wife, and Derrick Jackson's younger sister."

The woman was simply gorgeous with the most beautiful butter-biscuit-brown skin, long curly dark-brown hair, and eyes on a face that should be in ads for Dark and Lovely. She was also pregnant KiLe noticed when she reached to shake her hand. "I haven't, no, but I watched you land the helicopter. That is so cool," KiLe enthused.

Instead of shaking her hand, Kadijah pulled her in for a quick squeeze. "I'm so glad to finally meet you, KiLe. I've heard about you for years from Whitney and what an incredible voice you have. I hoped that my husband and I could get down to Uncle Chucky Pie's birthday party, but Martin got hung up on a job in Manhattan and we couldn't get away. Still, I saw your performance online and you were phenomenal."

"Thank you, Kadijah. It's a pleasure to meet you, too. It's fascinating to know there are female flyers. I've flown with Whitney several times and it seems so complicated, but you make it look so easy."

Kadijah laughed. "It can be, but if you're ever interested in learning, I'm a flight instructor here in Monroe County. I'd be happy to teach you."

"Wow, thanks. I may take you up on it."

"Come, all. Breakfast is ready," called out Althea and they went into a salon with hot, steaming trays on the buffets.

Brian occasionally watched and listened as KiLe and Kadijah conversed about a wide variety of things. He liked that KiLe could so easily fit into his family and become an active and lively participant in the discussions underway. She was also an active listener and remembered the family connections, even down to the remote detail of the names of Grandfather Stephen's dogs, Butch Cassidy and the Sundance Kid. Most women he dated couldn't remember clearly the names of his siblings, which indicated to him that they weren't paying attention. Admittedly, there were a lot of them to keep in mind, yet KiLe had no trouble whatsoever.

"So, Kadijah and Martin picked me up in Maryland late last night and flew me to Philadelphia," Stephen was saying.

"You got tires from Philadelphia before dawn this morning?" asked Pierce of his granduncle.

Stephen shrugged. "I know a guy," he said and continued eating. "He met us at the airport and he and his people loaded the tires I needed. He wants the damaged tires in partial payment for the tires he sold to me. He has a paving company and contracts to pave roadways, streets, and driveways. He cuts up the damaged or old tires and turns them into asphalt for his paving business. He's always on the lookout for old tires. I usually have a good supply of them at my garage in town. He really likes the oversized ones which come off of dump trucks, eighteen wheelers, tractors, trailers, backhoes or other farm equipment. So, when I called him at three in the morning and told him what I had and what I needed, he hopped right on it. His sons work in his business and have a warehouse full of new tires which weren't sold in the year they were manufactured. He gave me a deal on tires which were manufactured last year."

"That's pretty good," said Liam. "The tires I had on my truck were three years old."

"Mine were older than that," said Brian.

"When someone hands you lemons, make lemonade," commented Althea.

"Works out for me, too," said Kadijah. "Now, I have a new connection for the tires I need for my aircrafts."

Everyone was able to laugh it off, but the fact remained that they were no closer to discovering who was responsible for the vandalism or why it happened.

"Well, I need to get to the garage and give my people a hand with changing tires and pulling out gas tanks. I'll bring in a second crew and work overnight if I have to, but it's still going to take a couple of days to put everything to right," said Stephen.

"Start with the employees first, Granddad," suggested Brian looking around the table and getting a nod of agreement from Liam, Pierce, and Danny. "I can wait. If it's all right with you, Grandaunt Althea, I need to use your truck to go over to the barns for a few hours to start a recount and to take a look at the stock and the new horses I purchased."

"It's fine with me," said Althea. "In fact, I might ride over with you and take a look at the horses myself."

"Kadijah is going to give me, Pierce, and Danny a lift to Pierce's place to pick up some of his snowmobiles."

"Pierce and I will head up to the logging base camp and see who made it in. The workers were going to share rides into work," said Liam.

"I'll drop Stephen at home to get his truck so he can get into town. By then, I'll circle back to the barns and pick up you, Danny, and we'll do a grid search for your missing animals," said Kadijah.

Everyone nodded agreement, cleared their dishes, and went about preparing for their appointed duties.

"You're with me," Brian said to KiLe as he started for the stairs to suit up for the cold weather.

"Works for me," she said and hurried to catch up to him.

KiLe had never been in a horse barn or riding arena before, but these spaces were enormous. There was so much to see; she was full of questions. "What's the stuff on the floor?" she asked Althea.

"It's a mixture of pure silica sand, a select combination of synthetic fibers, shoe sole rubber granules, and a specialized wax. We are able to produce a stable yet supportive footing for horse and rider. The rubber granules help to resist compaction and hardening by absorbing the impact of a landing or stride and allowing the horse to rebound off the surface.

The fiber and wax combine to virtually eliminate tracking by creating a web-like lattice that is both flexible and resilient."

"Do you have to wet it down?"

"There is no need to water the arena or track, ever. The wax is a key component to make a completely dust-free arena footing that is also low maintenance. It is very hydrophobic, meaning the majority of outdoors rain and other liquids sheet off the surface or wick immediately through the footing, making it ready for riding and training after rain events. Creating a dust-free environment has significant benefits for the lungs of both horse and rider, producing better conditions for riding and training. Overall, our blended arena footing offers more riding time, better riding conditions, and an extended season for training."

"*Wow*, you really know a lot about this." KiLe was impressed.

"I grew up on a farm here in the mountains. Nothing as fancy as this, but I learned to ride and take care of my mount when I was very young. Back then, my sister and I rode a horse to and from school."

"I've never done that before; ride a horse, I mean. I know everyone in Brian's immediate family rides. Even the young ones ride the ponies."

"They do," Althea looked up as a woman approached. "Arabella," Althea warily acknowledged.

"Althea," she returned and then focused on KiLe. "You must be KiLe Hakamora." She extended her hand. "I'm Arabella Cascioferro Montgomery. I believe you've met three of my sons, Liam, Pierce, and Danny and my daughter, Molly."

"I've met your sons, but I haven't been introduced to your daughter." KiLe accepted her hand for a shake and believed she was looking at the reincarnation of a young screen star Elizabeth Taylor. Her mother collected classical Hollywood cinema of popular stars of the 1950s and every film the British–American actress, businesswoman, and humanitarian ever released. *Arabella Cascioferro Montgomery was simply stunning*, thought KiLe and didn't look as if she was out of her twenties or that she had four grown sons and a nearly grown daughter. Rather she looked like she belonged on the cover of **Bellisima Italia** or ***Vogue Italy***.

"Then, perhaps, I am mistaken. I was given to understand my daughter was ill-mannered to you last night."

"She was rude, yes, however, Ms. Hardyston forced her to apologize for her behavior."

"I see." Arabella turned toward the older woman. "I understand that you laid a hand on my daughter."

"I did, yes, and if you expect an apology for it, you will be sorely disappointed."

She nodded and looked into Althea's eyes. "I do not hold with corporal punishment involving my children."

"Generally, I don't either, but she's not a child and her behavior would not have been as boorish if she were aware of the fact of her parentage. For that, I lay the responsibility at your feet. I don't care who you sleep with, Arabella, nor do I have a dog in this hunt. I don't have children of my own, but if I did, I think I would not be ashamed to tell them where they came from."

"You are right. You do not have children. Therefore, I suggest you keep your opinion to yourself or tell someone who gives a damn about what you think. I am not one of those people. However, if I hear you have hit any of mine again, I will have you arrested for assault and battery."

"You certainly have the connection to do so. Yet, your *'children'* are all adults and have the right to decide such things for themselves. However, I give you fair notice here and now, Arabella, that should I have provocation again, I will act on my threat to slap the taste out of Molly's mouth."

"Ms. Hakamora, I add my apology to that of my daughter and promise her poor behavior toward you will not be repeated. I hope you enjoy your stay here."

KiLe nodded but was silenced by the enmity between the two women. Still, she wondered at Althea's comment that Arabella has "the connection to" have her arrested. It seemed such an odd thing to say

"I believe we understand each other, Althea."

"We do, yes, Arabella. Good day to you."

When Arabella inclined her head, turned, and walked away, Althea said, "I'm sorry you had to witness that discussion, KiLe."

"It's all right, Honorable Aunt Althea."

"Was that Arabella Montgomery?" Brian asked as he rode up to the guardrail where KiLe and Althea stood talking.

"It was, yes, Brian. If you need to speak with her, she's probably in the office."

"No, I'll catch up with her before we leave," he said and noticed how KiLe's attention was fixed on his horse, Pegasus. "Have you ridden before?" he grinned.

She shook her head, awed. "She's beautiful," KiLe breathed.

Brian leaned forward as if whispering a secret into the horse's ear, "You'll have to forgive her Pegasus. She didn't notice your impressive male parts. Will you forgive her this time?"

The pure, white stallion seemed to think about it and reluctantly nod his large head as if he shrugged.

"Do you think she deserves a ride?"

The horse shook his head and sidestepped away from the guardrail.

"Oh, come on, Pegasus, give the woman a break. If she says she's sorry, will you take her around just once?"

The horse looked sideways at KiLe and snorted.

"I don't know, KiLe." Brian shrugged. "Maybe if you apologize to Pegasus for mistaking a stallion for a mare, he'll forgive you."

Smiling broadly at Brian and his horse, KiLe said, "I apologize, Pegasus. Can we be friends now?"

The horse regarded her for a few moments and then nodded yes. He sidestepped back closer to the guardrail. Brian slid smoothly from the saddle, helped KiLe climb up and over the rail, and then onto the horse's back.

KiLe grinned from ear-to-ear as Brian shortened the stirrups to fit the length of KiLe's legs and then handed the reigns to her.

"What do I do now?" she excitedly asked.

"Tell him 'once around the park.'" Brian grinned.

KiLe did as directed and Pegasus walked on.

"How bad was it?" Brian asked Althea when KiLe was out of earshot.

"It could have been worse. We didn't come to blows and kept it civil because KiLe was standing here."

"I'm sorry for it."

"It's not your doing, Brian. Arabella needs to be truthful with Molly before someone slips up and tells her who her father is."

"Or someone could be vindictive and want to hurt her," Brian offered.

"You're right, but nothing Arabella must do but keep the child in the dark. I think it hurts Molly more not knowing."

"You're right, too," Brian agreed as he leaned back, stretched his arms out along the guardrail, hooked one booted foot on a lower rung, and watched KiLe and Pegasus circle the arena. She was still grinning from ear-to-ear, but he wondered at the difficulty some parents experienced with raising children. It made him more appreciative of his own parents. He learned, at an early age, there was nothing he couldn't discuss with his parents and grandparents. They offered advice only if he specifically asked for it, a vital trait he emulated. Even if he didn't take their advice, which was rare, they were respectful of his decisions and encouraged him along any path he chose. Yes, he always felt lucky for the parents in his life.

"Do you ever wonder about where you come from?" Althea asked.

He shook his head, his eyes still on KiLe and Pegasus. "No, not for one moment," he said and meant it.

CHAPTER 14

When the helicopter flew in over the indoor arena, the twelve wild horses jolted and startled running in all directions. Danny and Brian, on horseback, steadied their own mounts watching to ensure none of the wild horses panicked and tried to jump the guardrail. They rode around the oblong ring on opposite sides, cutting back and forth to block a frightened colt, calling out in gentle tones as they circled tighter and tighter. Eventually, the animals calmed but were still wary of their new situation.

"That is so cool," commented KiLe, almost reverently, as she stood outside the guardrail with Althea watching Danny and Brian work with this new group of horses. This was the fourth group they ushered into the arena that morning. *The way Brian handled his horse was almost as if man and mount were of one mind,* she thought.

Althea laughed at KiLe's exuberance. "Tina and Nico always send a good group to us. Just after the new year, Brian went to Argentina for ten days to see and select the horses he wanted. These are more beautiful than the last lot. That golden palomino is stunning. As soon as Dena and Petra get a look at him, they'll each be begging Brian to let them have him."

"They work for the Montgomerys?"

"Dena and Petra? No, they're Brian's younger sisters. They're both accomplished riders."

"No, I meant Tina and Nico?" KiLe clarified.

"Oh. No," Althea answered and smiled. "Constantina Justice and Nicholas Collins don't work for anyone. They married a few years ago and have a young son and another baby on the way; a girl this time I think Brian told me. Tina owns the Sweet Justice Communications Network and Nico owns the satellite that distributes her network and hundreds of others."

KiLe snapped her fingers in recognition. "I think I've heard of them. They're this couple who also race yachts, right?"

"Sometimes they do, yes. They're both business people who live half of the year in either New York or Chicago and the other half of the year in a remote area of southern Argentina where they raise wild horses. Tina's maternal grandparents are Argentinians. Her grandfather is a descendant of Spain and he's Spanish royalty. He's a businessman and a trusted advisor to the Argentinian government; a diplomat."

KiLe nodded. "Tina and Nico are close friends with Brian's parents, I think. They were at the birthday party for Brian's father. I remember being introduced to a number of people named Justice."

Althea nodded, too. "They are, yes. Tina is from a large family of Justices on her father's side of the family. As I said, her mother's side of the family is Argentinian nobility. Vivian and Tina were in undergrad school together at Spelman College. Tina and her family will soon be in New York City to prepare their J-class yacht, *The Outlaw Justice II,* for the Americas Cup regatta. Vivian and Chuck will sail her yacht, *The Vivian Lynn,* and JaiHonnah and Roderick Baylor will sail *The Navajo Princess* out of Washington, DC, and the three yachts will form a flotilla. JaiHonnah's brother, Adam Hawkins, is entering the race this year on his new J-class, sailing yacht, *The SeaHawk,* designed and built by Joyce Montgomery Calloway's husband, Peter. Adam usually races Formula One cars in the Fédération Internationale de l'Automobile World Championships. Are you familiar with it?"

"No, I'm not."

"The Formula One car season consists of a series of races, known as the *Grand Prix*, which are held worldwide including in the United States and maybe even in Japan. Instead of racing his cars, this year, Adam will join the flotilla in Galveston Bay or somewhere in the Gulf of Mexico and sail with them to Buenos Aires, Argentina. That's where one of the J-Class yacht races is held for the Americas Cup.

"Some of us will fly down to Buenos Aires to participate or to observe and give moral support. It's a lot of fun."

"What's a lot of fun?" asked Kadijah as she joined KiLe and Althea at the guardrail.

"The Americas Cup J-class yacht race."

"Ah, yes," Kadijah agreed. "Regrettably, this little person," she said, rubbing her baby bump, "will be born during that time so I won't be able to join in this year."

Althea laughed. "No, we wouldn't want to have a repeat performance of a birth during a hurricane on Vivian and Chuck's island in Bimini."

Kadijah laughed and nodded, telling KiLe, "Fortunately, Uncle Chuck and Aunt Vivian's mother, Sylvia Alexander, a registered nurse, were there to bring Peter and Joyce's daughter, Joy Calloway, into the world."

Althea laughed, too. "Although Joyce didn't relish the idea of her brother seeing parts of her anatomy previously viewed only by her husband."

"Chuck delivered his sister and brother-in-law's baby?" asked KiLe.

"He did. You see, Peter Calloway designed and built **The Outlaw Justice II** in a boathouse on the Hudson River in New York City. He and Joyce live on the upper floors of the boathouse, which they converted into a bi-level condo. That made it easy for Peter to be available to help parent their toddler son, Alex. Joyce was also pregnant at the time. She wanted to make the trip to the races with Peter and Alex, and Peter didn't want to leave her at home alone for the month it would take them to sail from New York to Argentina. They took the chance and made the trip. They were delayed on Vivian and Chuck's island because of a hurricane for almost a week. They expected to be in Miami around the time Joyce was due to deliver, but the storm hit before that and little Joy came early. She was nearly born at sea. A day earlier and she would have been."

"I'm surprised Brian's parents can get away to participate in the races."

"Well, with Chuck, he makes sure his schedule is flexible because he's the primary childcare provider in their family. His medical office is literally right across the road from their ranch in Maryland and his hospital is a mile away as the crow flies so he can usually make himself available to spend time on family matters and vacations.

"It's different for Vivian. The U.S. Supreme Court term or session begins the first Monday in October and ends the first Monday in October of the following year. Usually, Court sessions continue until late June or early July. Vivian's annual family reunion is held in Summer County, South Carolina, for ten days around Juneteenth and she tries never to miss it."

"I apologize for interrupting, but what's Juneteenth?" asked KiLe.

"It's an American holiday, also known as Freedom Day, which commemorates the June nineteen, eighteen sixty-five, announcement of the abolition of slavery in the United States. More generally, it's known for the emancipation of enslaved Americans of African descent throughout the former Confederacy of the southern United States. The word is a portmanteau of 'June' and 'nineteenth,'" explained Kadijah.

"Okay," KiLe nodded. "I've read about slavery in America, but I didn't know about the holiday celebration. So, you were saying?"

For a moment, Kadijah drew a blank. "What was I saying?" she laughed. "Oh, yes, now I remember. I was talking about Vivian's tight schedule and vacations. The Supreme Court's term is divided between 'sittings,' when the Justices hear cases and deliver opinions and intervening 'recesses,' when they consider the business before the Court and write opinions. Sittings and recesses alternate at approximately two-week intervals. The U.S. Supreme Court rises at the end of June but does not remain in recess long. Over the summer, they review cases for the upcoming term, then hold a conference in late August to discuss which cases they want to hear. It's called granting Certiorari."

"American government is so complicated it seems to me," said KiLe. "Whitney spent a lot of time helping me understand how it works."

"It can be complex, yes, but I studied to be a paralegal before I learned to fly. Then I joined the Army Air Corps. When I left the military, Vivian helped get my charter service off the ground, so to speak," she chuckled. "She always puts a priority on her family's needs. Chuck and their children are her first priority, so she makes time to be with them for family vacations."

"So it seems. They're away together now," said KiLe.

"They're a team. That's why they'll have a forever kind of love," contributed Brian as he came up behind KiLe with Danny.

Where had she heard that phrase before? KiLe recalled. However, she was so engrossed in the conversation with Kadijah and Althea, she hadn't noticed other ranch hands were working with different horses in the arena.

"From what I could see from the sidelines, you've got a nice herd of wild horses," commented Kadijah.

"I'm pleased with the possibilities," said Brian. "Most of the mares are a year or two old and will be perfect for breeding. We've got a few racers Dad may want to put in his lineup for regional trial races. I'll get Thomasina over to take a look at them."

"Thomasina?" asked KiLe.

"Yes, she's a former professional jockey who now trains other jockeys and horses for various tasks, including racing. We have trainers working on all three of our ranches," he said, answering KiLe's question before continuing. "Doc's reports indicate they're healthy and have been well taken care of. They made the trip up from Argentina without any lingering effects of the sedatives they were given. I'll start paring the mares with certain stallions, including Pegasus and Lucky."

"Pegasus and Lucky sired several beautiful colts with the wild horses Tina and Nico sent to you last year," Kadijah commented.

"They did along with several of Dad's racehorses and my sister, Dena's quarter horse, Quick Silver. I believe we'll have about twenty-two foals this year from last year's herd."

"I'd love to stay and talk horses, but we've got to get in the air and start the search," interjected Kadijah. "I have a few other jobs this afternoon."

"I have an electronic map on the wall in the office, which should give us some idea where the cattle were last spotted," said Danny and led the way.

The offices were not spacious or elegant, but comfortable enough, thought KiLe. They piled into Danny's office and stood looking at the electronic board, which lit indicating where their cattle were at any given moment. It surprised KiLe to see the little dots no larger than a pinhead slowly moving around the board.

"We put out bales of hay, so we have parts of the herd congregating in the southwest quadrant and the northwest, here, here and here." Using a laser, Danny pointed out the GPS locations. "If we fly over these areas, I can determine on my iPad whether any of the missing cattle are or have been in any of these groups."

"What about your pastures over here?" Taking the laser, Kadijah pointed to a different location.

Danny shook his head. "We haven't used that pasture for a few years. We've had roundups since then and we didn't have any cattle go missing.

Also, if they were over there or on any of the other pastures, they would show up on the map and they haven't. These cattle went missing in February and probably in the last month. If Brian hadn't called for the inoculations, we wouldn't have known for another month that the cattle were missing.

"Here," Danny continued pointing to another much larger pasture, "is where Brian is currently grazing his buffalo in this valley. His ranch hands have been moving them from one valley to another, but didn't report that any were missing."

"Okay, we'll focus on these pastures," said Kadijah. "Let's saddle up. The sun is directly overhead, which is a good thing. We won't have any glare." She turned to KiLe. "Would you like to ride with us?"

"I would, yes."

"Great. It'll give you a bird's eye view of the mountain ranges. It's always good to have another pair of eyes. What about you, Brian?"

"I'm working on the recount, so I've more than enough to keep me busy here. I'm also going to look for a more secure way to protect our herds."

"Okay, we'll be back in a couple of hours," Kadijah said and left with Danny and KiLe.

Brian waited until he heard the helicopter lift off before he went to Arabella's office down the hall from Danny's. She was on a call with a potential buyer, which she ended when he knocked on her open door. Arabella handled the consortiums' marketing and sales part of the business and was very good at her position.

When she spotted him at her open door, she waved him in. "I thought you might stop by," she said by way of greeting and stood to close her door after Brian entered.

"How is Molly?"

"Sullen." Arabella wrapped her arms around her waist and went to the window, looking out on the spectacular view of the mountain range. "She wouldn't come into the office today. I don't like to leave her alone when she's upset."

"Isn't Andy at the house?"

"No, he had a medical appointment today. Frankly, I just think he wanted to get out of harm's way."

"You know what needs to be done, Arabella."

"Not you too, Brian."

"I've never thought you should keep Molly's father's identity a secret from her. Too many people have ideas about who her father is and could tell her."

Arabella shook her head full of lustrous, long, thick, black hair as she continued to stare out at the beautiful, snow-covered landscape.

When she didn't say anything, Brian said, "I hope you and Grandaunt Althea can find a way to bury the hatchet."

"She hit her, Brian!" Arabella railed, her eyes flashing as she turned her head in Brian's direction.

"I know. I was there. You wouldn't have tolerated her behavior either if you heard what she said."

Arabella turned away, seemingly silenced by the truth in Brian's statement.

"I've got things to do. I just wanted to see how Molly is doing."

"Thanks, Brian."

"You're welcome," he said and made to leave.

"Brian, she loves you, you know."

"Yes, I know. Maybe a little too much. She's been coming on to me and I don't want to hurt her. There isn't a drop of blood between us, but I don't think of her in any way other than as my cousin," he said and left Arabella's office closing the full-view, wood-framed, glass door behind him.

It was all so awesome, thought KiLe sitting in the front seat next to Kadijah as she expertly flew over the mountain range. They scared birds from their nests, but she was careful to avoid flying anywhere near the large flocks or the geese returning from their winter retreats. There were thick forests and mountain lakes which looked like glass from the air. Farmhouses and log cabins sat on what appeared to be patchwork quilts in some of the most improbable locations on the landscape. However, each residence took full advantage of the incredible views.

"That's my place," said Danny pointing to a log cabin partially covered by wooded forest. "There's Liam's place and Pierce's place near the ridge."

"You live within what looks like a mile of each other," commented KiLe.

"We do, yes. Mom, Andy, and Molly live over there where our three-times, great grandfather built our ancestral home. Granddad Seth and Granduncle Charley live there now. That's where my father and his siblings grew up. He was a military man and, while in Italy, he met our mom, Arabella. He told us she was still very young, only sixteen at the time, but for him, it was love at first sight. He had to sneak her out of Italy because her family had plans to marry her off to someone else the same year they met. The man was much older and she didn't even know him, but she loved my father and agreed to run away with him."

KiLe thought about her own situation with her parents, who wanted to marry her to a man of their choice. She understood Arabella Montgomery's need to escape being forced into a lifelong commitment to a complete stranger.

Danny continued. "My parents got married in a little church in Italy where no one knew them and again by a military Chaplin so that Mom would receive military benefits, including an American passport. Dad brought her here to live where no one could find her, but he was career military, so he was away a lot. We all grew up here while our father was away in the service."

He didn't mention that his father's death was ruled a homicide, which was never solved. Speculation had it that Arabella's mafia family put a hit out on him. It was entirely possible since Arabella is the great-great-granddaughter of Tomaso Cascioferro; Don Tomas, the boss of mafia bosses. He's a man in his nineties in the Cosa Nostra in Palermo, Italy, who still rules his family with a tight fist through his six sons, all of whom are in their seventies. Everyone in the Montgomery family knows that one of Don Tomas' grandsons is Diego Valachi Cascioferro, and would have been the perfect prototype for ***The Godfather's*** Michael Corleone; the head of the largest Italian mafia family. Even years later, the Montgomerys lived with the concern that Arabella could be kidnapped, returned to Italy, and forced to marry whomever they chose to fulfill a debt. As a result, she stayed close to home and rarely traveled. That is partially why her sons chose to live close to her.

"Those are really nice homes," KiLe commented, breaking into Danny's thoughts. "So, your mother, brother, and sister live with your grandfather and granduncle?"

"Yes," said Danny and let the subject drop.

They were flying up high over a ridge KiLe thought she recognized. "Isn't that where we were working?" she asked Danny.

"It is, yes. That's where Liam usually trains his birds."

"What's that on the ridge above it?"

"My brother's, Derrick's, and our father's, Grover's gravesites," said Kadijah as she circled back closer. Then she went up over the graves to a higher elevation."

"WOW!" KiLe said, reverently breathing the word as they flew over a huge mountaintop lake surrounded by peaks of rugged, yet breathtaking landscape.

"Brian's favorite place," said Kadijah. "He sometimes has me fly him up here so he can camp for a while and go fishing and swimming in the summer. He loves it up here. Sometimes the clouds are so low in this area, I can't safely fly up here. So, he'll climb up. Still, it is a beautiful spot."

"I'll say," agreed Danny. "We've camped here when time permits."

KiLe knew she would never forget the sight or the beauty of the isolated location.

Road crews were out clearing away snow and laying down ash to identify the curbside boundaries, Kadijah told her, in an area where there were sheer drop-offs into deep ravines. Yet, when KiLe looked up, all she could see for miles in any direction was the bright sunshine reflecting off the unrelenting snow. That is until she spotted something incongruent with the bright, white snow. "What's that?" she asked no one in particular.

"I'm not sure. Let's take a look-see," said Kadijah as she swung the helicopter in that direction.

"Damn it!" Danny cursed.

"What is it?" asked KiLe again, until they got closer and recognition dawned.

"Slaughtered cows," said Kadijah as she flew lower. She hovered over the roadway blowing away the snow sufficient for her to land, but not too close to the crime scene.

"There's bright red blood congealed all along the fence line and into the trees. These cattle have been slaughtered recently and I think it's more than the six we thought missing," Danny said into the cellphone.

"I was afraid of that," said Brian. "I believe it's connected to the vandalism. The thieves knew we were doing a headcount and would miss the cattle. Of course, we would send out a search party, but we couldn't use the horses because the snow is too deep. We would have to use our trucks so they disabled them so these thieves would have enough time to slaughter the cows and make off with the meat before we were up and operational again."

"I agree. I'll call Granddad and let him know. His deputies need to be on the lookout for the thieves."

"They won't try to sell in this county. They would be too easily identified, so, they'll take it to a larger market like Philadelphia, New York, or points west, like Pittsburgh or states like Ohio or Illinois. They may even have a way to store it until the heat is off before they try to sell it."

"You're right, but I sure wish I could get my hands on them."

"This is a gang, Danny. We've got to keep a cool head and try to outsmart them. They got away with it this time, but they'll be back. Other ranchers in the area need to be put on alert, too. We'll talk about it later tonight."

"Yeah, there's nothing to be done now. As soon as Granddad and his deputies get here, we'll come back in and meet you at the barns. Kadijah has other obligations this afternoon."

"See you shortly."

Later that evening, "How are you holding up?" asked Brian of KiLe as she sat reading in one of the mansion's salons on the main floor.

"I don't understand why someone would do that to your cattle."

"Greed, that's why. They couldn't rustle the steers and sell them on the hoof. It's too risky and easy to trace the cattle. Meat, on the other hand, would be difficult to identify. So they slaughtered them and will probably butcher them somewhere else. They'll sell the meat to unsuspecting souls. They would be none the wiser about where the meat originated or, for the right price, they probably wouldn't even care."

KiLe nodded her understanding. "Has this ever happened before?"

Brian shook his head. "No, not that I'm aware of. Certainly not since I've taken on the task of managing the ranches after I finished grad school. I think Dad would have mentioned it if it had."

"What are you going to do now?"

"I've already done it. We filed a police report and I've made a claim with the insurance carrier."

KiLe's brows drew together in confusion. "Insurance? Your cows have insurance?"

Brian laughed. "They do, yes."

"They're cows," she averred as if the idea is completely foreign to her. "You insure the cows?"

He took out his smartphone and dialed up the website for the National Association of Securities Dealers Automated Quotations, commonly known as NASDAQ, a computerized system for trading in securities. "This is how much each cow is worth on today's market." He passed his phone to her.

KiLe's eyes grew wide. "You can't be serious," she said skeptically.

"Very serious. Ranching is a business and what we do has monetary value attached to every aspect."

She shook her head in disbelief. "You have thousands of cows," she said in wonder as understanding began to register. "The cows are only part of your business, right?"

He nodded. "The Alexander Montgomery Consortium or AMC is diversified, yes." If he told her what AMC grossed on a daily basis and the depth and breadth of their holdings, she'd probably faint, so he kept that bit of information to himself.

As a private company, not traded on the New York Stock Exchange, information about AMCs operation is not available for public consumption. However, they invest heavily in a wide range of businesses. He could tell her some of it without being too revealing. "My Uncle Gregory Alexander is a founding partner in a stock-and-bond, brokerage firm, Alexander, Atterly, Chandler, Chase, Jackson, Lightfoot, McAlister, and Montgomery, PA, which constitutes Compliant Trading and Investment, Inc., or CTI. The Wall Street brokerage house not only trades stocks and bonds on the New

York Stock Exchange, but it's also a banking institution, business insurance underwriter, and a highly respected member of the financial community. Uncle Gregory handles the AMC portfolio exclusively.

"The CTI partners are loosely connected as friends and some as relatives. Margo Chandler is Bill Chandler's younger sister. Bill and my mother are former law partners; Troy Jackson is Mom's brother-in-law, my uncle, and the brother of my first father, Derrick. Jeremy Lightfoot is the brother of another one of Mom's former law partners, Alan Lightfoot, Attorney General for the United Indigenous American Nation or UIAN. Jeremy is a Stanford grad. He handles the treasury for the UIAN exclusively. One of the Nation's regions is located not far from here and one of my fraternity brothers heads the operation for the Shawnee and Susquehannocks. China McAlister was one of Mom's former client's comptroller and business associates. She's CTI's managing partner. Joyce Montgomery Callaway is my dad's younger sister and CTI's comptroller. Joyce and Troy are also related through their siblings. Aunt Joyce's older brother, Bob, and Troy's sister, Sheila, are husband and wife.

"As young industry titans, they quickly expanded their talent base with the addition of Jackson Chase, a well-known commodities trader taking the industry by storm. Adam Atterly is Janice Atterly Dixon's younger brother. She's the wife of Cousin James Dixon. James' twin brother, Donald, is the legal representative for CTI and the Alexander Montgomery Consortium. Adam is a west-coast trader showing incredible savvy in the insurance market. He is touted as an insurance guru which is surprising, considering that he's just a little older than me. Adam's branch of CTI handles the insurance plans for all of the businesses they represent. Troy, Adam, and Jeremy are so successful the industry has tagged them The Golden Guys.

"All of the CTI partners have solid academic backgrounds and gained valuable experience working in various aspects of the financial industry. The collaboration of their combined talents and family connections gave them a leg up over their competitors. Close friends and family members were involved in making both CTI and AMC successful concerns. I depend on CTI for cutting-edge advice on market trends."

As she listened, KiLe surmised that Brian never took for granted the contributions everyone in his family and close friends made. Clearly, he was honored to be a member of the family and the team. There didn't appear to be anything he needed or wanted. He had a lifestyle that, although it could be difficult or challenging at times, suited him. At some point in the future, when he decided to marry and have a family, he would want to continue this way of life; teach his children to appreciate making life better for the next generation as his parents had done for him and his siblings. She was awed by his sense of who he is and his comfort in his own skin. That was the type of self-awareness and confidence she could admire.

As Brian thought about his life going forward, he could imagine someone, like KiLe, in it. He looked at her now as she continued to read about NASDAQ on his smartphone. *She is like a sponge*, he thought, *soaking up information. Her thirst for knowledge is even more pronounced than his*, he realized. That alone intrigued him and simultaneously turned him on. When she looked up at him after she finished reading, there was nothing more he wanted than to kiss her. He looked at her mouth and she smiled knowingly, meeting him halfway. He could still feel the smile in her kiss.

CHAPTER 15

KiLe had once wondered how it would feel to kiss Brian Montgomery and now she knew and was gaining more experience by the day. *His kiss is everything great and wonderful*, she thought. He made her *feel* things she never knew existed. When she was in his strong arms, like now, everything seemed to settle down and was right in her world. *It was never like this with Payton*, she thought as she deepened this kiss and pressed her body against his. She could feel his passion and wanted something, but she knew not what.

"Hey, Brotherman," came the interruption from Pierce. "Unhand my woman," he joked. "Dinner is ready."

"Yeah, yeah, yeah," Brian raggedly responded, still looking at the smile on KiLe's face. He liked that about her. She smiled while they kissed. Hell, there wasn't anything he didn't like about her. "We'll be there."

"Not if you keep looking at KiLe like that, you won't. Come on, man. I'm hungry," Pierce complained. "You know we can't eat until everyone is seated at Aunt Althea's table. Also, Ned brought over six sweet potato pies from Ms. Sophie."

"I needed one of those long hugs where I kinda forgot whatever else is happening around me for a minute." KiLe gazed up into Brian's eyes. "Brian's really, really great at delivering those kinds of hugs," she told Pierce.

Brian sighed and unlocked the visual hold he had on KiLe, lest he devour her instead of his dinner. Though he thoroughly enjoyed Ms. Sophie's sweet potato pies, he'd make KiLe his dessert instead of the pies. "Come on, KiLe, before Pierce starts crying like a baby over a missing meal." He slung an arm around her shoulders and she placed her arm around his waist.

"Aunt Althea made shrimp scampi, Brian," Pierce whined as he tried to hurry them along through the halls to one of the dining salons.

"Well," said Brian. "That's something to rush for," he told KiLe. "We're in for a real treat: Aunt Althea's shrimp dish and Ms. Sophie's pie."

When they arrived, Liam, Danny, and their younger brother, Andy, were already assembled.

"*Yo,*" Andy hailed from his wheelchair. He popped a wheelie and scooted over to KiLe. "I heard how beautiful you are, KiLe, but those comments are gross understatements. Hi, I'm the sane brother, Anderson Montgomery, but everyone calls me Andy. You can call me anything you want as long as you call me. Want a ride?" he offered, grinning.

KiLe laughed and sat on his lap while he popped another wheelie and spun around several times before he wheeled them to the table.

"You really don't have to get up," Andy wiggled his eyebrows at her. "I'm harmless."

"Don't believe a word of that," said Seth Montgomery as he entered the salon drying his hands on a paper towel. "Scallywags, the lot of them. Come sit next to me, Ms. KiLe."

"Somehow, I think you might be the most dangerous one of all," KiLe teased.

"She sure has your number, Seth Montgomery," said Althea.

"There is that," the older man admitted and grinned, making KiLe laugh.

"Settle down, boys, and give the young lady a break," cautioned Althea and they did. She served white wine with dinner and everything from soup to nuts.

"That was mighty fine, Althea," commented Seth at the end of the meal. "Where did you find fat shrimp like that this time of the year?"

"Brian brought them up from his Maryland fishery."

"I think you ought to build a fishery up here," suggested Andy.

"One in Maryland and one in South Carolina are plenty for me at the moment. We ship to restaurants in the area with same-day service. If that becomes burdensome, I'll consider expanding. However, you could build one yourselves. I wouldn't mind a little healthy competition," he laughed.

"Not likely," Pierce spoke up. "We're spread thin as it is, Andy. Don't start thinking we can add another venture."

"That's right, Pierce," said Liam. "I have enough on my plate. I'm not a workaholic like Andy and Brian. I want a life at some point before I meet my maker."

Andy shrugged. "It's just a thought," he said, but Brian could see the seeds of a new venture were taking root in Andy's very active brain. Of the four brothers, Andy was the most innovative.

"For the time being, let's figure out how to keep what you already have," suggested Seth.

"I don't want to string wire on all of the meadows we use for the animals. For now, I suggest we keep them close to the barns. If we get lucky and get a thaw sometime soon, we'll be able to get out on horseback again and ride the areas. Maybe put on some night crews. Until then, I suggest we put people on snowmobiles and make sure the stock doesn't wander far from the barns."

"My deputies will make regular runs on the back roads leading to your ranches and stop anyone driving large trucks for a look-see. This area has been generally safe, so we didn't patrol out this way. Now we've put it on our regular rotation," said Seth. "Since you boys own the roads out that way between your pastures, you'll have to put a crew on to patch up any potholes once the snow melts."

"Will do, Uncle Seth. I talked with my Uncle Kenneth and asked him whether there is anything electronic we can do to increase the security. He suggested we put up drones with night-vision lenses and have someone monitor twenty-four/seven."

"That's doable," said Liam. "I'll let you know when and where I'm working with my birds. They would mistake a drone for another bird and attack it."

"Good thought. I'll ask Uncle Kenneth whether he can outfit the drones with sounds which would make your birds stay away."

Liam nodded in agreement.

"He's working on this as a priority. I expect to hear something from him in less than a week. In the interim, with Granduncle Seth's increased patrols and our crews' increased presence, we may be able to hold off any more attacks for a while. Once we get the drones and Uncle Kenneth gets us trained on how to use them efficiently, we'll have another security tool in our toolbox."

"Whatever you decide to do, keep word of the new security measure down to a trusted few. I still want to catch these varmints. For sure, if I don't, they'll try to do this again," said Seth.

There were nods of agreement around the table.

"I'm also working with a canine security force. This area is much larger than my Maryland ranch. Also, there are more wild animals here, like bears, wolves, bobcats, and coyotes. Bears flourish in these mountains, so I'm not sure whether the canines would work here. My canine leader and I will have to give it more consideration and soon. I'll give her a heads up. Also, as I mentioned before, I'll start recruiting for more hands to work this ranch, maybe as many as ten more. There are a number of military veterans and wounded warriors who may not be averse to living in this area."

KiLe noticed that Seth gave a nearly imperceptible nod to Brian, who seemed to know what he was referring to and nodded in return.

"Okay, now that that's settled, let's go play ball," said Andy enthusiastically. "I brought the van. KiLe can ride with me."

"Not on a bet," Brian snorted and smirked.

Less than a half-hour later, they pulled into the parking lot of the junior college gymnasium and joined the group of people heading inside. Once inside, Pierce, Liam, Danny, Brian, and Andy put on blue, numbered jerseys and selected wheelchairs. They met up with others wearing blue jerseys already practicing on one end of the regulation-sized basketball court.

The other team wore red numbered jerseys and the referees wore traditional black and white.

Althea and KiLe found seats on the bleachers while greeting people, some of whom KiLe remembered from the bowling lanes and the base camp.

"This is interesting," said KiLe to Althea. "I've been to basketball games before. Whitney regularly plays with a group of female attorneys, law school students, and judges, including her Aunt Vivian, but I've never seen a game played in wheelchairs."

"Some of the players are physically challenged, so to even the playing field, everyone has to get in a wheelchair at the very beginning and cannot get out of the chair until the very end. When I was much younger, I played basketball in junior and high school. I wanted to play in college, too, but, back then, there weren't that many colleges or universities with female teams. Thank goodness Title IX changed all of that."

"Title IX?" KiLe asked.

"Title IX is a portion of the United States Education Amendments of 1972, renamed the Patsy Mink Equal Opportunity in Education Act in 2002. It requires that no person in the United States shall, on the basis of sex, be excluded from participation in, be denied the benefits of or be subjected to discrimination under any education program or activity receiving federal financial assistance."

"There is so much to learn here in America. My parents don't understand why I don't want to leave."

"Your parents want you to leave America?"

"They and my grandparents want me to marry one of the seven men they have chosen for me to become engaged to and finish my education in England. Then I am to come home to Japan and marry so that I can have children."

Althea stared for a moment before looking out onto the basketball court where Brian and the others were warming up before the start of the game. "Does Brian know about your parents' wishes?"

"Yes, we talked about it."

"What were his thoughts?"

"He told me 'Don't fret. Where there's a will, there's a way.' Whatever that means."

"Nothing more than that?"

"He asked me a lot of questions, but otherwise, he just listened."

Althea nodded. "He's good at that. He pays attention to details."

He does, KiLe thought, but for some reason, she expected more. For now, she was intrigued by the many facets of Brian Alford Montgomery. When one of the referees, also in wheelchairs, blew a whistle for the start of the game, Brian had her undivided attention.

She never noticed Molly and her mother, Arabella, sitting up higher on the bleachers. While KiLe focused on the game, Molly focused on her.

No one noticed the man sitting on the opposite side of the gym, snapping pictures.

Damn! They just couldn't catch a break, thought Brian, the next day as he checked the weather report again. Another heavy snow-producing storm was predicted to race up the coast, starting from as far south as Florida. It wasn't unusual to get snow in March in Pennsylvania and even April in the Poconos, but this was crazy. They had three snow events since arriving on Sunday morning. The next one is predicted to be like a late-winter hurricane making spring break at the beaches in the south untenable.

Still, it was one of the reasons winter tourism was a top industry for Pennsylvania, but it was hampering their efforts to protect their cattle. They had all hands working to erect temporary shelters for the livestock before the storm hit. Like helium-filled balloons, the dome-like structures would keep the cattle from freezing, yet it would be a messy undertaking. They didn't have nearly enough cat litter to keep down the stench. They would have to continuously lay down beds of hay and keep the troughs full of flowing water and feed. They also had cows to milk. Brian wasn't looking forward to the effort.

Yet, he stopped momentarily to look over to where KiLe was helping to feed the baby calves whose mothers were slaughtered. She pulled the animals to the artificial teats with purpose and determination. Those animals weighed in at more than her in some cases. No sooner than she got one animal situated, she would have to go chasing after another one. *She's a real trooper*, he thought, as he watched her loose her grip on a calf and plop down on her bottom. She hopped right up and went charging after the animal and finally got it to an available teat. Then she was scurrying off to find another baby calf. He laughed, shook his head, and went back to work, securing the lines as the domes rose.

He remembered last night at the basketball game hearing KiLe's voice cheering them on. They lost by three points, but their defeat didn't dampen her spirit. She came off the bleachers and distributed towels and water to the players while offering encouragement.

He was truly off his game last night, sinking only five shots. Too much on his mind, he knew, but none of them were up to their usual coordinated routine. This thing with their slaughtered cattle bothered all of them far more than anyone wanted to openly admit. Then to have their vehicles vandalized didn't help the situation. No one liked feeling vulnerable and unable to protect the legacy handed down through generations of their ancestry. Admittedly, ranching had its challenges, but this theft struck at the bedrock of their foundation. Nothing ever so adversely affected them than this robbery.

When they got home after the game, he only wanted to swim, take a turn in the sauna, and sleep. However, KiLe wouldn't let him be. She stuck to him and forced him to teach her a little more about swimming in deeper water. Then, in the sauna, she gave him a massage which loosened his tight muscles and took the tension out of his shoulder and back to the point he nearly fell asleep.

She had good strong hands and forced him to think of things other than the loss of the cows and the basketball game. She told him about growing up in Tokyo, Japan, the daughter of wealth and privilege. As a good teacher, she taught him some words and phrases in Japanese while she worked on him from head to toe. Of course, she was wrapped in a terrycloth robe and he wore a towel around his waist. It was a good thing she worked on only his shoulders and back or she would have seen the evidence of her ministration on his body. He had massages before, but KiLe seemed to know just where his body needed the most attention. Her hands were small but talented. As a result, when he woke this morning, not one ache or pain accompanied him when he left his bed. More importantly, his mind was clear and ready to process whatever came next.

It was the storm which occupied everyone's mind now. His grandfather and his mechanics worked like demons changing tires and cleaning gas tanks until well after midnight, but all of the trucks and cars were finished and picked up. The consortium paid a bonus to the mechanics for their swift and efficient work in getting the task completed in record time. Kadijah flew granddad Stephen back to Maryland to resume spending the week with his grandchildren and relatively new wife, Harriet.

They were back to full strength on each job site again, but the coming storm forced them to divert some of their time to erect the temporary shelters. Yeah, no, they couldn't catch a break.

KiLe's feet stuck in the mud with every step she tried to take. More than once, she was hauled out of one muddy puddle or the other by one of the ranch hands. They seemed to get a kick out of rescuing her and started calling her "Little Bit." Well, she did weigh in at only a little over a hundred pounds. Most of the guys and many of the women lifted twice her weight with ease. She was beginning to believe she was more trouble to the effort than she was worth.

As the shelter went up, heat caused the ground to thaw. With hooves moving from place to place, mud and muck mixed. She was wearing someone's hip boots usually used for fishing in lakes and streams, but they were like lead weights on her feet when she tried to move around.

She didn't know how everyone else seemed to be able to move with ease while she struggled. Of course, she didn't have the leg and thigh muscles Brian had or the upper body strength. She had her hands on his body the night before and luxuriated in how he felt under her palms. She gave him a full-body scrub—well, almost a full-body scrub—in the sauna after they got out of the pool and then a hot-oil massage. She was curious about whether she could execute a "happy ending," but thought better of it. She had been taught how to administer a deep-tissue massage, but her instruction was limited. Her mother said her education in how to please a man would continue when she returned to Japan for the summer. That was one lesson she hoped to avoid by being permitted to stay in America until she completed her doctorate . . . and maybe even beyond that. Actually, she liked living in America more than she liked living in Japan. There was so much more to see and do here and she wanted to explore more areas of the country. The way Tucker talked about Maine, she wanted to see it herself in the fall when he said the trees were the most beautiful. She lived in a house where the other students were from different parts of the country.

Everyone had interesting stories about his or her home state. She wanted time to see it all.

KiLe looked up and around the rapidly inflating structure. Brian was helping to lash it down. She understood the engineering. Because of its shape, snow wouldn't be able to stand on the barrel-back roof. It would slide off to the sides. They were stacking bales of hay both inside the structure and outside of the tarp to prevent air infiltration. They were going about this task so efficiently it was clear to her this was not the first time they were forced to take these measures.

It was fascinating to watch, but she accepted the task of keeping the baby cows corralled in a pen she helped to erect—at least when she could stay on her feet. She looked away from the structure going up to one of the heifers who kept trying to get out of the pen. "Don't you even think about it," she said meanly to the calf. "I've got my eyes on you, pal," she said, pointing two fingers to her eyes and then to the cow's eyes.

"Now if that isn't the sight," said Althea laughing. "If you're talking to the livestock, you need a break."

"I wish I could, Honorable Aunt, but this little heifer is sneaky. Every time I look away for a moment, it tries to get out of the pen."

"He's looking for his mama," said Althea. "It will take a few more days of artificial feeding before he forgets her."

"Oh," sighed KiLe, instantly sympathetic. "I didn't realize. The others seemed content to feed from the bottle."

"Don't worry, he'll be okay. Come now and sit a spell. You've been at this since before sun up this morning."

KiLe tried to pull one foot and then the other up out of the mud but threw up her hands in frustration.

Althea laughed and threw a rope to KiLe. She latched on and Althea pulled until KiLe was free of the mud.

KiLe climbed up on the bale of hay and sat beside Althea. When she was seated, Althea passed a thermos of hot coffee to her. They sat in companionable silence, just watching the activity going on around them.

"How many tarps do they have to erect?" KiLe asked.

"Enough to ensure they can contain the entire herd. The problem is the twenty-three bulls. They can be aggressive so they have to be held in separate pens. We group each one of them with a certain number of cows to let nature take its course. The Consortium has saved a lot of cows by erecting these temporary structures in severely inclement weather and produced a lot of calves because of the close proximity of the papa and his ladies. The cattle are accustomed to cold weather, but when you add ice and snow and they can't move freely, they could freeze to death standing still. These barns are in the valley, but it's still a lot of moisture in the air when the temperature drops like this and the wind picks up racing down from the mountains. It's a good thing when they have a few days to prepare for the worst."

"Brian really works hard, doesn't he?" KiLe acknowledged while watching him and others lash down another set of ropes until a front loader could maneuver another big bale of hay into place. His muscular arms enticingly flexed as he pulled on the ropes with gloved hands. She could also see his thigh muscles move in his snug jeans.

"He does, yes, but he wouldn't have it any other way." She looked at the concentration on KiLe's face. "You seem to enjoy this type of challenge, too."

KiLe turned her head and looked at Althea, nodding. "I'm afraid that I do. I love being out in the open air and not cooped up in a cubicle."

"Why afraid?" asked Althea.

"If I were at home—in Japan, I mean—my parents would never allow me to do this type of manual labor. This," she said while looking around at all of the people working hard together to save a herd of cows, "would not be tolerated. To them, this is the type of work people who can't do any better, are expected to do. They are not expected to rise above their lower station in life. With my academic acumen, they expect me to achieve great things and take what they expect will be my rightful place in Japanese society as my husband's handmaiden and helpmate."

"Does your family want what's best for you?"

"They want what they *decide* is best for me. You see, when I was very young, I trained as a gymnast. I even placed with my team during the Olympic Games, but because we didn't win the gold, my parents wouldn't allow me to train for competition anymore. I still do it for exercise, but it is their opinion that, if I couldn't win the gold medal, I was wasting my time and theirs.

"They permit me to train as a vocalist, but only to sing traditional Japanese songs in my native language. If they heard me singing a Grace Jones ballad, I'd be sent to my room for a millennium. I can play the flute and the harp, which are acceptable in Japanese society, but my parents don't know I can whale on the tenor sax, too, to some gut-busting jazz and blues. I can do all of the things I like to do here in America with the friends I've made here. They accept me just as I am. When I go home, all of that will end and, once I'm married to their choice of a proper husband for me, I'll never be permitted to return to America again."

"What will you do, KiLe?"

"I don't know. I'll try to convince my parents to let me stay here to receive my doctorate, but they want me to go to England for that. I just have to find a way to convince them otherwise." She checked her herd of heifers and found one missing. "I'll be back, Honorable Aunt." Setting aside her thermos, she climbed down off the bales of hay in search of her cow.

CHAPTER 16

"A Friday night fish fry?" asked KiLe of Brian as they dressed after a swim and light meal.

"Yes, at the fire station. It should be a lot of fun. We've had a couple of rough days and the storm will probably hit over the weekend. If there are white-out conditions, we won't be able to get out of the house much. Hopefully, it will end before you leave on Sunday afternoon."

"You're not coming back to Maryland with me?"

Brian shook his head. "I've arranged for Whitney to pick you up on her way back home. I need to stay and help get us back on track. We've got orders for fifteen timber-frame homes and the deadlines are approaching fast. Most of the trees we haven't even identified yet. We'll have to run two shifts at the mill to get all the lumber cut, kiln-dried, and then dry-fit the parts together. After that, we have to package and ship. We send two crew members with each home to ensure the building is assembled correctly. In two cases in upstate New York, the footings couldn't even be dug because the ground is frozen. We've identified a few warehouses to store the timber on flatbeds until work can begin, hopefully, next week, but we're behind schedule.

"I also need to deal with the security issues for our herds. I don't want a repeat of what happened before. I also have a new group of wild horses I need to work with. My dad is going to want to look at a few, which seem to have thoroughbred championship qualities. Others, broodmares, I like for mating with my stallions, including Lucky and Pegasus. I have other projects I need to get underway.

"Now let's get a move on. I don't want to be late."

KiLe pulled on all of the heavy weather gear she had come to appreciate since coming to the mountains. Even though they would be riding in a heated truck, Brian insisted that she suit up in case something happened and they ended up having to walk.

KiLe could hear the music even before they pulled into the protected fire station lot with others. The scent of fish and fries wafted on the cold, brisk air. There was a noticeable police presence in both the front and the back of the large fire station building. The emergency vehicles were moved out of the building, making plenty of room inside for the partygoers. Heavy-weather clothes came off in a nanosecond, once they entered the large, heated space and were exchanged for claim tickets.

A young band was accepting applause and gearing up for another little hoedown. This led to the introduction of jugs, spoons, guitars, and washboards to provide the rhythm section. Upside down, round washtubs were pressed into service as drum sets for an original Zydeco-like sound. With the addition of woodblocks, cowbells, and cymbals, people were tapping out the beat on tabletops, handclaps, and voice calls. *These homemade instruments and ordinary objects, like the washtub bass, washboards, spoons, bones, stovepipe, and comb and tissue paper, adapted to or modified for the making of sound, could have been a full orchestra concert in Carnegie Hall,* thought KiLe.

She hadn't heard music like this before and she strained to hear and understand the lyrics of the trio of singers.

"Come on, Althea, let's show 'em what they're up against," a middle-aged man said, grabbing Althea's hand and leading her into the thick of the dancers.

"*WOW*, this is something, huh?" asked KiLe awed.

"I bring you to only the best places," Brian joked. "It's country living. Most of the people here grew up together. Their families have lived in these mountains for generations. Friday night fish fries are somewhat of a tradition. They've been held twice a month on the second and fourth Fridays for more years than I've been alive. Money is raised from the sale of fish dinners, ticket sales, and raffles. After expenses for each event, the proceeds are donated to a worthy cause."

"What's the dance they're doing?"

"It's the Texas Two-Step. Come on, I'll show you," he said and swung her into his arms.

She tried to follow his footfalls, but the cadence was off to her and then someone tapped her on her shoulder.

"Hello, Brian, KiLe. May I cut in?" asked Gayle Hightower.

"Hello, Gayle," said KiLe. "Sure. Brian was just trying to teach me the Texas Two-step, but I'm getting nowhere fast." She stepped back and headed for the sidelines.

She hadn't quite left the dance floor when she heard, "Hello, KiLe," from Officer David Turner.

"David, how are you?"

"I'm fine. I saw you on the dance floor with Brian. I noticed Ms. Hightower cut in. Looks like Brian is going to have a busy night. I saw his girlfriend, Haylie, a few moments ago."

"Yes, he's a pretty popular guy."

"Would you like to dance?" he asked her.

"Aren't you on duty?"

"My partner is in the radio car out back if anything happens. How about it?"

"Well, yes, I'd like to dance, but I can't do what everyone else is doing."

"I'm happy to help you learn the steps. Now stand beside me and I'll teach you how it's done."

"What's up with you, Brian?" asked Gayle.

"What do you mean?"

"You're dancing with me, but you're watching KiLe."

He turned his attention to her while they danced, looking her in her eyes. "When are you going to stop trying to make Liam jealous, Gayle?"

"If you hadn't noticed, Liam is dancing with someone else right now. She doesn't look familiar. Do you know who she is?"

Brian turned his head and looked in his cousin's direction. It took a few moments for Brian to recognize the woman in Liam's arms. "She's a client who purchased one of our larger timber-frame homes. She wants it to be constructed in the Catskills. Her name is Catherine something," he remembered. "She asked to come to see the logs being cut for her get-away home."

"What does she do to be able to afford one of your homes as a vacation spot?"

"As I recall, Catherine is an advertising executive of her own firm . . . Boyd, her last name. Boyd Advertising, New York City. Catherine Boyd," he now remembered. Oh, yes, there was definitely an interest on Catherine's part where Liam is concerned, Brian knew.

Liam must have called her a few days ago when they began cutting the trees needed for her project. Catherine is certainly an attractive woman, the kind of woman who could sell ice to Eskimos. Gayle had every reason to feel pea green with jealousy, thought Brian, as he continued to dance with her. Still, his attention was on KiLe, who was now dancing with the Sheriff's Deputy, David Turner. As he watched them, he recognized that Gayle wasn't the only one feeling a little off-center.

"So, how did they meet?"

"Uh, I believe it was at my sister, Linda's annual fundraiser for her dance academy. Boyd Advertising handled the publicity and ad campaign for the event. Liam and all of us went to New York to support Linda's efforts. We stayed over a few extra days. Catherine joined us one night at The Run Way, Angelique's nightclub adjacent to her restaurant, and we went out to parties around town she knew about."

"Is she single?"

"Gayle," Brian said on a windy sigh. "I'm not the four-one-one Answer Man on Liam's life. You have questions, ask him. Now, thanks for the dance." He said it and walked away before the music ended. Instead of going directly to where KiLe danced with David, he detoured to the bar for a beer for himself and his aunt and a bottle of water for KiLe. It gave him time to think about what he was feeling seeing KiLe in the arms of another man. Geez-oh-flip, it hadn't even been a full week and he was obsessing about KiLe and who she spent time with.

"Hello, Brian," a woman said behind him.

He turned and smiled at Susan Atwater, an antique dealer from Stroudsburg. "Susan, this is a surprise. I didn't know you were in the area."

"I came down on a buying trip. It got too late to drive back tonight, so I'm staying over at a bed and breakfast near here. How are things with you?"

"Fine. I came up from Maryland on Sunday."

"So I've heard. Your name has been in the news quite a bit lately. I also saw an article in a high-fashion magazine which featured you. Very impressive."

"Believe me when I tell you that if I could have avoided that article, I would have. How are things in the antique industry?"

"Slow. The only reason I would come this way in the dead of winter is for a chance to spend a little quality time with you." She stepped a little closer into his personal space. "If you're free later tonight, I'd like for you to join me at the B&B. I understand they have a great breakfast buffet."

"Under ordinary circumstances, Susan, I might take you up on that offer. However, my schedule over the next few days will be extremely tight. I'm sure you've heard the weather reports."

"I have, yes. In fact, I was hoping we would get snowed in together for a few days. You have to go to bed sometime and rumor has it that you have a very comfortable bed at the Montgomery Mansion and a great deal of privacy. I'd love to get a look at your home. Perhaps you have some antiques you'd like to part with."

Brian chuckled. "Again, very tempting, Susan, but no to both offers. I'm behind schedule as it is. I can't afford the time right now. I'll have to pass."

"That's regrettable, Brian." She kissed his cheek. "I want to sleep with you, but if you're using the weather as an excuse, then it's obviously not going to happen. Take care of yourself," she said and walked away.

Strike Two, he thought. First Haylie, now Susan, but Susan isn't a gamer, he knew. She was a few years his senior, but she has brains and beauty. A lethal combination. Real curb appeal and not the type of woman to sit around waiting for a man to make a move. With Susan's departure, that left Joelle. However, now there is KiLe.

"You're doing fine, KiLe, so relax," said David when she stumbled.

She did relax, marginally, but David was holding her a little too close for her comfort. Maybe it was her imagination or he was just making sure she wouldn't fall. Yet, it just felt different from the way Brian held her, which seemed dissimilar. More likely, it was the kiss a very stylish woman planted on Brian. In any event, she was glad the music was ending.

"I, uh, thought about stopping by to follow up on your initial statements about the robbery, the vandalism, and the slaughtered cows. What would be a good time for you?"

"Really, David, I've told you everything I remember happening in each event. I don't think I have anything else to offer in the way of eye-witness information."

"You never know what might come to you after a few hours. I'll call you tomorrow and set up a time. I can make it convenient for you. You're staying at the Montgomery Mansion, right?"

"Yes, I'm a guest there, but if you think I can be of further assistance, I'll do whatever I can to help. I can come to your office."

"That won't be necessary. We're patrolling out in your area these days, so it would be convenient for me to drop by. What time will Brian be there?"

"I really don't know his schedule. He usually leaves before sun up in the morning. I can ask him to make himself available if you know what time you can come by."

"Oh, no, that won't be necessary. I can see him at another time. I'll call when I'm in the area."

She shrugged. "That's fine." When the music ended, she stepped back. "Thanks for the lesson. I'll try to remember what you taught me."

"I enjoyed it, too. Anytime you need a lesson, I'm your man," he said and moved away melting into the crowd.

She stared after him and wondered whether he was hitting on her. Something definitely seemed different. Mentally, she shrugged, dismissed the thought, and looked around for Brian. When she spotted him, she moved in his direction.

"Having fun?" asked Althea when she joined Brian and KiLe.

"I am, yes. There always seems to be something to do here," KiLe remarked.

"If there wasn't, we'd have cabin fever. It seems we're getting more winter than usual," said Althea.

On stage, the young band was packing up while another band prepared to carry the music in a different direction. KiLe listened to the canned music played through the transition. "I've never heard this music either," she said to Althea.

"The Doobie Brothers. They were popular in my grandparents' era."

"Oh," KiLe said and continued to listen as the new band finished assembling on stage.

"Evenin' ladies and gents," said the bandleader. "Are y'all ready for a hot time in the ole town ta nite?"

The crowd roared *"yeah,"* along with hand-clapping and shrilled whistles.

"Then, let's have at it!"

When they led off with "On the Road Again," the crowd went wild. Through several successive songs, the crowd clapped, danced, and sang along before the bandleader came to the mic and cupping his hand above his eyes, said, "I know them Montgomery brothers are out there in the audience somewhere."

"Here's one!" someone shouted.

"Here's another over here!" someone else shouted.

"Okay, boys, you know what we want," said the bandleader and again, the crowd roared.

Pierce, Liam, Danny, and Andy headed for the stage and lifted Andy up in a contraption that had him standing to his full height.

"See, all we wanted to do was come and have a little fun," joked Danny into the mic and then looked around. "Someone is missing. Who's missing, y'all?"

"Brian!" the crowd called out.

"Yeah, y'all know he was tryin' to hide back there, but are we going to let him get away with that?"

"No!" the crowd responded.

KiLe turned and smiled up at Brian, who was indeed trying to become invisible, but it was not to be.

The crowd pushed and prodded until he made his way up on stage and the women went wild. Mics were quickly positioned in front of the five men and the band picked up with *"Take Me in Your Arms" (Rock Me A Little While)* with Andy as the lead singer.

"He's fantastic!" KiLe enthusiastically said to Althea as she clapped and swayed to the foot-stomping music. She was even more impressed with Brian. With her ear for sound, though they all blended and harmonized beautifully together, she could clearly distinguish Brian's richly, creamy voice from the others. She had heard him sing in his cabin before he knew she was there to escape Payton.

"Yes, they all are. They started singing old songs from the fifties and sixties together when they were preteens at family gatherings to appease the older folks. They've been at it ever since. Every once in a while, they'll get together and just have a marathon sing-along."

It showed, thought KiLe as they segued into "What A Fool Believes" to the crowds' delight this time with Danny providing the lead. No sooner had that song ended than the crowd shouted for "Black Water," and the Montgomerys obliged with Brian taking the lead. KiLe was mesmerized by Brian's smooth, sexy sound, but was thrilled when the band stopped playing and the Montgomerys went acapella and Brian let it rip. The only accompaniment they had was provided by the audience who clapped in rhythm with the song and sang the chorus:

"I'd like to hear some funky Dixieland
Pretty mama come and take me by the hand.
By the hand, take me by the hand, pretty mama.
Come and dance with your daddy all night long. I want to honky-tonk,
honky-tonk, honky-tonk
With you all night long."

When they ended, the crowd went ballistic. KiLe, too, found herself shouting in approval.

"The Montgomerys!" the band leader bellowed into the mic and again the crowd roared. "One more, boys! *Give me the beat, boy, I want to get lost in your rock and roll*," he began and the Montgomerys picked up the song "Drift Away."

When they finished, Danny said into the mic, "We have in our midst, ladies and you jokers who call yourselves gentlemen, another talented vocalist, Ms. KiLe Hakamora! Come on up here, KiLe, and give us something to talk about."

She rolled her eyes, but, with Althea's encouragement and that of the crowd, joined the guys on stage. "What am I singing?" she asked the guys as the music built. The band leader handed a page of sheet music to her, which she quickly read.

"It's a Bonnie Raitt song, 'Let's Give Them Something To Talk About'," said Andy.

"Okay," she huffed out a breath and stepped to the mic someone set up for her. She got the cadence of the music by patting her right hand against her thigh to the rhythm, and, after the first few lyrics, stepped into the lead singer's role with the Montgomerys as her backup singers. She was having fun and just relaxed.

She was still singing the Bonnie Raitt song when she and Brian climbed the interior steps at the mansion.

"I think you had a good time tonight," observed Brian as they walked in tandem up the staircase with their arms linked around each other's waist.

"You know I did." She was smiling as they reached the final step. Brian opened the heavy metal door to the hallway that led to their bedroom suites.

"You wowed everyone when you sang Whitney Houston's 'I Will Always Love You'." He smiled at her as they walked the hall.

"It's one of my favorites, along with 'Giving You the Best That I've Got' as sung by the great songstress Anita Baker."

"Mine, too, but then you ripped it up with 'Queen of the Night'."

"Another favorite as such by the incredible Whitney Houston, but I liked it best when we sang that duet together. It's good practice for when we sing those duets for Tucker's and Whitney's wedding."

He snorted a laugh. "You did that tonight to get back at me for getting you up on stage."

"I did, yes," she smiled cheekily. "Are you sleepy?"

"Why?" suspicion in his question.

"Nothing special. I'm just not sleepy yet. My adrenalin is still coursing through me. It happens when I've had a good set like tonight. I just don't want to go to my bed yet."

He shrugged. "Okay, you can come in for a while." He opened the door to his suite, ushering her into the living space.

They took off their outerwear and KiLe took off her boots and settled tailor-style on the sofa while Brian lit the fireplace and started the Keurig in the kitchenette for hot cocoa for two.

KiLe watched him move around the space, his actions economical. "Brian?"

"Yes?"

"What is 'knowing' supposed to feel like?"

"Knowing what?"

"Knowing when something is right. When someone is right for you."

He turned from his tasks and looked at her. "I suppose it can be different for each person. For example, I knew from a very early age that I loved farming. I started out in an orphanage in the city, but the moment I got an opportunity to live in a rural area on a farm, I knew this is what I wanted to do for the rest of my life. I like the city, but only for visits. I don't want to live the rest of my life in that kind of chaos."

She nodded as she accepted a mug of hot chocolate Brian handed to her before he sat down beside her with his own mug.

He toed off his boots, put his feet up on a hassock, and put his left arm along the sofa back behind her.

"I thought I was in a pretty serious relationship with Payton for nearly two years. He was my first real long-term liaison. Sometimes, when I'm with friends, they talk about how they *'know'* the person they are with is who they want to spend their life with. I try to ask how they **know**, and they mostly say they *'just feel it.'* I don't think I really felt it with Payton, but I also have no idea what I was supposed to feel in the first place. I felt Payton was amazing and such a good match for me in so many ways, especially because we clicked when we sing together. We talked about marriage, but neither of us felt in a rush. Was I doing something wrong by staying in a relationship where I didn't necessarily *feel* this magical 'it'? Or is there no such thing and being happy is good enough?"

"I hope you won't be disillusioned by one disappointing relationship, KiLe. I believe that the number one mistake many women make is wasting years of their lives waiting for the men to change. When you get to know a man, rely on your instincts. He'll reveal who he truly is in little or no time.

Just don't go into your next relationship with rose-colored glasses. Each experience will make you better prepared to handle the next one."

"Brian?"

"Yes?"

"Would you want to make love with me?"

"Sure," he said and shrugged as if the question was academic.

Snuggling into his left side, she grinned up at him.

His brows furrowed until recognition dawned. "You mean right now?"

"Yes," she nodded.

He shook his head, smiling and unbelieving until she leaned up and kissed him. *Daaaammnn!* He thought as his pulse ratcheted up and he blindly put his mug on the side table. She nimbly climbed on to his lap facing him and placed her mug next to his. As she began to unbutton his shirt, he stayed her hands and took a deep breath. "I'm not into one-night stands, KiLe, or rebound interludes."

She moved his hands away and said, "Good, because I want something more than that with you, Brian." She continued undressing him.

Again, he stayed her hands. "What is it you want with me, KiLe?"

"I want someone to love me for who I am. I don't know whether we can get there, but I like very much where we've been together as friends. I'm very attracted to you, not just because you're drop-dead handsome, but because you have the type of character I can trust and respect. To use your phrase, you push all the right buttons for me. I don't want to wait. I want to take it to the next level. I want you, Brian. I would want you even if there were no strings attached."

At her honest and forthright words, Brian felt something electric click into place and then surge through his system. She trapped his arms in his sleeves while ravaging his mouth. Then her hands were in his hair while she seated herself more intimately against his arousal, her breasts to his chest. It took time and effort, but he finally freed his arms from his shirt and pulled her shirt from her jeans running his hands up the soft skin of her sides and the warmth of her breasts. He opened her bra and palmed her pebble-hard nipples hearing her breath catch and her breathless moan. He was able to free her upper body of clothes as she continued to ride him through their jeans.

When Brian sucked one of her breasts into his mouth and then the other, she could feel the synapses firing in her brain. However, as she rocked back and forth against the impressive bulge between Brian's thighs, the lower regions of her body became more and more insistent for something…she knew not what. Still, with Brian's calloused hands and clever mouth on her, her body torqued up to a level where she was nearly mindless. So mindless that she was moaning and trying to chase the heat building to the point where her legs began to tremble and shake.

Brian could feel KiLe was reaching her peak and kept her in a state of heightened anticipation while attempting to tamp down his own needs. This was her first time, he realized, and wanted to make it as pleasurable for her as possible. When completion came for her, she squeezed her arms tightly around his shoulders. He effortlessly lifted her, carried her to his bed, and quickly relieved her of the rest of her clothing. She was still in the throes of her first orgasm when he disrobed and found a foil-wrapped condom in his nightstand. Then, hiking her legs on his shoulders, he began to kiss the insides of her thighs. When he latched on to her and suckled, she was loudly moaning his name with a death grip on the bed linens.

KiLe didn't know what was happening to her body; it wasn't under her control anymore. Brian had taken over, causing her body to erupt at least three times. She was still quaking with spasms when he kissed his way up her torso to her mouth. She welcomed the feel of his weight on her. She was lax and languid and still responsive to his fingers between her thighs.

"This is going to hurt, KiLe," he warned soothingly in her ear.

"It won't, no. I had my hymen broken by Dr. Savannah Logan-Flack a few years ago," she said and lifted her hips, welcoming the feel of him inching his way inside her.

Brian closed his eyes and gritted his teeth. She was so soft and tight; he nearly lost control before he was seated to the hilt. She was so small, but agile as she continued to lift her hips to greedily meet his thrusts. He leaned on his forearms and knees not wanting to crush her and letting his pelvis do the work. She kissed him and wrapped her legs around his waist pumping slowly, but firmly.

He felt her orgasms crash through her again several times before he permitted himself to fly off the next precipice with her. Rolling onto his back, he brought KiLe onto his chest without breaking the intimate connection between them. Then they slept.

It had to be morning, Brian's internal clock told him, but all he could see from his bed through the floor to ceiling doors was blinding white, energetically dancing snow. Bending his wrist, he confirmed the time to be five on Saturday morning. *A lot of good that would do his schedule,* he thought.

Next to him, KiLe slept in his arm. He kissed her forehead and eased out of bed to tend to his needs and shower before dressing. When he entered the kitchen, Althea was coming in from the pool towel drying her hair.

"I've already let your dogs out," she said and went to the coffeemaker. "Are you ready for breakfast?"

"I'll have coffee and a bagel in my room for now. I can smell the ones you must have baked this morning," he said yawning. "I was just coming down to see to Starsky and Hutch. Thanks for taking care of them."

"You're welcome. When I got up this morning, I could see we weren't going to be doing anything outside today. We've got a complete whiteout situation. According to the news reports, this weather system should keep up until late this evening. I plan to pull out a good book and read most of the day. Let me know when you're ready for something more substantial to eat."

"Thanks, Aunt Althea," he said as he watched her leave the room. She was right. He would need a rope line to guide his way in the blinding snow. So, he bagged a bunch of assorted bagels Althea made fresh that morning from the bread bin, small pots of homemade jams and jellies, lox, and a tub of soft cream cheese. From the fruit bowl, he grabbed a few grapefruit, bananas, and strawberries before he went back to his suite. He entered quietly and laid out the food on the bar in the kitchenette. Slicing a few bagels, he slipped them in the toaster and started the coffeemaker. After peeling the grapefruit and separating it into quarters, he added the strawberries. When all was ready, he put it on a rolling cart and took it into the sleeping area where KiLe still slept. For a long moment, he just watched her sleep and remembered. She woke him during the night and climbed onto him inserting him into her body. He enjoyed teaching her what turned him on and she took advantage of her lessons, delighting him with her eagerness.

Admittedly, their relationship developed rather quickly, but he would take it slowly with her. He genuinely liked her and felt they were off to a satisfying friendship and a good basis for an intimate rapport. As he continued to study her features, her eyes opened and locked on him. Slowly, she sat up, put her arms around him, and kissed him, forcing him to lay back on the bed. She tunneled her hands under his sweatshirt and rubbed his nipples between her fingertips making him instantly harden. One of her hands slipped down his body and inside his sweatpants to find him heavy, hard, and hot.

"Mmmmm," she hummed while smiling and kissing him. She was fondling him and simultaneously tweaking one of his nipples.

"I think I've created a sex fiend," he flipped her naked body onto her back. She was already damp and responsive to his touch. "No pain or discomfort?"

"Not a bit, but I want you inside me again right now."

He reached into the nightstand and retrieved another condom, the fourth he'd used in the last eight hours, before disrobing in a nanosecond. Moments later, he was balls deep inside her, listening to her moan his name in ecstasy.

Later, KiLe nibbled on a bagel while she watched Brian on the phone talking with Danny Montgomery. They were sitting at a small, round table in Brian's suite beside the floor-to-ceiling, glass, accordion door. He wasn't wearing a shirt and had only a towel around his waist and his bare legs and feet up on a chair across from him. His upper body was beautiful, a masterpiece of sculpted muscles, washboard abs, and broad, straight shoulders. When she sighed audibly, Brian looked her way and smiled. *He is such a handsome guy*, she thought, even with his hair still damp from the shower they took together where he again rocked her world up against the shower walls. She could develop an addiction to Brian Montgomery. She never had a lover before, but she didn't think anyone else could instantly trigger her body into action the way he did. He didn't even have to touch her to have her salivating for him and going damp.

She nibbled more of the bagel and noticed when Brian's eyes dropped to her mouth while he continued to carry on his conversation. She licked the jam from her thumb and his eyes followed her movement with increased interest. Standing from her chair, she straddled Brian's lap and, digging her finger into the small pot of jam, she spread it on his nipples the way he had done to her. Then, with her eyes on his, she leaned forward and slowly licked the jam from his pecks.

"Uh, Danny, let me give you a call back in a little while. Something has come up that I need to take care of right away," he said and immediately disconnected the call. "Ms. Hakamora, you promised to be good and not distract me."

"Am I distracting you?" she asked as she spread jam in his belly button. "I thought I was having a snack.

When she leaned down to lick away all evidence of the jam, her ministration didn't end there. Fifteen minutes later, he was grabbing for another condom mindless of the sticky residue of jam and jelly, which coated his member and would be trapped inside the prophylactic on the skin of his rigid phallus. The race was on to get himself covered and inside her before he erupted.

It was past lunchtime when Brian and KiLe made it into the salon where a meal waited for them on the steam trays. Althea was sitting comfortably in a double-wide chair with her feet up and a book open in her lap. She took off her reading glasses and smiled at the young couple. "Hungry?" she asked.

"Starving," said Brian as he went to the buffet and retrieved a wide bowl handing it to KiLe.

"This smells delicious, Honorable Aunt." KiLe sniffed deeply and smiled.

"Chicken and dumplings. Just what a body needs on a day like today. I put peas, chopped carrots, onions, and celery in it because I'm all out of fresh field greens."

"This will be fine, Aunt Althea." Brian seated KiLe and then retrieved bottled water from the free-standing cooler and a small bottle of chilled white wine. "I spoke with Danny. He and Pierce slept in the office at the barns last night. According to him, so far, everything is all right. They were making rounds periodically through the tents and to the outbuildings. They were able to keep the temperature above freezing and didn't expect to lose any cattle to frostbite. The horses are in the arenas and calm. They were able to string rope lines to check on the other animals in the outbuildings."

"The forecast says this thing is really strange for this late in the season, but it has blanketed the east coast from Florida north. Kadijah and Martin got Stephen back to Maryland and decided to ride out the storm there at your Maryland ranch rather than try to come back here. She would only have to turn around and pick up Stephen and Harriet on Sunday when Chuck and Vivian get home anyway."

"I spoke with Dad and Mom. They're not coming in until after the storm passes. The seaplane will pick them up on Monday or Tuesday and fly them into Miami. When the airports are open again, they'll fly into Maryland."

"Did you speak with Whitney?" Althea asked.

"I spoke with her," answered KiLe. "They've got snow there just as we have here, but so far they've been able to make it to Tucker's school reunion. The worst of the snowstorm seems to be going east of them out to sea. As soon as they're clear in Poland Springs, Maine, and can land here, she'll fly in to pick me up. The storm has shut down schools in DC, Maryland and Virginia, so she and I won't have to miss classes because we're out of town. Tucker is excused from his residency program during the snow emergency, too."

"Well, that's a relief." Althea lifted her book to continue reading.

"This is really good." KiLe rose to get another helping of the chicken and dumplings. "Would you like more?" she asked Brian.

"I would, yes." He rose from his seat, taking her bowl with him. "You relax. I've got this."

"Thanks, but I'm really all right, Brian," she said quietly for his ears only.

"I know, but save your energy. I hope you're not finished with me yet." He grinned at her.

A blush spread across her cheeks. For sure, she wasn't finished with Brian Montgomery.

After lunch, they swam in the pool, this time with Brian's dogs joining in. Later after they tended to the dogs, they spent most of the afternoon with Althea playing a board game. After dinner, they spent the night in naked abandon discovering new and interesting things about each other.

CHAPTER 17

KiLe checked her phone for the umpteenth time. *Could this day move any slower?* she wondered. She was sitting in the lecture hall with a hundred other students listening to Professor Whosit drone on and on about the Molecular Construct of Biodegradable Plastic: Its Promises and Consequences? She was acing the class as it is, but she felt honor-bound to attend the lectures. After all, her parents were paying for her to be here. Still, her focus strayed repeatedly during the two-hour session. The professor was extremely knowledgeable, but he wasn't the most inspiring speaker. Nevertheless, she had a clear sense of the bullet points sufficient to retain her position in the advanced honors' group of seniors and grad students.

She had a study group meeting that evening at the Georgetown house and she knew everyone would be there. They liked it when it was her turn to host the group because Anna Jones, the house majordomo, made sure they were well fed during their sessions. Still, all she wanted to do was go to her bedroom suite and wait for her nightly call from Brian.

She had been back in class only a couple of weeks and she was already bored out of her mind. It was so much more interesting to be with Brian as he went through his daily routine and then to spend exciting nights in his bed, learning what he taught her about being a woman. She closed her eyes recalling the memory of his kisses and lovemaking. Her body flushed hot with the recollection. It felt so natural to be in his arms while he attended to all of her needs and fantasies. It is mind-boggling how he knew just what to do; how to touch her to bring her to a cataclysmic orgasm. At first, she didn't even know or understand what was happening to her body until he explained it to her and then proceeded to demonstrate how he could repeatedly take her to that special place in ecstasy.

"Ms. Hakamora?" a voice asked.

She opened her eyes to see Professor Whosit, well his name is actually Professor Stan Donnelly, standing before her holding his briefcase. She looked around the lecture hall and noted it was empty.

"Are you ill, Ms. Hakamora?" Concern evident on his face.

"Ill?" she asked stupidly.

"Yes, you had your eyes closed and you were moaning."

"Oh." She flushed with embarrassment. "Uh, no, uh, I'm fine."

"Good. I meant to speak with you about a summer internship. You will be here for the summer before you begin your graduate studies, am I correct?"

"I plan to, yes. However, my parents want me to continue my education in England."

"Oh," he said, but she could read the disappointment in his expression. "Well," he seemed to breathe unsteadily. "I had hoped to have you join our advanced studies science and technology program. We'll be working under the auspices of Mensa. Have you heard of it?"

"I have, yes. It's the largest and oldest high IQ society in the world. My parents are members."

"Yes, it's a non-profit organization open to people who score at the ninety-eighth percentile or higher as you have on standardized, supervised IQ and other approved intelligence tests. As you probably know, Mensa is comprised of national groups and the umbrella organization, Mensa International, with a registered office in Caythorpe, Lincolnshire, England. It is separate from the British Mensa office in Wolverhampton. The minor in Science, Technology, and International Affairs offered by the College, in connection with the School of Foreign Service, is designed to provide policymaking training to students who already have a strong math and science background. You perfectly fit the requirements.

"All students, majoring in a program offered by the Department of Biology, Chemistry, Computer Science or Physics, are eligible to pursue the minor. The interns will focus on Science and Technology in the Global Arena, Principles of Microeconomics, International Relations, Energy; Business, Growth and Development; Biotechnology and Global Health; and Science, Technology, and Security. This internship will be counted toward any master's degree program you choose to follow. It could also provide guidance for your doctoral study."

KiLe had to admit to herself that she was intrigued by the possibilities. This is exactly what her parents wanted for her; to be counted among the elite in her field of study. Perhaps this would help her convince them to let her continue her studies here in America rather than go to England. That perked her flagging spirits up a notch. "I will speak with my parents about your kind offer, Honorable Professor."

"Good!" he said enthusiastically. "You're one of the best and brightest students to ever come through my program. I want to see you continue to succeed. This opportunity would be highly beneficial for you. So, I'll hold a spot open for you in the internship program. Please let me know as soon as possible whether you'll be able to participate. Have a good rest of your day."

She nodded her agreement, shut off her recorder, and gathered her things. He gave her a lot to think about. As she walked out of the lecture hall, Roland Harrington, one of her housemates, fell into step with her. A bit surprised, she asked the tall, gangly law school student, "Were you waiting for me?"

He shrugged and pushed his dorky glasses up on his narrow nose. "I was on campus and thought I'd catch a ride to the house with you."

Her eyes widened a bit in surprise. The Georgetown Law campus was located in a different part of the city. He had to pass the house to reach this campus, but hers was not to reason why. "Sure," she said, though she wondered how he knew which class she was in and her schedule. They amicably chatted as they went to the student parking lot where her compact, four-year-old Prius was located. Once she unlocked the car, he slid the passenger-side, front seat back and folded his tall frame inside. He was practically kissing his knees.

"So, you went to the mountains for Spring break," Roland said conversationally.

Though she thought the subject odd, she nevertheless answered. "I did, yes. What did you do?"

"I, uh, stayed in town, saw a few movies, caught up on my reading assignments, and hung out on campus. Of course, we had that heavy snow event which closed the campus for three days."

"Weren't you planning to go home to Michigan to see your folks?"

"Minnesota, and no, I did that for Christmas and New Year's."

"Oh," she absently said as she drove through the heavy traffic. "I thought I was the only one who didn't have plans for spring break."

"Your friend, Payton, thought you'd be in town, too. He came by the house a few times while I was there. He was looking for you."

"Oh," she said, again, not surprised at the news. After their talk at the Montgomery birthday party, Payton had been blowing up her phone, sending text messages and calling wanting to talk. No doubt, he saw the kiss she shared with Brian that night. So, he'd want to talk about it, but she'd essentially ignored him and finally blocked his number. She didn't know he resorted to stopping by the house. This was the first time she heard of that ploy.

"So, I gather you and Payton are no longer singing the same tune." Roland awkwardly chuckled.

"We are still both members of the band Changelings," she absently said as she scooted through a yellow light, which was about to turn red. She hoped there were no traffic cameras at that intersection.

"No, I mean, are you still dating?"

KiLe's brows bunched. She and Roland lived in the same house for the past three years, but in all of that time, they never discussed personal matters. They took their meals together with the rest of the housemates, but other than a few house parties and group outings, they weren't intimate pals with each other. He was in the advanced scholars' program in law school and the same study group with Whitney. So she found his question strange. "Why do you ask?"

"I thought that maybe, if you and Payton weren't an item anymore, you'd be willing to go out with me sometime."

She was taken aback. She never suspected he was interested in her in that way. In fact, she never thought of him as dating material. Sure, they played board games during downtimes, shared popcorn when the group of housemates watched movies together or went to concerts in the city, but those were all group events. She lived in the house for four years and he came to live there when she began her sophomore year, but, in all of that time, she never thought of dating any of the guys who lived in the house. She'd been pretty much oblivious to them as males. The only male person who lived in the house and caught her attention was Bill Chandler, but, of course, Bill caught any woman's attention with a heartbeat. After all, in addition to being one of the top sports and entertainment lawyers in the country, he was a world-class movie actor and internationally ranked male model who owned and published several magazines. When he was in a room, as he often was during meal times, all other males paled by comparison.

So, this question from Roland seemed to come out of left field. She wasn't sure how to answer him. She'd never been put in this position since she and Payton were always together. Or at least she thought they were together. She didn't want to be rude, but she was really confused. She pulled into a parking spot near the house and cut the engine. "Let me get back to you on that." She unbuckled her seatbelt, opened her car door, and grabbed her backpack from the back seat as did Roland.

"Look, KiLe, my light is green where you're concerned," he forthrightly admitted as they walked toward the large brownstone on the corner at the edge of Rock Creek Park. "I've wanted to ask you out before, but I knew you and Payton were close. I want to get my bid in before you reconciled with Payton or moved on to someone else. We're both graduating this year and I'm planning to stay in the area. When I pass the bar exam, I've been offered a position with Bill's law firm."

He unlocked the front door of the house and stepped back to let her enter before him. "Think about it, okay? I'm not going anywhere and my interest in you won't change."

WOW. That took some getting used to, she thought, as she climbed the steps to her bedroom suite. His bedroom was on the lower level of the house, so they headed off in different directions. As she reached her door, Whitney was descending the wide, grand staircase from her top-floor bedroom suite.

"Hi, Kiddo," Whitney said and started to continue down the rest of the stairs.

"Hi, Whitney, do you have a moment?"

"Sure," she said and stopped on the stairs before coming back up a few steps to follow KiLe into the sitting area of her bedroom suite. "What's up?"

"Roland Harrington just asked me to go out with him." She sat on one of the love seats that was also a sofa bed.

"You're surprised by that?" Whitney sat on one of the side chairs.

"Aren't you?"

"No, not really. He's been interested in you for a while. You didn't know?"

"No, it seemed unusual to me."

Whitney shrugged. "There have been several guys who would have asked you out, but you were being faithful to Payton, so they backed off. Now that you're free, single, and disengaged, you have the time to explore."

"That's the thing. I don't consider myself single."

This time it was Whitney's brows which bunched. "Oh? Did you reconcile with Payton or is it just too soon for you to start dating again? I mean, I know Payton's been trying to reconnect with you. He's asked Tucker and me to intercede on his behalf. We've both told him no."

"It's not Payton. It's Brian."

"Brian? *My* Brian? My cousin?" Whitney asked, her eyes wide.

KiLe nodded, a grin widening into a broad smile.

"Tucker thought something was going on between you two when we stopped to pick you up to come home. I didn't think anything of it at the time."

"Is it okay with you, Whitney?"

"Sure, KiLe, but you don't need my permission to date my cousin. Are you over Payton? I mean, you two were together for quite a while."

"We weren't **together**, in that way, if you know what I mean."

"You mean you didn't have a sexual relationship."

"That's right, but he was having sex with Stephany from the band."

"Oh, I'm sorry, KiLe. Initially, Tucker and I didn't know."

"It doesn't matter. Whatever it was with Payton is nothing compared to what it is to be with Brian."

Whitney readjusted in the seat and sat tailor-style while she studied KiLe's face. Then she knew what was going on. "You've had sex with Brian?"

KiLe enthusiastically nodded. "We made love and it was…I don't know. I can't explain how wonderful it's been to be with him."

Whitney's jaw dropped. *"WOW,"* she said, breathing the word in wonder. "I thought you planned to stay celibate until you married."

KiLe giggled and hid part of her face in her hand. Her eyes were alight with joyful tears, she knew. That's how she felt whenever she thought of Brian Montgomery. "I did, but I couldn't help myself. Your cousin is just so wonderful. I couldn't wait. He didn't coerce me or anything like that," she hastened to assure Whitney.

"That goes without saying, KiLe. Brian would never take advantage of a woman. He's not built that way."

"You're right. He gave me plenty of time to back out, but I didn't want to. For the first time in my life, I acted on something I wanted; not something my parents wanted me to do."

"I hope that's not why you did it, KiLe. I know your parents are traditional Japanese, but I hope you didn't do this as retribution for their dictates."

"No, I did it because I wanted him, and only him. It feels right. When you and others said you 'just knew when it was right,' I never knew what you meant. I enjoy talking with Brian far more than I ever enjoyed conversations with Payton. Brian and I never run out of interesting and enlightening things to discuss."

"How does Brian feel?"

"Wonderful."

Whitney chuckled. "No, I mean, how does he feel about your relationship?"

"He said when a man is into a woman, he leaves no question in her mind about his intentions. I have no question in my mind how he feels about me."

Whitney nodded. "Good. You're working with a man who I know you can trust and respect. I'm happy for both of you. I'm sure Tucker will be, too."

"Where is Tucker? I haven't seen him at any of the house meals since we've been back."

"He's pulling long hours at the hospital on the night shift. He sleeps during the day and has his military obligations taking up more of his time in the afternoon and evening."

"This has got to be hard on your relationship."

"No, we still talk all the time. We knew this would be tough in the home stretch. I'll be done with law school in a few months. Then I have to study for the multi-state bar exam. After the exam, Tucker and I will work on the final plans for our wedding. We finalized the guest list while we were in Poland Springs with his parents and grandparents. His high school reunion was a big success and he was able to connect with the friends he wants to invite to our wedding. We were able to mail the 'save the date' announcements while we were there."

"Yes, I received my invitation. June nineteenth in Goodwill, Summer County, South Carolina."

"It's during my family's ten-day reunion. Tucker posted everything on our bride-and-groom website right away. We have a number of events leading up to the wedding to fit into the schedule."

"I know. I'm working with your cousins and planning one of your bridal showers." KiLe smiled.

"So I've been informed." Whitney laughed.

"Have you decided where you're going to live after you're married?"

"We're not sure, but we believe Tucker will be posted to **the Landstuhl Regional Medical Center. It's the largest American hospital outside the United States. Uncle Chuck and Aunt Vivian have a close friend, a former Marine, Dr. Mark Brooks, who is stationed there now. Tucker and I also spoke with Claudia Shaffer. She's a former Army Ranger who recuperated at the facility before returning stateside and working on the Maryland Alexander-Montgomery Ranch. They've both given us very good information about the facility and the city. The military doctors' quarters are actually on the hospital grounds.**

"Landstuhl is located in the German state of Rhineland-Palatinate eleven kilometers west of Kaiserslautern and five kilometers south of

Ramstein Air Base. So, we decided not to put down roots in the U.S. for a while. Tucker has to fulfill his military obligation before we can settle down and start thinking about having a family."

"What will you do while you're in Germany?"

"I'll open a law office there for Alexander, Carter, Chandler, Charles, Lightfoot, and Towson, PA." She laughed, excited about the future. "The senior partners asked me to join the firm and focus on international law cases, just like Aunt Vivian did before she became a judge. I'll be taking on some of the casework for Aunt Vivian's friend, attorney Thomas Ashton Marshall, too. He's of counsel to Alexander, Carter, so it's a good fit for me."

"Whoa!" said KiLe. "Mr. Marshall is always in the news. Isn't his wife the judge who stepped into your Aunt Vivian's judgeship at the Appellate Court level when your aunt was selected for the Supreme Court?"

"She is, yes. Judge Kristen Catherine Bryant-Marshall."

"I remember meeting them at the party for your Uncle Chuck."

"Yes, they've been friends of my family for many years. I'll learn a lot about international law working with Thomas Marshall. That specialty may involve multinational organizations, international courts and tribunals, and humanitarian issues. I'll have to quickly master new languages and court procedures, so I know I'll be busy while Tucker is working at the hospital.

"I've also been vetted by the Judge Advocate General's Corps, also known as JAG or JAG Corps."

"I've never heard of this. What is it?"

"It's the legal branch or specialty of the military concerned with military justice and military law. Officers serving in the JAG Corps are typically called Judge Advocates. Tucker and I haven't had an opportunity to discuss much about the possibility of me joining the JAG Corps. Still, considering my parents are both in the military, it may be something to consider. Tucker's dad is an attorney and we talked it over with him and Tucker's mom. When Dad returns from his current mission to SPACEHOME, Tucker and I plan to discuss it with him and Mom to get their thoughts on the possibility. Joining JAG is certainly one way to serve my country."

"I wish it was that easy for me."

Whitney frowned. "What do you mean?"

"My parents have started plans for me to continue my education in England. They want me to come home for the summer and meet the seven men they've picked for me to consider marrying. I'm to be engaged to one of them before the end of summer. Then after I finish my doctorate, I am to marry and return to Japan to live."

"Oh, I didn't know that, KiLe. How do you feel about it?"

"I don't want to go to England. I don't want to marry my parents' and grandparents' choice for a husband for me."

"Have you discussed this with them?"

"I've tried, but they're not allowing any discussion. I'm to do as they say and that's final." Speculatively, she looked up at Whitney. "What would you do?"

"Mind my own business." Whitney huffed out a breath. "Look, pal-of-mine, this is not something I would advise you on, KiLe. It's one thing for me to advise you to try out for a part in a school musical, but this is between you and your family. You have to make your own decision about what to do and try to work it out with your parents and grandparents. Tucker and I will have your back no matter what you decide. So will Brian, I'm sure. Now, let's table this discussion. I'm hungry and dinner will be served shortly."

"You're right." KiLe stood up. "I have to freshen up. I'll be down shortly."

"Okay." So saying, Whitney left the room, closing the door behind her.

CHAPTER 18

Brian stretched and yawned hugely. He admitted to himself that he was weary. He worked long hours since KiLe left and hadn't slept well since she wasn't next to him in bed. It was difficult not to miss her too much.

He checked the time. She should be finishing work with her study group shortly. He needed to finish work on his accounts and shower before he called her. They talked for hours each night, sharing their day and plans for the next or anything of interest they found to talk about. They never ran out of conversation and had to put a limit on the time they spent talking or they wouldn't get a decent night's sleep. Even after they ended their conversations, the adrenalin rush he felt after each encounter with her could keep him awake and in need of her softness for hours more.

If the situation with the vandalism and rustling weren't a top priority, he'd take a night off and drive to DC, to take KiLe out for dinner and a movie. Instead, he needed to be available to handle several business meetings in this area. One of those meetings involved representatives from Richardson Investigations and Security and his Uncle Kenneth, who would arrive the next day. He was bringing a prototype he developed to address the security issues. They also were scheduled to discuss the e-mail addressed to Brian Alford in his suspense file.

Meetings with his cousins were also on his schedule for the next few days. The weather cooperated enough so that they were able to complete the cuts for seven project homes they were contracted to design, deliver, and construct. For the next few months, the Montgomery Mill would be working three, ten-hour shifts to meet their deadlines to package and ship the timber-framed log homes to the building sites. They would dispatch two of their own people to work with those they hired at the job site in each area to complete the construction. Fortunately, there were enough skilled carpenters in the family and in the area to get the prefabricated, timber-framed homes built and dry-fitted before shipping. Once under roof and weather-tight, a different crew of craftsmen and women would take over to complete the interior design and exterior landscaping.

The Montgomery family members were mostly artisans who worked their farms and were in the building trades. They sponsored a combination junior high, high school, and junior college trade school facility, Monroe County Vocational. It focused on training future carpenters, plumbers, electricians, welders, framers, and landscapers. They coupled the vocational programs with a first-rate education in math and science typically used in the building trades. Scholarships were made available for those graduates who wanted to continue their education in business and economics toward their goals of business management and/or ownership. Both males and females came through the Montgomery-sponsored vocational school, and there were many success stories of which they were proud.

Their students and graduates were in high demand in the construction industry. Each spring after graduation, they held a fund-raiser and job fair. Large and small building companies bought space to set up as vendors to attract the best and brightest graduates to sign on. The graduates, both past and present, had their pick of some of the top positions in construction companies in the country. Experienced graduates could easily be hired on with firms paying six figures for masters-level workers in each specialty. Every year more and more students signed on to train in the building trades and more companies came to the job fair eager to hire the trade school's graduates and get a look at the remaining promising students in the program. The vocational school generated so much interest from students outside the county; they were considering adding a boarding school component.

Lately, the school was offering classes in architecture, interior design, and interior decorating. These new endeavors were proving to be as enticing for students and companies alike. Brian needed to get by the school to spend time talking with the administrators about the new technologies' curriculum they planned to institute in the fall. There was a lot of innovation exploding in the building trades, particularly for homes built off the utility grid. His ranches were all self-sufficient and off the utility grid. They were green-built or converted to green homes and businesses. Both the structures and the application of processes that are environmentally responsible and resource-efficient throughout a building's life-cycle: from planning to design, construction, operation, maintenance, renovation, and demolition, were used in their completed products. Their homes were powered by geothermal energy, solar panels, and windmills. They used rain-barrel systems for water and bottled gas, where necessary, primarily for cooking. They had to use innovative ideas since their timber-framed homes were rarely built in populated areas where utility services were readily available.

New and innovative applications were being developed every day and the Montgomerys wanted the vocational school to stay on the cutting edge of the building trades. It was his contribution to work toward that objective with the school's administrators. There were several trade shows scheduled around the country he believed would be beneficial and necessary for administrators and some of the top students to attend. He worked out a budget which should allow the maximum amount of participation by faculty and students. Thus, the need to meet now that the schools were open again after the last heavy snow event.

He was proud of their accomplishments, but he couldn't take credit for the ideas. He simply mimicked what Roderick and JaiHonnah Hawkins Baylor did with their Baylor Park Academy in Washington, DC. The Baylor and Baylor Company built shipping container homes for mere pennies on the dollar and had cornered the market. They were out on the cutting edge of that aspect of the construction industry and became the prototype all others in the trades followed. He planned to add the container-home aspect to the vocational school's curriculum, too. Although they'd made a reputable name for themselves in the timber-framing aspect of the industry, he didn't want Montgomery Builders to lag behind the next generation of home-building innovation. He had to be diligent to ensure that didn't happen.

Brian had to fit that aspect of his tasks in with his work to pair his stallions with the new mares to guarantee a goodly number of foals. He needed to meet with Thomasina, who handled matters involving his horses. As in his Maryland operation, his stables here in Pennsylvania provided horses for riding the bridle paths and for training young and older students to learn to ride. Some of the people from the cities liked to board their horses with the Montgomery Stables and come to ride periodically. There were a few private boarding schools close enough that the Montgomery Stables provided riding lessons to their students for equestrian events and polo. Lately, polo lacrosse was catching on and making it into the arena of new sports. As a horseman and collegiate lacrosse player, Brian was enthusiastically encouraging and promoting the relatively new sport. He had plans to complete the polo field he began to build the year before in time to host the first annual polo lacrosse games this summer in August.

He let his sister, Dena, a rodeo star, talk him into hosting a rodeo in connection with the polo and polo lacrosse events. In exchange for that, she had to spend time on the marketing and sales aspects for all events related to the exhibitions. She had invaluable connections in the rodeo world because she started participating in the event when she was a preteen. Now she was working on her doctorate at Massachusetts Institute of Technology in Boston. Two of her favorite rodeo horses, Butterscotch, so named for his coloring, and Piccolo, were stabled there. All of their siblings rode and some were even rodeo participants. Dena succeeded in getting Linda's husband's nephew and niece, Eugene and Violet Hamilton, involved in rodeo riding, too. Since it would be a three-day event, they had a lot of work to complete in preparation for the occasion.

One of the things he had to address was the possibility of flash flooding in the area of the polo field. Now that the snowmelt in the mountains was rapidly approaching, he had to find a way to curb the water and collect it or divert it so as not to ruin the parking area for his polo and rodeo fields. He needed to consult with a civil engineer to determine what measures to take to avoid a disaster. Chanel Fuller, a top-rated civil engineer with Baylor and Baylor Design and Development, usually was his go-to person. However, her interest in him went beyond a professional relationship. He didn't want to open the door to that possibility. Especially not now when he and KiLe were exploring their intimate and sexual liaison. He could contact Roderick Baylor discretely and ask for a referral to a different civil engineer in his company who would have time to take on this flash-flood project. He'd made the call first thing in the morning.

As if his time wasn't already divided between several major projects, he just received a text message from Andy, who wanted to talk more about constructing a hydroponics farm and fishery on their land. Brian took the time to forward a load of informational material to Andy via his laptop. He, like KiLe, was a sponge soaking up every tidbit of data he could get his hands on. Brian blocked out the time on his calendar Andy suggested for an in-depth discussion of hydroponics farming. They'd meet over lunch to answer any questions Andy had.

For now, he shut down his laptop and got up to take a shower before he called KiLe.

>>>>><<<<<

"Hi, Uncle Kenneth," Brian said the next day as he entered one of the mansion's salons.

"Hi, Brian." Kenneth Alexander shared a warm, manly embrace with his nephew.

"Hey, I'm here, too," declared Kevin, one of Kenneth's eldest twin sons, as he returned from the rest room.

"Hey, cousin, I didn't know you were coming." Brian was truly happy to see his cousin. "Where's Kenny? You two usually travel in packs," Brian joked.

Kevin laughed. "He took advantage of the pool. He'll be up shortly. He can't pass up Grandaunt Althea's good food."

"Brian," Kenneth said just as two more people entered the salon. "You've met Slade Richardson, owner of Richardson Investigation and Security before, I believe."

"Yes, I have." Brian extended his hand to the tall man who could have passed for the actor Sendhil Ramamurthy. He had always felt an undercurrent of something about Richardson. He dressed like someone who stepped off the front cover of *GQ* magazine, but he had an aura of a warrior just below the surface. Strangely enough, Brian got the same vibe from his Aunt Stacy Greene Alexander, Whitney's mother; Donald Dixon, his and his mother's cousin; and from Bill Chandler, his mother's friend and former law firm partner. In a physical altercation, Brian knew he would want to have any one of them covering his back.

"Good to see you again, Brian."

"You also, thanks. I have to admit I didn't expect you to come in person to meet on a matter like this."

"Anything which involves the Alexanders and the Montgomerys will always get my undivided attention, Brian. I've brought one of my top operatives, Avilla Montenegro, to consult with you and the local authorities about both the vandalism and the slaughter of your cows. Avilla, this is Brian Montgomery. He's the General Manager of the Alexander-Montgomery Consortium, also known as Alex-Mont Ranches."

"Mucho gusto, Señor Montgomery."

"De nada. It's a pleasure to meet you as well." Brian noted the stunningly attractive security agent. "Please, make yourselves comfortable. I've been at the barns working with the cattle and horses. If you'll give me a few moments to freshen up, I'll be right back."

"Take your time, Brian," said Kenneth. "We arrived earlier than we were expected."

"Yes, Brian, don't hurry on our account. I haven't finished showing Avilla around the house yet and familiarizing her with the security measures we have in place," said Slade. "Ms. Hardyston went to select a suite for Avilla to use while she's here."

"Okay, it shouldn't take me long." He departed for his suite to shower and change his clothes. *He hoped he wasn't going to be responsible for entertaining Ms. Montenegro. If so, he would have to convince one or more of his cousins to take up residence in the mansion to keep her company,* he thought, as he climbed the steps two at a time to the second floor. When he opened the heavy door to the hallway, Althea was leaving the suite on the opposite side of his.

"Oh, there you are, Brian. I didn't know Mr. Richardson was bringing one of his operatives to stay here. I put her things in the suite on the other side of yours. Is that okay with you?"

"It is, yes, Aunt Althea. You don't have to check with me." He distractedly smiled at her.

"She's a beautiful woman. I wasn't sure where you would want her."

He laughed. "Yes, she is very beautiful, but I'm interested only in her professional security skill and ability."

Althea nodded. "I had no doubt, but still, I had to check."

"I'm going to take a quick shower, then call Granduncle Seth, Liam, Pierce, Andy, and Danny before I join you and the others for lunch. Will there be enough to feed all of us?"

She nodded. "There's plenty. Don't worry about making the calls. I'll do it while you shower and change your clothes."

"Okay, thanks. That'll save me some time. I'll see you shortly." He went into his suite.

Brian was just entering the kitchen when he noticed Althea standing and looking at her iPhone. "What is it? Is something wrong?"

She shook her head, but her brows were still bunched in question. "No, I don't think so. Deputy David Turner was at the gate. I granted him entrance. He should shortly be out front. Did you ask him to come too?"

"No, I didn't. Did he say why he's here?"

She shook her head. "He didn't, no."

Brian shrugged. "Do you need help with anything?"

"No, you go on into the salon. Lunch will be served shortly."

"All right." He left to join his uncle, cousins, and other guests.

"You must have been to Gregory's house lately, Brian," said Kenneth as he poured wine for everyone.

Brian laughed. "I have, yes. Uncle Greg let me have a couple of cases of the new wine he received from the old winery Linda found in France and he bought. There were several different selections the winery produced. I've been working my way through a bottle of each of them. I'm planning to buy more cases for when the family comes here in August."

He settled down with his glass of wine and joined the conversation. For the most part, they were filling Avilla in on the history of the mansion and the property while waiting for the others to join them. When Althea got his attention, he excused himself to join her.

"Sorry to interrupt," she said quietly, "but the deputy is here to interview KiLe again."

"KiLe? Why?" Brian asked, confused.

Althea shrugged. "When I told him she wasn't here, he was going to leave. I asked him to wait to speak with you. He's in the vestibule of the front lobby."

"Okay," Brian said and moved off in the direction of the front of the mansion. The deputy was standing with his hat in his hand, looking up as if in wonder at the Frescoes on the ceiling four stories up. The mansion had the same awe-inspiring effect on most people who saw it for the first time. When he heard Brian approaching, the deputy straightened his shoulders, a neutral expression on his face.

"Hello, David. My grandaunt says you're here to interview KiLe Hakamora?"

"Uh, yes. I spoke with her a couple of weeks ago. I mentioned that I would stop by to see her…about the robbery and other crimes, of course."

"Did you make a specific appointment?"

"No, I thought…well, it doesn't matter. I understand she's back in Washington, DC, in school at Georgetown University. I thought she was still here visiting."

"She left after the storm passed through. I can provide her contact information if you need it." He looked at his watch. "She's in class until three this afternoon, but you should be able to reach her after that."

"I have that information in the files."

"Okay, is there something I can do to help?"

"No, I've taken up enough of your time."

Brian thought the deputy's behavior odd, but didn't question it as he lit on a different thought. "Why don't you join us for lunch, David? I'm meeting with a new security specialist about the vandalism and the cattle rustling."

"I wouldn't want to intrude."

"It's not a problem. Come on back. We're in a salon at the back of the house." He led the way through the long, wide hallways.

"Well, if you're sure." David looked curiously all around as they walked.

When they reached the salon, the rest of his Montgomery family were present and amicably chatting. David drew to a noticeable halt when he saw the sheriff and all of the others assembled in the salon.

"Deputy Turner?" Seth said. "Is there a problem?"

"Uh, no, sir. I was here on other business…"

"He was here to re-interview KiLe. He didn't know she returned to school," Brian offered. "Since we are going to discuss the vandalism and the theft of our livestock, I've asked him to join us."

Though Seth looked a little confused, he accepted Brian's explanation and nodded. Shortly thereafter, the buffet lunch of French Onion Soup, Waldorf salad, Chicken Florentine on a bed of sautéed garlic and buttered spinach, and angel-hair pasta was served. White wine and crusty, individual, small seasoned loaves of breads accompanied the meal. A raspberry sorbet with fresh raspberries and sauce was served for dessert, along with coffee.

After lunch, they got down to business describing the events for Slade, Avilla, Kenneth, and his twin sons. The deputy described the measures taken by the authorities subsequent to each event. Still, Brian was surprised that his Granduncle Seth didn't mention the surveillance measures they planned to institute until after Deputy Turner left.

Apparently attuned to Brian's confusion, Slade said, "I've asked the sheriff to keep the information about the drones to himself. Nothing against the deputy, but for the protection of the security measures, the fewer people privy to this information, the better. We fully expect that you, if not others in this county, will be subjected to other thefts. It's a big county and most of it is mountainous with large farms like yours. The measures we plan to take may be expanded later to other farmers, but for now, the prototype is new and the patent is pending. Come with me." He led them toward the floor-to-ceiling salon doors, which opened out onto a terrace overlooking the mountain range. Near a lake on the property, a flock of geese rose in unison and headed toward the mansion. They were flying so low, Brian thought they would crash into the house, but just before they did, they did a one-eighty and returned to the lake.

Suspicion covered Brian's face as it did on the faces of Seth, the Montgomery brothers, and Althea.

"That can't be real," Andy said from his wheelchair.

"You're right," said Slade, "but for a while, you thought they were, right?"

Andy nodded. "I did," and his brothers also agreed.

"How did you do that?" Brian asked.

"Look around you," Slade directed. "Who's missing?"

"Avilla," Andy was the first to say before the others caught on.

"Where is she?" Liam asked.

"In the Security Control Room," answered Slade, who then spoke into what is apparently a mic in his left arm cuff. "Bring up five for inspection."

As they watched, five geese rose, flew to the terrace, and set down in the outstretched hands of the brothers Montgomery and Brian.

"Damn," said Liam, critically inspecting the machinery. "They look and feel real. If I didn't know better, I wouldn't believe they're drones."

"You're right," agreed Pierce. "At a distance, no one would know."

"That's exactly right," said Slade. "Kenneth designed and engineered these drones and equipped them with day and night vision video cameras. You also didn't hear them coming even when they set down on your hands. Their stealth capability is exactly what you need to covertly cover such a large area.

"We arrived early to test their capabilities in this mountainous terrain. We were able to maneuver them over this mountain range without any problems. Let's go inside and I'll show you what we've done."

For the next hour, they watched a video of Brian, the Montgomery brothers, and Seth going about their regular routines via drones and interfaced with internal security equipment. Brian admitted he never noticed the drones while he went about completing his tasks at the barns with the horses.

"Even in an area like this," said Slade, "you can be captured on any number of video cameras. Most satellites in geostationary orbit can read the date off of a dime on a sidewalk. My company has a contract with Kenneth's company and Nico Collins' company to use transponders on his satellites to conduct security operations for our clients. With Kenneth's help, we're just beginning to explore the possibilities. These birds will give us a good test of whether they will work in other situations. Most people, except bird watchers or hunters, don't pay a great deal of attention to birds in the sky, so we believe your vandals and robbers won't either. When they come back, and we believe they will, you'll be ready."

"Uncle Kenneth, this is awesome," said Brian.

"I can't take all the credit. Kenny and Kevin came up with the idea and sold me on it. They helped with the engineering work too."

"Our youngest sister, Kristine, researched the kinds of geese typically found in this area and then painted the prototype to look realistic," said Kenny. "Then she found feathers, painted them, and fashioned the lifelike prototypes which can operate within close proximity to people to listen to their conversations. She has ideas about other types of birds too, but it will take time to miniaturize the equipment to fit into a smaller model or it won't have the same functionality as these larger models do."

Kevin laughed. "She wants to do hummingbirds next."

"That's a little ambitious, even for me," said Kenneth, laughing.

Brian had no doubt Kenneth and Kristine, the father-and-daughter team, in league with Kenny and Kevin, would have a patent pending on a prototype security hummingbird sometime in the very near future.

After the meeting and demonstration, Slade Richardson, Kenneth and his sons flew to Washington, DC. Slade had an east coast office in the city and Kenneth and his sons would visit JeNelle Towson Alexander, his wife, and his sons' mother, who is the current junior senator for the state of California. When she was in town, JeNelle lived in the same Georgetown brownstone with KiLe and Whitney. Since Kenneth's company handled the security system for the house and Richardson Security provided bodyguard protection, it was more advantageous for all of the protected family members to be in close proximity. Brian liked that KiLe was also a part of the ones protected.

Seth left too, but the Montgomery boys stayed and Avilla continued to educate them on the capabilities of the new equipment. They had seven flocks of geese to learn to handle. The birds were programmed to fly different patterns over remote parts of the farms. The operator could change the pattern if something suspicious showed up. For the next few days, they would take turns monitoring activities day and night. Once the birds were linked and on-line with the satellite service, people in Kenneth's home office in San Francisco would take over the surveillance duties until the thieves were caught and successfully prosecuted.

Brian rested a little easier that night after his conversation with KiLe. He hoped he would be able to see her soon. He missed being with her.

It was the end of Brian's fourth week at Point of View North. Spring was starting to bud the trees and the crocuses were peeking out of the moist ground as the snow continued to melt. The days were steadily warming, getting longer, and, occasionally, the sky was cloud-free. Still, they were on the cusp of the March winds and moving into the April showers time of the year. Though he communicated with his family daily, he missed being there with them. KiLe also took up a great deal of his thoughts during downtimes in his schedule.

He accomplished many of his major tasks, but there was still much to do. He kept busy and now that the monitoring would soon be in the hands of his uncle's company, CompuCorrect Global, he, the Montgomery brothers, and Avilla wouldn't have to spend as much time in the security office at the mansion. They were able to plan to re-engage their regular routines, including attending the Monday night bowling league, Wednesday basketball games with Andy, and the Friday night fish fry.

They took Avilla Montenegro along to the various job sites and community events. She wanted to meet the people in the area and gauge what she could of their character. She spent time with Seth Montgomery in his office going over crime and incident reports, but, thankfully, Andy became her primary point-of-contact and guide around the community. As a result, Avilla and Andy spent a lot of time together. *That was a good thing*, Brian thought, because he didn't have the time to entertain her during his down time. Andy virtually moved into the mansion and kept Avilla company.

Despite Andy's attention to Avilla, she seemed to be in his space more frequently than necessary. He wasn't dense and knew when a woman was sizing him up, but he wasn't in the market for another relationship, so he made sure not to be alone with her.

It was times like those when he thought of KiLe the most. Although they talked and laughed together each night, for him, it wasn't enough just to hear her voice. He wanted to feel her in his arms; kiss that smiling mouth of hers; sink himself into her warmth.

"Son?" Chuck said when Brian seemed to drop off their conversation.

"Oh, uh, yes, Dad." Brian got himself back on track. "You've read the reports?"

"We have," Chuck and Vivian said in unison. "There is a steady increase in the profit margin," Chuck noted.

"There is, yes, and I think it's sufficient enough to start planning for the school mom wants." Pride and a smile were evident in his voice.

"Really?" Vivian asked, obviously thrilled.

"Really. There is an old farm about a mile from the ranch that would be ideal for construction. Initially, I wanted to buy it for a tree farm, but I think locating the Alex-Mont Academy there would be a better use of the property."

"I think I've seen the land you're referring to. It's overgrown, isn't it?"

"It is, yes, but I know the great-granddaughter of the original owners. She's handling the sale for her family and offering the land to me at market rates before she puts it on the real estate market. "What do you think, Mom?"

"I think I couldn't be more proud of you, babe!"

"Thanks, Mom. Dad?"

"You put a smile on your mother's face that's a mile wide. Go ahead and purchase it and then the next time we're all together, we'll bring it up during the family meeting."

Smiling, Brian said, "I'll alert Uncle Gregory to handle the financing through his bank and talk with Donald about the terms and conditions of the sale and the settlement agreement."

"That's perfect, Brian," said Vivian. "How long do you think it will take before the school is ready for occupancy?"

"I've had some preliminary conversations with Roderick and JaiHonnah Baylor; the last one during your birthday party, Dad. I'd like to use their firm to construct the school. If we can work it out, we may be able to open in approximately twelve months.

"I'll have to work with Dr. Greenfield about the curriculum and staffing. Then there's the question of whether to refurbish the old farmhouse and outbuildings to use as residences. I'll talk with Wesley Greenfield about that aspect of the build."

"Fantastic," said Chuck. "I can't wait to get started."

"This is wonderful news, Brian. You've made me very happy."

"Thanks, Mom."

"You sound tired, son," said Chuck. "It's late. Let's call it a night for now."

"Thanks, Dad. Goodnight. I love you both."

"We love you more," Chuck and Vivian said in unison and then ended the call.

Brian turned out the bedside lamp and eased under the covers. He wanted the forever kind of love his parents shared. More and more, he thought of KiLe as a woman he would want in his life as his partner. She was on his mind as he let sleep take him.

"Please, Whitney," KiLe pleaded.

Whitney sighed and looked up over her shoulder into her fiancée's handsome face.

Tucker shrugged. "Why not? I'd like to go with you. After all, I didn't get to spend much time there when we picked up KiLe a few weeks ago. I'm not scheduled for duty this weekend. It seems a perfect time to make the trip."

KiLe crossed her fingers and begged with her expression.

"Okay," Whitney relented while KiLe whooped with joy. "I'll file a flight plan and have the plane readied. Pack a bag, KiLe, we're going to Pennsylvania."

It didn't matter to KiLe that Whitney invited Brian's parents and siblings to go along. It just meant Whitney had to take a larger jet for the forty-five-minute hop from the airport near the Alexander-Montgomery Maryland ranch to the Monroe County Municipal Airport in Pennsylvania. They were met by one of the ranch hands who drove the big coach bus right onto the tarmac to load them up. They were keeping their arrival a secret from Brian and the rest of the Montgomerys as a surprise. It was Friday night and they headed straight to the fire station for the fish fry.

When they arrived, Brian was standing with his cousins, clapping to the beat of the music and apparently having a very good time. His paternal grandparents, Stephen and Harriet Montgomery, were dancing the two-step and doing a good job of it. KiLe noticed a stunningly attractive woman standing with the Montgomerys, but she wasn't clapping. She kept turning to Brian as if asking questions and pointing out something to him. KiLe watched for a while until Brian's siblings found him in the crowd and descended on him full force.

"*What? Whoa!* Where did you come from?" Brian asked with a broad smile as he hugged and kissed his siblings.

There was no question he was glad to see them. KiLe waited while his parents approached him.

"Hey, Mom, Dad," Brian's face wreathed in a smile a mile wide.

"Hi, son." Vivian hugged him and relinquished Patrick, who was wide awake, reaching for Brian, and looking around at all of the activity.

"Hey, little brother." Brian kissed the baby boy and made him smile. "Look at you! You've got two teeth now," he exclaimed. "I go away for a few weeks and you try to grow up on me."

"You were missed, babe." Vivian hugged him around the waist.

Brian put his arm around his mother's shoulders and kissed her temple. "I can't tell you how much I missed all of you. I can't believe you're here."

"When Whitney Ivy called to say she was flying up for a visit, we took a vote and decided unanimously to tag along," said Chuck. "You were missed, son."

"Thanks, Dad. Where is Whitney?"

"Oh, she's around here somewhere. She and Tucker got waylaid just as we came in."

"Well, this is a wonderful surprise," said Althea as she joined them and shared hugs. "Wow, will you look at Patrick!" she exclaimed, taking the baby from Brian's arms. "Chuck, I think this boy is going to be taller than you are. He's growing like a Georgia pine."

"And eats almost as much as a starving lumberjack," Stephen said of his grandson as he and Harriet joined the group. "The week Harriet and I spent taking care of him, we thought he would eat us out of house and home."

"Hey, Dad, Mom." Chuck hugged his father and step-mother in turn. "That's why we live on a working ranch. Otherwise, we wouldn't be able to feed my posse."

Everyone laughed and continued to chat while the children scampered away to dance or renew friendships with the other children in the fire station.

"Hey, Chuck, Vivian," hailed Liam. His brothers followed, giving Chuck an exploding fist bump and hugging Vivian.

"I'll tell you, Vivian, we're sorry we didn't get down to Chuck's birthday bash because you looked smokin' hot on the video," said Danny.

"Boy, you ain't never lied," Chuck said, laughing and causing everyone else to join in.

"Oh," said Andy, "This is Avilla Montenegro. She's with Richardson Investigations and Security."

"Mucho gusto, Señorita Montenegro," said Vivian extending her hand.

"De nada." Avilla shook Vivian's hand and then Chuck's.

"We had lunch with Slade last week," said Chuck. "He mentioned that you were advising on the series of problems we've been experiencing. Have you come to any conclusions?"

"Nothing concrete, yet, but Brian has been very helpful." She touched his arm and warmly gazed at him.

"More Andy and Danny than me," Brian was quick to correct. "I've had my hands full with several other projects."

"That's for sure," Althea inserted. "I can hardly catch up with Brian these days to feed him. He's out so early in the morning. I wonder whether he even makes time to sleep."

"Yeah," agreed Pierce. "Then, he doesn't come in until we've all turned in."

"Hey, is that KiLe over there?" Danny bobbed and weaved to get a clear view through the crowd.

Brian quickly turned around, and when he spotted her, he wasted no time weaving his way to her.

KiLe saw him coming, met him halfway, and leaped into his arms.

Grinning, Vivian elbowed Chuck in the solar plexus. "Well, now, I didn't see *that* coming."

"Neither did I, but our son certainly knows class when he sees it." Chuck grinned while watching Brian and KiLe kiss.

"Hey, don't I even get a hello out of you?" Whitney teased. "After all, I piloted the plane that brought her here."

"Kisses." Brian hugged Whitney. "Many kisses. Hey, Tucker, welcome back to Pennsylvania." He shook Whitney's fiancée's hand.

"Thanks, Brian. I'm glad we could make it up here before all the snow melted."

"You ski?"

"I do, yes. Downhill and cross country."

"I think there may be enough pristine snow left on the North Slope to get in a few good runs early tomorrow morning. If you're game, we can head out at first light? Liam and I have a few things to see to at the mill at six, but after that, we can hit the slopes."

"That works for me. Whitney?"

"Not me, but you go ahead." She smiled. "I'm going to ask Aunt Althea to show me how to make a nice lunch."

"She's on this cause to learn to cook. I keep telling her that as long as there are on-line cookbooks and menus, we'll be fine." Tucker smiled at Whitney.

"As long as there are restaurants, we'll be fine," Whitney joked.

"Oh, no, babe. I'm game to learn to cook if you are," Tucker countered.

"Okay, at least as a full-fledged physician, you know how to pump my stomach," she teased.

"I've got you there," Tucker responded with a wink.

Obviously, their wedding date couldn't come soon enough, thought Brian, and then looked at KiLe. He couldn't wait to be alone with her.

Later that night, KiLe whispered in Brian's ear what she wanted him to do to her. She didn't have to ask him twice as he torqued up his thrusts into her tight, wet portal.

"Yes! Yes! Yes!" she moaned.

CHAPTER 19

Very early on Saturday morning after breakfast, but before dawn, Liam and Brian went up to the Montgomery Mill to put in a few hours of work taking Tucker Cavanaugh with them. Because of the delays, they were running three round-the-clock shifts. Their primary task was to ensure that the progress on each home they contracted for was on schedule for completion and delivery. The night crew was diligently working when they arrived. The early morning workers would come on duty at seven.

The rest of the family planned to go to the barns to see the new wild horses and to ride before going skiing later in the morning. When Liam, Brian, and Tucker arrived at the mill, they immediately put on their headphones to block the noise and to be able to communicate with one another. As they took Tucker on a tour of the facility, Brian noticed how Tucker cast critical eyes on the process each craftsman used to ensure perfect dimensions when dry fitting the pieces together and forming the frame for a house. Tucker was an active listener and asked pertinent and probing questions.

It was what Brian expected of the younger man with a genius-level IQ. Tucker was in his early twenties and should have still been in college. Yet, he was already a medical doctor finishing his residency program. A real-life Doogie Howser. He was also a captain in the Marine Corps and a genuinely nice guy. Brian liked him for Whitney and believed they were a great match.

"You can do this with any floor plan?" Tucker asked.

Brian and Liam both nodded and then guided Tucker into the office where male and female drafting technicians were working on computers and displaying the work on wall-mounted monitors. They took off their headgear and walked Tucker through the open-concept space.

"In here, initially work comes in through our website. We work with CADD programs," said Liam. "That's short for computer-aided design and drafting. Kenneth Alexander, Whitney's uncle, designed the hardware and software you see in use here. We use the software for the house design and create documentation for each project. It replaces manual drafting with an automated process. It also saves us a great deal of time, resources, and work. Customers or architects can select one of our packaged designs or link their designs directly to our software. Our equipment prints out a pattern in a miniature plastic scale to ensure that every tolerance will work together for a solidly built home."

Brian interjected, "Again, Uncle Kenneth's computer programs make this work. We send the scale model to the customer for review. If the customer is satisfied, we start looking for the right wood species to harvest for each aspect of the home's construction. Uncle Kenneth is a carpenter hobbyist, so his design helps with suggestions on the species of lumber to use."

"Can you do it for a house plan that's not designed by an architect?" Tucker asked.

"Sure." Liam nodded. "Generally, we need to know only how large the structure needs to be and a description of what the finished product's exterior should look like. We can design the interior to suit the client's needs and budget. When we work in the architecture or the structural engineering fields, we use the 2D or 3D CADD software Uncle Kenneth also designed. The program lets us investigate every aspect of the design/build process before we cut the first piece of lumber."

"Why do you ask?" Brian questioned Tucker.

Tucker scratched the back of his head and sheepishly regarded Liam and Brian. "Well," he hedged. "I have this land my many-times great-grandparents owned and I inherited. When I was a little kid, we used to go there and camp in tents as often as we could. It's a beautiful spot right on the water where we could see whales, porpoises, and seals from the shore. If we were lucky, we would see some of the seals resting or sunning on the shore with their pups. It's great for hiking and fishing, even mountain biking. Since I inherited it, I was thinking about maybe building a place there for Whitney and me. I, uh, like very much what I've seen here today and wondered whether you might consider building a cabin for us."

Liam shrugged. "Sure, Tucker, you're going to be family. Of course, we'll design and build it for you."

"Uh," Brian said, looking at Tucker critically. "Where is the land you want the cabin erected on?"

"Well," Tucker said uncomfortably. He dug his hands in his pockets and rocked back on his heels. "That may be a bit of a problem. You see, it's off the coast of the Grand Marian Island near Seal Cove on an island in the Bay of Fundy."

Both Liam's and Brian's eyebrows noticeably rose.

"An island?" asked Liam, "Off the coast of Maine?"

Tucker nodded.

"I don't know that area, but my sister, Geneviève, is a Coast Guard pilot. It's her old stomping grounds," Brian shared. "She flies a Sikorsky MH-60T Jayhawk for the Coast Guard. You're in the military, so, you may have heard of it. It's a multi-mission, twin-engine, medium-range helicopter operated for search and rescue, law enforcement, military readiness, and marine environmental protection missions. Geneviève is deployed to the First District. Her area is from northern Maine to Lake Champlain and from Western Massachusetts to Rhode Island, Cape Cod, and the islands, like Martha's Vineyard. That is her area to do aerial patrols. I'll ask her about it. Is there a bridge to the island?"

"Uh, no," said Tucker. "The island is out in the middle of the Bay on the eastern side of Grand Marian, maybe a third of the way to Nova Scotia. The only way to reach it is by boat."

Liam rubbed his face with both hands. "Okay, let me get this straight. The land is not **on** the Island of Grand Marian, but on an island **off the coast** of Grand Marian?"

"Yes, that's right."

"How large is the island?" Brian asked.

Tucker shrugged. "I have no idea. Probably thousands of acres. To my knowledge, it's never been surveyed."

Liam rolled his eyes to the ceiling and shook his head. "So, does this island have any infrastructure at all?"

"Uh, no. It's completely off the grid."

Both Brian and Liam just stared at Tucker.

With his hands still stuck in his pockets, Tucker hunched his shoulders and grinned at them.

"You're joking, right?" asked Liam.

"Uh, no." Tucker was still grinning. "I kind of want this to be my wedding gift to Whitney and the place where we'll spend our honeymoon."

This time, both Liam and Brian rolled their eyes to the ceiling.

"Does this island have a name?" asked Brian while taking out his iPhone to Google it.

Tucker shook his head. "No. As far as we know, no one has ever named it. It's only referred to by longitude and latitude lines on a grid. We just call it the island. Since I inherited it, I think I'll call it Whitney's Island."

"Tucker," began Liam. "You and Whitney are getting married during the Alexander family reunion this June, right?"

"Yep, Saturday, June 19," he said, grinning proudly.

"If you want to spend your honeymoon there, unless you're camping, that gives us only four months to get this done." Brian's brows beetled. He turned his head and looked at Liam, who negligibly shrugged. "Yeah, no, we'll definitely have to talk with Geneviève."

"Geneviève is Vincent's twin, right? She's the one everybody calls Eve?"

"Yes, that's right. Eve and Vincent are a few years younger than me. I'll ask her about the area when I go back to Maryland. What do you think, Liam?"

"It's doable if the stars align." Liam looked to Brian and then to Tucker. "Do you know what you want? What type of structure and amenities?"

"I do, yes. Do you have paper and a pen?"

Liam handed over what Tucker needed and he began to sketch floor plans.

Liam sat down to a computer terminal and began to draft the basic floor plan as Tucker sketched it. An hour later, with various tweaks here and there and a bit of discussion, a two-thousand-square-foot, timber-frame cabin on two levels floated across the wall-mounted monitor.

"That's it!" Tucker agreed, pleased by what he saw. "That's exactly what I have in mind and even better with the robotic features. It's a combination of contemporary and rustic influences. The outdoor spaces are perfect for relaxing and watching the sun rise and set. The view from the wrap-around deck will be spectacular. The structure doesn't take up a lot of space on the site and built into the hillside like that, it will blend nicely into the forested landscape. I can't believe how quickly you designed it."

"It's an open-concept plan for a structure that's designed for homes to be built completely off the grid, but it will have all of the modern amenities." Liam pointed out several spaces as he talked. "We'll have to put in a geothermal system, solar panels, here, here, and here--to take full advantage of the sunlight, particularly during the winter months. Maybe even a windmill for power further back in the forest to keep the batteries charged." He pulled up a map of the prevailing winds over and around the island. "Yes, see here. It's an ideal location to take advantage of the jet stream. We'll also have to dig a well and put in a septic system using compost toilets. A propane system will work if you need it only for cooking or you can use battery-powered electric. The topography map helps, but I'll know what will work best once I see the site. I need to core the soil to see what the cabin's concrete, brick, and block will be resting on. Still, a couple of backup generators should be the first things installed so that the workers will have a source of electricity for power tools and battery operation."

"It's a good design," agreed Brian, nodding. "It's easily expandable, too."

"It will be a great place for us to get away to for long weekends. Since the island is more or less uninhabited, Whitney and I can keep dirt bikes, ATVs, canoes, fishing gear, and other outdoor equipment there in the garages. Maybe even put in exercise equipment on the ground level."

"I can design it large enough for you to store that equipment and a motorboat there in a garage if you don't need a particularly large boat."

"That would be perfect if you can include a dock, too."

Liam nodded in agreement and placed it on the preliminary site plan.

"That's a lot of baby-making time," remarked Liam, with a wide grin. He set the program in motion and waited while the computer created a miniature replica of the home they just finished designing.

A warm flush rose on Tucker's cheeks. "We plan to hold off on having children for a while. Maybe eight to ten years until we're in our thirties.

Whitney and I initially will be stationed in Germany. She'll be opening a law office there, and I'll be working some pretty long hours in the Landstuhl Medical Center, probably working on the night shift. We want to be well settled into our careers before we have children. Once the babies come, we want to be able to spend a great deal of time with them."

"You'll have a lot of practice time then," commented Liam. "Okay, since you're okay with the design, when can I go see the construction site?"

"Any time your schedule permits, but as I said, it can be reached only by boat."

"Or seaplane," suggested Brian. "I can talk with Eve about taking some time off to fly us up there, but her schedule is so unpredictable. If not Eve, then maybe Kadijah can take us up one day this coming week."

"That's a good idea," agreed Liam. "We'll have to put together a crew who won't mind roughing it for a couple of months preparing the job site and completing the construction."

Brian scratched his chin in concentration. "I'll work on getting the additional workers through the homeless shelter and securing a barge to take the materials, supplies, and equipment to the island."

"*WOW!* You guys really think you can get this done in time for our honeymoon?" Surprise and excitement were in Tucker's voice.

"Yep," Liam and Brian said in unison.

"I'll have the prototype for you in a few moments. You can study it and the plans while Brian and I attend to a few other projects. Jot down any questions or changes you have and we'll sit with you to finalize the project.

"We'll give it top priority. Now that the weather is cooperating, we can get the timbers cut and milled before the end of the week. Once the frame is packaged, it's going to take at least three eighteen wheelers to truck everything up to the Maine coastline where we'll need to have barges and a tugboat waiting with rafts large enough to handle the loads." Liam theorized aloud.

"It's a better idea if we can just offload the shipping containers so the crew can use them to protect the material from the elements," Brian suggested. "I'll see to it. We can also look at what type of lumber is already on the island and whether we can mill any of it onsite."

"Agreed," said Liam. "I'll have to change a few things around, but I think we can do this on an expedited basis, Tucker."

"Great. When you've had a chance to work up an invoice, you'll let me know, right?"

"Sure." Brian shook the hand Tucker offered. He knew hell would freeze over before Tucker would receive a bill for their services. Whitney was their family and this would be a perfect wedding gift from the collective Montgomery family to her and Tucker.

They left Tucker sitting and smiling at the home plans and scale model he designed for his bride-to-be.

Later that afternoon, as some of the family members sat in one of the lounges talking and playing board games, Liam, Brian, and Tucker talked quietly with Kadijah. They were waiting for the rest of the family to assemble for dinner.

"This sounds like I will need to use an amphibious plane if there isn't a landing strip."

"Probably." Tucker looked around to ensure their conversation wasn't overheard or drawing attention as they played Poker. "There are a few places where there is a sandy beach, but in most areas around the island the forest comes up close to the water's edge. There are other areas where there are outcroppings and sheer drop-offs into the Bay."

"Then we definitely need to take one of my seaplanes. The problem is that I'm booked solid. The only day I have available is tomorrow. Is it possible that we can make the flight early tomorrow morning?"

The three men looked to one another, nodding in agreement.

"I think that's doable as long as we can get back here before lunch," offered Brian.

"I can do that." Kadijah nodded. "We're just going up for a look-see, right?"

"Yes," said Tucker. "How early?"

"If you can meet me at the airport at five, we can be there by seven. That should give you enough time to see the terrain by air and then explore your preferable area on foot."

Just then, the salon filled with the excited voices of those family members who had been riding or skiing most of the afternoon. As Whitney came in, Tucker ducked his head and paid closer attention to the cards in his hands.

Brian noticed that Whitney came to the table, suspicion written all over her face.

"Well, hello." Whitney sat on the arm of Tucker's chair, eyeing the people at the table.

"Hello," they all chorused, but they continued to play.

"So, what did you think of the mill, Tucker?" Whitney asked.

"It certainly was busy even on a Saturday morning." He played a card at random. "I thought I'd go back tomorrow morning when it's not so noisy."

"Humm," Whitney intoned, casting her eyes on the foursome. "Okay, what are you four up to?"

"A quiet game of Poker." Liam's face was unrevealing when picking up the card Tucker discarded. "Just what I was looking for." He laid down a straight flush before raking in the pennies in the pot.

Eden Ann came to the table and climbed up into Brian's lap, leaning back in his arms against his chest to get comfortable. "Brian, may I have Ginger Snap?"

"You want a cookie?" He picked up the cards dealt to him by Tucker and studied his hand.

"No, a horse." She arranged the cards in his hand to the best advantage.

For a child soon to be nine-years-old, she was a master at Poker, Brian thought as he kissed the top of her bushy head of light-brown, corkscrew curly hair. "We don't have a horse named Ginger Snap, babe."

"Yes, we do. I saw her at the red barn today. I even got to feed her."

"She's talking about one of the new foals, Brian," Whitney offered.

"Well, then," he said, "If you help me win this hand, I'll see what I can do."

Dinner over, Brian drove his little sister to the stables so that she could identify the horse she wanted. When she took over his hand at the Poker table, she beat the pants off of Liam, Tucker, and Kadijah. At the stables, Brian gave a certificate of ownership to her. Eden Ann hugged Brian tightly around the neck and gave her new horse, Ginger Snap, a golden brown-colored palomino, a hug, as well.

"I want to do what you do, Brian," Eden Ann spontaneously said, sighing.

"What's that, sweetheart?" He watched her grooming the colt.

"I want to work with animals like you do. I've been reading about it."

"Really? I thought you wanted to be a great basketball player like dad and mom?"

"I can do that and take care of the animals, too," she confidently proclaimed.

Sufficiently chastised, he grinned at her. "Babe, you can do anything you want. Plan what you want to do—."

"And work my plan," she interrupted, finishing the often-stated directive. "Will you help me, Brian?"

"I will, yes. You can be my assistant."

"Good. Then I won't have to tell Whitney Ivy that Kadijah is going to fly you, Tucker, and Liam to Maine in the morning."

Stunned, Brian just stared at his sister until he found his voice. "Why, you little imp." He grabbed and tickled her.

Giggling, she danced away from him. "I wanted to work for you, Brian, so I made my plan and worked my plan just like you taught me. You already agreed so you can't take it back."

"Would you have told Whitney Ivy?"

"Nope, but you didn't have to know that."

"Sneaky, but I like that quality about you." He slung an arm around her waist, carrying her under his right arm like a football while she laughed like a loon.

"Good, 'cause I want to go with you in the morning."

Brian shook his head, opened the door of his truck, and hoisted her into the seat. His little sister was swift, he'd give her that.

He thought he had outsmarted her by getting up extra early and preparing to leave his suite. However, the little imp was sitting on the floor fully dressed outside his door playing a game on her iPhone.

"Good morning," she said, rising from the floor and leading the way to the stairwell. She never took her eyes off her game and continued to play as he fell into step beside her.

His aunt served them a hearty breakfast, and by four in the morning, they were on their way to the airport. By four-forty-five, they were airborne. An hour and a half later, Kadijah was circling the island.

"I'd say eight to ten miles squared," offered Liam.

Brian nodded in agreement. "Heavily forested and hilly, though. Not a lot of beach area. Can you set us down on the north side, Kadijah?"

"Can do," she said and brought them down to skim across the water. Turning toward shore, Kadijah piloted the plane until the pontoons bumped against the sand. Tucker and Brian scrambled out and tethered the plane to a couple of trees. Soon, Liam, Eden Ann, and Kadijah followed carefully stepping over moist soil.

"This way," Tucker said, leading the group through a trail no wider than a goat path and up a rise to a flat clearing. "This is where we used to camp when I was a boy." He turned and pointed to a large tree where he had carved his name.

Brian and Liam turned to regard the water view.

"Yeah," said Liam, "this is doable."

Brian nodded in agreement. "Cut away the undergrowth and they would have a panoramic view from this spot." Turning to his little sister, he asked. "What do you think, Eden Ann?"

She looked up at Brian and Liam and grinned. "It's perfect."

CHAPTER 20

"Welcome aboard, Mr. and Mrs. Campbell," Brian said, rising from the comfortable seat, shaking the woman's hand, and then her husband's. "Here is the signing bonus we discussed, your travel expenses, and your employment package. All employees are paid on the first day of each month. Andy Montgomery is expecting you in Pennsylvania tomorrow. You'll be housed at Point of View North near the mill until you decide on a permanent residence. Ms. Althea Hardyston is the majordomo there. She'll take very good care of you and your family."

"Thank you, Mr. Montgomery," the middle-aged man said, his eyes moist and his voice choked with gratitude. "We'll do good work for you."

"Of that, I have no doubt. Your experience in construction is exactly what we need at the Montgomery Mills, but the people I work with call me Brian. In Monroe County, you'll find that there are too many Montgomerys to rely on last names."

"Then we insist that you call us Bart and Bettina. This is a blessing for us," Mrs. Campbell said, her emotion apparent in her tremulous smile.

"I think you'll enjoy the area and the people you'll be working with, Bettina," said Brian. "My dad tells me that the medical facility in Stroudsburg, Pennsylvania, is one of the best in the country to deal with childhood illness. I was a patient there myself when I was much younger than your boy is now. As an experienced nurse, Bettina, the hospital is looking forward to having you join the staff since your son will be cared for there in the children's center."

"The fact that we'll have health insurance again…" Bart choked. "We'll be able to give our son and the rest of our children the medical, dental, and vision care they need. We thank you, again, Brian."

"You're welcome. Have a safe trip." Brian walked with them to the office door. When they waved goodbye, Brian noticed that his father was in the family homeless shelter talking with the manager. When their eyes met, Chuck ended his conversation and, with a big smile on his face, came toward Brian.

"I didn't know you were here, son." Chuck embraced Brian in a manly hug.

"I had scheduled meetings with the new hirers starting at eight this morning. The Campbells are the last ones I'm scheduled to see today. I hired all of the people you, mom, and I discussed. They'll be moving out of the shelter today and tomorrow. That should free up space for Betty to bring in more homeless families. I have six more families who haven't cleared Richardson's background checks yet, but that should happen by next week."

"Yes, so Betty told me. She asked me here to take a look at a few of her new families before they moved in. The Campbells are the ones who have a son with cancer?"

"They are, yes. He's the youngest of four stair-step children. Because of their high medical bills and the amount of time they lost from work to take care of him, Bart and Bettina Campbell lost their jobs, their home, and everything they owned except their car. Medical bills for their son's care were staggering. They needed both incomes to stave off bankruptcy. The Derrick Jackson Foundation has helped offset the medical expense. The Campbell's family members helped as much as possible, but found it difficult to take in a family of six. Especially, a family with a very sick child. They ended up living in their car on the street until someone told them about this shelter. So, they came here and have been here for the last three months."

"I'm glad we can offer them a fresh start," said Chuck.

"I am, too. Their son is in remission at the moment. Since school is out for the summer, they are anxious to move up to Pennsylvania and start their new jobs," Brian said distractedly.

Chuck noticed and asked, "Is something wrong, son?"

Brian shook his head. "Uh, no, dad. Nothing really. I was talking with the Campbells about the medical facility in Stroudsburg and I remembered that's where you said I spent time hospitalized."

Chuck shrugged. "Yes, that's where Derrick found you. As you know, he was a pediatrician and pediatric surgeon. He and I had credentials and hospital privileges to work at Stroudsburg Memorial when we came home for visits, but we lived and worked in DC. As I recall, you were already a ward of the state with severe medical challenges. Derrick examined you while on one of his trips when your cousin, Randy, developed Lyme disease from a deer tick bite. Derrick wanted to follow your progress. He had his attorneys work it out with the state so that he could have you transferred from Stroudsburg Memorial to the Children's National Medical Center in DC as one of his patients. He took over the expense for your care."

"I don't remember the Stroudsburg area. My earliest recollections are in DC and particularly when Derrick and Vivian adopted me and brought me to live with them at The Watergate Complex condo. They had already adopted Linda and then after me, they adopted the twins, Vincent and Geneviève, the twins, Ryan and Roger, Dena, and then Samantha. That's when we ran out of bedrooms." He laughed. "Then they bought the farm in Virginia and were in the process of renovating it when Derrick died the day Derrick Junior was born."

"I know, but your mother and Derrick already had plans and family court proceedings in place to adopt Andrew, Darren, and Spencer from the orphanage. You were still very young back then and may not know that she went through with those adoptions after Derrick's death."

"I didn't remember the details. All I remember clearly is that we were all hospitalized, lived in an orphanage, and Derrick was our doctor. Then, all of a sudden, we were spending time outside the hospital and orphanage with Derrick and Vivian. I enjoyed all the things we did on those outings and looked forward to each one. I couldn't believe it when Derrick and Vivian got married and asked us whether we wanted to be a family with them. I kept thinking I was in some type of movie and that it couldn't be real. Then we had an adoption ceremony with all of the relatives from both Derrick's and Vivian's family and Jackson was added as our last name. That's when everything got real for me."

Chuck laughed. "Yes, I remember that each time a new child was added, the adoption ceremony was held. Your parents adopted each of you and each of you adopted your parents and siblings."

"Did we all come from the Stroudsburg, Pennsylvania, area? Is that why Derrick picked us?" Brian asked.

"No, only you, as I recall. The only connection among all of you was that you were his pediatric patients. He volunteered his services to the orphanage, but the medical challenges and costs for all of you placed a hardship on the orphanage. He had been your doctor for many years. Because he cared so deeply for each of you, Vivian suggested that they adopt all of you and, with his wholehearted support, she got the ball rolling. You know your mother. Quit isn't a word she knows or even considers a part of the English language. Why?" Chuck asked.

Brian shrugged and shook his head. "No reason. The Stroudsburg Memorial medical facility came to mind because of the Campbells and their son, Jamey. They sacrificed everything for him and they have three other children. They could have given him up for adoption or let the state take over, but they didn't. They kept their family intact."

"You're wondering why your biological parents didn't fight for you and your health challenges."

"I'm not disappointed about that because Derrick and Vivian saved my life. I have the very best parents, siblings, and extended family with the Jacksons, Alexanders, and Montgomerys. I never questioned whether Derrick, you or mom would fight for me. You've shown me that I'm loved every day of my life. Even when you were still my Uncle Chuck, you were my best buddy. After you became my father, our relationship only improved. You've made it possible for me to have the best education and career. I couldn't be in a better place than I am now or have better parents."

"You're still wondering how your genealogy will impact your future," Chuck surmised.

Surprised, Brian looked up at his father and nodded.

"Because of KiLe, I suppose," Chuck guessed. "Your mother noted that you haven't been home for many meals of late."

"Yes, I've been spending time with KiLe. She's special to me, dad. These last months since we've been dating one another exclusively, I've begun to wonder what my DNA says about my history. Someday I want to marry and have children. That could be important if KiLe and I take this relationship to another level. Her biological history is unadulterated Japanese on both sides of her family back thousands of years. I haven't a clue about how adulterated my heritage might be."

"Ask your mother about that. Before she and Derrick adopted you, she did a thorough search for any living relatives or familial matches to your DNA. You were just a little kid back then. I don't remember the details, but when you agreed to let me adopt you as a preteen, we didn't do another search. If you're interested, I will run another DNA test for you. I don't think you have any Asian ancestry, but one never knows, does one?" Chuck joked.

Brian snorted a laugh. "I'd appreciate that, dad."

"You're welcome. By the way, your mother wants you home for dinner tonight. Roderick, JaiHonnah, and their children, as well as Wesley and Rosalyn Greenfield, and their children are going to be there. Linda and Will are already at the house with their boys. Dena's home, too. I believe that at last count, all of my posse has verified that they are going to be in attendance. They're all staying over until after the ground-breaking tomorrow. You know how your mother gets when she doesn't have an opportunity to look into the faces of her babies. So, we'll do the DNA test before dinner. By the by, did your Uncle Kenneth figure out who sent that e-mail to you under the name Brian Alford?"

"He's working on it along with Richardson's agents."

"Ah, yes, one of his agents being Ms. Avilla Montenegro. She's been out to the ranch and made a point of asking several ranch hands and family members about you." Chuck grinned.

Brian sighed and rolled his eyes, making Chuck laugh. "I know. I think she has some type of tracking device on me or my truck. She showed up a few times at the Georgetown house when KiLe, Whitney, Tucker, and I were heading out to dinner and a show. The first time it happened, Tucker and Whitney asked her to join us."

"They're swift. I imagine they didn't invite her to join the group outing the next time it happened."

"You're right, dad. Initially, I thought she was continuing her investigation of the Pennsylvania incidents. She or one of her agents interviewed everyone I know in Pennsylvania back to my college days at UPenn and all of the residents in the Georgetown house. I don't see a connection between what happened in Monroe County, Pennsylvania, and the people here except that KiLe was in Monroe County with me when the tires were slashed and the cattle slaughtered. However, when Avilla tracks me down, she asks questions unrelated to any of those incidents. I'm not dense and, perhaps if I were not in an exclusive relationship, I might be interested, but not now. I'll work with her toward a determination about these incidents, but beyond that, I'm unavailable."

"Your mother and I like KiLe for you. She's also made a lot of friends with our family here and in Pennsylvania, too. If you decide that she's it for you, your mother and I agree that she'd be welcomed into the family as a daughter-in-law. She's been coming around for the last four years with Whitney, so I think she rates high among your siblings."

"Thanks, dad. We're just getting started on a relationship. We have a way to go before I get down on bended knee. KiLe also has a problem to solve concerning her parents. Hopefully, she'll be able to convince her parents and grandparents to let her complete her education here in the states. They'll be here for her graduation and stay until after Tucker and Whitney's wedding."

"Speaking of after the wedding, how is it going with Tucker and Whitney's cabin? Eden Ann is fascinated with the building process. She talks of nothing else these days except her big brother, Ginger Snap, farming, and the building trades."

Brian chuckled. "She does, yes. She's my shadow whenever Eve and I can coordinate our schedules and make time to visit the construction site in Maine. Eden Ann is also with me when I'm working on projects involving the ranches or in Pennsylvania or South Carolina. She knows my schedule better than I do and takes on the responsibility of arranging for Eve or Whitney to fly us to wherever I need to be.

"Everything is going extremely well with Whitney and Tucker's cabin and it's still a secret we've kept from Whitney. It helps when we don't have to wait for government permits and inspections. As a result, the cabin will be completed a week before the wedding ceremony. They'll have four to six weeks to spend alone together on their island before they have to report to the American Regional Medical Center in Landstuhl, Germany. As you know, Claudia Shafer spent months there recuperating. Tucker and Whitney had lunch with her recently and got her perspective on the experience."

"Gezzeus, it seems like only yesterday that Benny called to say that Whitney Ivy was born at the military hospital in San Diego. She'll be twenty-one in September, an attorney opening an international law practice in Germany for your mother's former law firm, and the wife of a U.S. Marine physician. Your mom wasn't much older than Whitney is now when she and her law school pals opened Alexander, Carter, Chandler, *et al.*"

"Whitney and Tucker are excited about the future and stupid in love with each other. They'll have what KiLe calls 'a forever kind of love.' I think she's right."

"I do, too. From the first day they met through the time Tucker was targeted and nearly killed and Whitney was abducted, they have been tighter than twins in the womb." Chuck was glad that he could laugh about the past now. Things could have gone horribly wrong and they could have lost both Tucker and Whitney. "I hope someday you'll have 'a forever kind of love' with KiLe."

"I'd be a happy man if my relationship with a partner for life is half as successful as your marriage is to mom."

Chuck gave Brian a one-arm embrace and a soft smile. "Your mother is the very best person I've ever met. I want all of our offspring to have the type of love, trust, and commitment your mother and I share. Now, come on, son. It's your turn to buy lunch for me. You can tell me everything about your feelings for KiLe."

KiLe sat in the very quiet Human Resource office of the Japanese Embassy, listening to the sound from a water feature pouring over rocks. She was waiting for her turn to be interviewed for a position with the tourist department. She had completed her undergraduate studies and had only the graduation ceremony to conclude this part of her academic career.

When Professor Stan Donnelly again asked her about whether he could include her in the graduate program for advanced scholars, she readily agreed. Still, so far, she hadn't succeeded in convincing her parents to let her stay in America to complete her education. They still insisted that she come home for the summer to meet the men they selected for her and to continue her education in England instead of America. She was determined to stay and decided that it might help her cause if she had a job. It would appeal to her parents' and grandparents' work ethic and demonstrate her growth and maturity…she hoped. They would be in town with their new spouses and toddler sons in a week. So, she had to have all of her plans well in place before they arrived.

Momentarily closing her eyes, KiLe thought of Brian and the relationship they were building together. She had been uncharacteristically nervous about Brian meeting her parents, resulting in a queasy stomach. Taking a deep breath, she couldn't bear the idea of being away from him for the summer, let alone for the rest of her life. The thought of leaving him made her heart physically ache. Brian didn't want her to go, either, but he promised to give her his moral support for whatever decision she made. He stressed, however, it should be *her* decision. If she elected to go to Japan for the summer and England in the fall to continue her education, he agreed to make time to visit her as often as possible. After all, he had family in Japan; his Uncle Benny, Aunt Stacy, and their six children were in the military and stationed in Tokyo, where her family members lived. So, he would visit unless she became engaged over the summer at her parents' insistence. Regardless, he would respect her decision.

"Ms. Hakamora?" the assistant called out in the waiting area, peering over the tops of his black, horn-rimmed glasses at her.

"Yes," KiLe stood and slightly bowed to the man. Nervous jitters tightened her stomach. Taking a deep breath, she straightened her back and tried to mimic the confident strides which came so naturally to Whitney. The business suit she wore was stylish and well-tailored to her petite frame. She wore classic, low-heel pumps, small gold hoops in her earlobes, and carried a small, unpretentious handbag. Her hair was braided and twisted into a chignon at the nape of her neck. When she kissed Brian goodbye this morning, he said she looked like a professional woman off to conquer the world. She rewarded him with another kiss for that. She would have much preferred to take him back to bed and satisfy her need for more pre-dawn sex.

"This way," the assistant said and led her down a wide hallway and into an office where the Chief, Human Resources Officer sat going over an open file on his uncluttered desk.

"Ms. Hakamora?" he questioned.

"Yes, Honorable Sir," she said and stood until he gestured her to a chair before his desk.

"Congratulations. I see, by your school transcript, that you have completed your studies at Georgetown University with high honors. You've also been accepted into a scholars' program for the summer and at Oxford University for the fall term to study for your advanced degree."

"That is correct, Honorable Sir. However, I hope to remain here in the United States to complete my graduate degree and doctoral studies."

He frowned, turning several pages in the file. "You are the daughter of the Doctors Hakamora? Your mother is a member of the Royal Family?"

"I am, yes, Honorable Sir."

"It says here that it is their decision for you to return to Japan before the end of June. You are here in the United States on an F-1 Academic Student visa. It allows you to enter the United States only as a full-time student at an accredited college, university, or other academic institution or in a language training program. That's over with now and your parents have not authorized you to enroll in a graduate program here. Under these circumstances, you must know that your visa will expire and you will be required to leave the country."

"I have the hope of convincing my parents to—."

"No, no, you may not stay in the United States, Ms. Hakamora. Your parents were consulted when you applied for a position here at the Embassy before. Your appointment was canceled because it is your parents' decision to deny… Ms. Hakamora? Ms. Hakamora, where are you going? We have to discuss your return—"

KiLe couldn't stand to hear anymore. So, she stood and rushed from the office with a fountain of tears blurring her vision. Blindly, she stumbled into a restroom and into an empty stall where her stomach erupted. *Why would her parents do such a thing?* she silently questioned, aggrieved. Shaking with despair and impotent anger, she felt the misery descending on her with the agonizing realization that she would be forced to leave America before the end of June; to leave Brian. It was all too much as she was violently ill and the tears continued to flow.

Feet up on the sofa, relaxed after a hard day's work, Brian turned the page on his cousin's, Adelaide Jackson's, first novel in her Firefight Military Suspense series, which featured women as modern-day warriors. The series promised to be on the hot and steamy side of the romantic suspense genre and was climbing the bestseller's list. Reaching for his glass of wine, his hand stilled as he read a particularly salacious paragraph. *Damn*, he thought, *his cousin was a helluva writer*. He lifted the wine to his lips just as his cellphone chirped. After placing a bookmark between the pages, he lifted the phone and smiled at the readout on the small screen. "Hey, Whitney. What are you doing up at," he paused to check the time on his watch, "this time of night?"

"Hi, Brian. I've been going through my closets to clear out clothes and shoes I want to donate to charity before Tucker and I leave for our wedding."

"That reminds me that I need to do the same thing. I've got stuff in three or four different locations. Are you calling me because you need to take a break?" He laughed.

She laughed too. "You know me so well, but no. I wondered whether you spoke with KiLe this evening."

Frowning, he said, "No, I haven't. I called her earlier to ask whether she wanted to go out tonight, but my call went to her voice mail. I left a message, but she hasn't called me back. Why? What's up?"

"It may be nothing, but KiLe didn't come down to dinner tonight. When I checked her room, she was asleep in bed with the lights off. I didn't disturb her, but when I came up to start clearing my closet, she was still asleep. It's not unlike her to miss a meal when she studies, but her classes are done and graduation is coming up soon. If she misses a meal, she usually just makes a sandwich or a snack to fuel up."

"Okay, if you're worried, I'll come into town tonight and check on her."

"Oh, no, Brian. It's late and I know you've got to be up early in the morning to break ground on the new school. Aunt Vivian is so excited about opening AlexMont Academy that she's taking tomorrow off so that she can dig the first shovel of dirt. I'll check on KiLe in the morning. I just wondered whether you knew of something unusual going on with her."

"No, I don't. I think she only had an interview for a position with the Japanese Embassy today. I stayed with her last night. She mentioned it this morning before I left your place, but she seemed upbeat about it. I had five back-to-back meetings in town at the homeless shelter and didn't have a chance to speak with her. Then Dad and I hooked up for lunch. After that, we headed back to the ranch to meet and have dinner with the Baylors and the Greenfields about the construction schedule for the school. Since their children are out of school for a few weeks, they're staying here tonight so we can meet early tomorrow morning."

"Did you have a chance to meet with Uncle Kenneth about the incidents in Monroe County?"

"I did, yes, via Skype. After the ground-breaking tomorrow, I'll drive up to Pennsylvania to meet with the Richardson agents and Uncle Kenneth. They will both be in town for the conference."

"Hey, if you want, I'll give you a lift up to save you some time. I don't have anything important on my schedule for tomorrow except taking my clothes to the homeless shelter."

"I knew there was a reason I keep you around," he said, laughing.

"Wah wah," she teased back. "I'll drop off the clothes early and then see you in the morning at breakfast before the ground-breaking. Then after it, we can leave from the airport near the ranch."

"That'll work. I'll call KiLe in the morning and see whether she wants to come with us."

"I'll check on her, too."

"Thanks, Whitney. Love you."

"Love you more," she said before they disconnected.

Checking his watch, Brian realized that it was much too late to drive into town and then be back in time to have breakfast with his family, the

Baylors and the Greenfields before the scheduled ground-breaking. The Baylors owned the construction company that would build the school using shipping containers. Wesley Greenfield, the Baylors' site manager, and his wife, Dr. Rosalyn Hunter Greenfield, the director of the prototype school in DC, were close family friends. While Brian was working on the plans, he spent as much time as possible with KiLe still getting to know each other. The time they spent in bed learning to please one another wasn't as important to him as the times they spent talking and socializing with others as a couple. KiLe was still learning about her own sexuality and often took time performing a hands-on study of his body.

    He smiled to himself. Just that morning, she woke him with warm hands and her mouth on him under the covers. It was a challenge to hold on to his sanity while she experimented and explored him at her leisure. When she finally let him put on a condom, his body was flushed with moisture, the sheets were damp, and his muscles were drawn as tight as guitar strings. She was still so achingly tight, he had to take his time inching inside her. In any event, with each encounter, he was learning more and more about what pleased her while staving off his own release until she was completely sated and satisfied.

    This was not the time to think of their last encounter that morning. If he did, he'd never get any sleep and he needed to sleep fast because tomorrow promised to be a very busy day. With a last look at his schedule for the next few weeks, he would likely have very little time to spend with KiLe. He hoped that she would understand.

CHAPTER 21

"I don't understand, Uncle Kenneth," said Whitney, confused, her brows bunched.

"You're not the only one," said Brian, just as perplexed about the information they received. "You believe that Mr. Hightower instigated the trouble we've had?"

"The e-mail you received addressed to Brian Alford came from a server in one of his guest registration call centers. Reasonably, it could have been sent by any number of people who have access to the corporate level of his headquarters' building in Stroudsburg," offered Kenneth.

"Richardson agents have discreetly interviewed the employees who are in the upper echelon of Hightower Hotels and Resorts, including Mr. Gaylord Hightower and his daughter, Gayle. It appears to be common knowledge that Mr. Hightower doesn't care for you or your association with his daughter," stated Agent Avilla Montenegro.

Brian shrugged. "I'm aware of that, but his opinion doesn't concern me. Gayle and I had an affair in college that is long over with. I don't see why this would be problematic now."

"It has to do with the fact that as a much younger man, he may have had an affair with the woman who was your biological mother. The question may be whether Gaylord Hightower is your biological father instead of Brian Alford, Sr."

That put a frown on Brian's face as he shook his head in incredulous denial. "Are you telling me that Gayle could be my half-sister?"

"It's possible," Avilla said. "Initially, your mother, Paula Smith, worked for Hightower Hotels as a cocktail waitress in the flagship hotel. She was reported to be very young, a teenager, brick-house shapely, and very beautiful. Hightower took an interest in her and elevated her to his office staff, and later to his personal assistant. She traveled with him to his hotels in Pennsylvania, often with overnight stays and to other locations in the Caribbean reportedly to scout hotel locations for weeks at a time. His wife, Gayle's mother, was deceased, so he was a widower then as he is now.

"At about the same time, Paula was known to be dating a musician, Brian Alford, who did studio work as a backup singer and played guitar with a band that frequently traveled to gigs outside Monroe County. From time to time, he could be gone for weeks, which—surprise, surprise—happened to often coincide with the business trips Hightower and Paula took together. Over time, Brian senior got caught up in the drug culture and brought Paula into that lifestyle. That's why you were born addicted to methamphetamines. You were taken away from Paula by social services, but she never recovered from using the drugs. Ultimately, Paula and the man who may have been your father, both overdosed and died. The authorities didn't collect a sample of their blood to test for DNA and there doesn't appear to be any other relative for either of them.

"As you know, Vivian and Derrick did have DNA tests done, but did not find a match."

Stunned at the revelations, Brian just shook his head.

"Can you get a sample of Mr. Hightower's blood for testing or Gayle's?" asked Whitney.

"Legally, if Brian wants to clear up the question of his paternity, then he could take it to court and get an order to compel Mr. Hightower to submit a sample."

Whitney shook her head. "Hightower's Fifth Amendment right against self-incrimination would be called into question. He would never agree."

"Perhaps Gayle would be curious enough to want to know," Kenneth suggested.

"Frankly, Uncle Kenneth, I don't think I want to know. It would make it much harder for someone else who cares for Gayle."

"Ah, you're referring to your cousin Liam Montgomery," said Avilla.

Surprised, Brian raised an eyebrow. "Yes, Liam. He has this long-term strategy to marry Gayle. He knows about Gayle and me in college. In fact, I introduced them to each other."

"Yes, Richardson's agents are aware of that, too. We interviewed the people who were closest to you on your college lacrosse team and your fraternity. Again, we did it very discreetly. None of your friends knew that they were being interviewed. However, in our investigation, we turned up evidence that Hightower Hotels plans to attempt a hostile takeover of Point of View North."

"What?" Brian asked. "How could they do that? It's not traded on the open market. Derrick and Chuck bought the hotel and ski resort from the state years ago, before I was born. Upon his death, Derrick's share of the property went into his estate, which mom inherited."

"Hightower plans to challenge the state's right of eminent domain. His grandfather was one of the original investors who built the property and then lost it to bankruptcy."

Brian looked to Whitney for an explanation.

"It's based on the question of the right of a government or its agent to expropriate private property for public use, with payment of compensation," she supplied. "It's a stretch, but there have been challenges to the state, municipal, and private persons' or corporations' power to take private property. A municipality exercises its power of eminent domain through the process referred to as condemnation. The state condemns the property so that it can take it." She shrugged. "There are court cases which may be on point. Cousin Donald should be notified about this, Brian."

"I've already made him aware of the possibility," offered Avilla.

Brian turned to her. "Have you concluded that all of our problems are a result of someone in Hightower's operation?"

"Actually, the vandalism to your and your employees' vehicles and the slaughter of your cattle were in retaliation for capturing the three robbers." She looked at her watch. "I think your Granduncle Seth Montgomery and his deputies are likely arresting the rest of the gang members about now."

"How did you identify who killed the cattle?" asked Brian.

"A traffic camera at an intersection approximately a mile from your property. It's the only way the UNSUBs could have gone after the theft and it was the only truck to cross the intersection at that time of night. We followed from camera to camera until the truck crossed into New York State. Because they crossed state lines, we notified the FBI. Apparently, you and your family have friends in high places there. The FBI picked up the trail and followed the truck to a meatpacking facility. They sold the meat wholesale to a food chain in New York City for a tidy sum. A helluva lot more than the jailed gang members almost got from robbing the convenience store. They definitely would have been back to slaughter more of your cattle. The gang didn't think to wash the blood out of the truck or to erase their fingerprints. We already had them on camera," she shrugged, "but it still helps to be thorough. We compared the blood in the truck to the blood at the kill site and what you had on file and *voila*, game, set, match."

"They'll be away for a while because of the high dollar amount of the cattle and because they crossed state lines, it's a federal offense. Some of the criminals have prior convictions, which will keep them locked away for quite some time."

"Well, this seems to wrap things up nicely," cracked Whitney.

"Perhaps," said Avilla, "I'll know the final piece in a week or so. I'll see you in Maryland before I turn in my final report."

Brian extended his hand. "Thanks. You and your agents have done an admirable job."

Avilla accepted his hand and held it a little longer than was necessary. "You're welcome."

After Whitney landed at the small airport in Maryland, they sat in the plane not talking. Finally, Whitney asked, "Do you want to talk about it?"

Brian shook his head. He and Whitney had been quiet since they left the meeting with their Uncle Kenneth and Avilla Montenegro. "I need to let this information settle a bit," he said quietly, looking through the windshield.

Whitney reached across the cockpit to squeeze Brian's hand. "We can sit here for as long as you want and not say another word."

Brian leaned toward her and kissed her on her nose. "Thanks, Pal. I know you have things to do. I'll be fine."

"I do, yes. Tucker sent a text to me. His parents and grandparents are coming to town tonight. They've never spent an appreciable amount of time sightseeing in DC, so I'm going to play tour guide for the next few days before we head to South Carolina, but I'm only a phone call away."

"Okay, I know. Thanks for the lift."

"You're welcome. Are you coming into town tonight? If so, you're welcome to join us for dinner."

Brian shook his head. "No, not tonight. I have paperwork to do and I need to talk with dad and mom. I'll call KiLe later after dinner."

"Okay, I'll let her know."

"You won't mention what we learned today, will you?"

Whitney's brows beetled. "Of course not, silly rabbit. You know that I don't play tricks."

"Thanks, Whitney. You're the best," he said, smiling at her.

"I'm your best bud, and don't you forget it."

They deplaned, got into their trucks, and parted ways.

It was dinnertime and the housemates, Tucker, his parents and grandparents gathered for the evening meal. KiLe set the table for all and helped put ice in the tumblers while the rest performed other tasks.

"So, KiLe, what are your plans for the weekend?" asked Roland Harrington.

She shrugged while placing napkins at each place setting. Roland followed her with the silverware. "I don't have any specific plans. Why did you ask?"

"I, uh, plan to go home to Minnesota for a few days to visit with my family. They want to throw a party for me for graduating from law school. I'm the first one in my family to graduate from college. So, in my family, graduating from law school is a pretty big deal."

"That's great, Roland. I'm sure you'll have a great time."

"I, uh, wanted to ask you whether you'd like to come to Minnesota with me. I mean, just as a friend. I know you said that you wished you had spent more time traveling to different places in America. So, this might be a good time to travel before graduation."

Surprised, KiLe stopped setting the table and looked up at Roland. "I, um, yes, I did say that, but I don't think that now is the right time—."

"I know it's short notice and all, but just think about it…okay? We would be gone for only a few days…just long enough to see another part of America," he hastened to add before he moved on.

KiLe stood, not knowing what to say. She watched his retreating back until he was out of sight.

"KiLe? Is something wrong?" asked Whitney as she entered the formal dining room.

"Roland just asked me to go home with him to Minnesota for an extended weekend." She was stunned by the invitation.

Whitney's eyebrows elevated. "What did you tell him?"

"I didn't really say anything other than I didn't think it was the right time. I was surprised that he asked me." She looked at Whitney with a perplexed expression.

"Do you want to go?"

KiLe shook her head. "Graduation is coming up and my parents and both sets of grandparents are already in the states. They're in San Francisco. They plan to do Los Angeles and your parents said that they can use your family's condo in San Diego. My parents and grandparents want to see Chicago and New York City before they come to Washington, DC, for the graduation ceremony. I'm just surprised that they're traveling together. I mean, my parents are divorced and married to other people now. They both have toddlers!"

Whitney shrugged. "It's good that they can still get along with each other, isn't it?"

Anguished, KiLe just shook her head. "I don't know what to think anymore. I can't get them to understand that I want to finish my education here, not in England."

"They're still insisting that you go back to Japan?"

"They are, yes. They made sure that I couldn't stay by alerting the Japanese Embassy that my visa should not be extended beyond the end of June," she said, remorsefully. "I can stay until a few days after your wedding because they want to visit Miami before we all fly home together."

Whitney knew of a few legal ways that KiLe could stay in the United States, but she wouldn't offer her opinion unless or until she was asked. She didn't want to influence her friend to make life-altering decisions KiLe might later regret. For now, she could see how miserable this situation was making KiLe feel, but Whitney decided to keep her own counsel.

Whistling to a tune on the radio, Brian shut off the engine of his truck and climbed out of the seat. Just as he shut and locked the door, he turned at the sound of his name. "Avilla?"

"Yes, how are you this evening, Brian? You look very handsome."

"I'm well, thank you. How are you?"

"Very good. May I speak with you privately?"

"I was planning to take KiLe out to dinner. Can this wait?"

"I don't think that it should. Can you spare me a few moments?"

Brian shrugged. "Sure. Let's go inside. We can talk in the library." He escorted her up the steps of the Georgetown brownstone. He keyed in his code on the door and stood back to let Avilla enter before him. Closing and locking the door, he said, "This way," and led her into the library where he turned on a light and partially closed the door.

He wanted to surprise KiLe and didn't want her to leave the house without him seeing her. He had been so busy with the construction schedule for the new academy and the other tasks which needed his undivided attention. That included a snafu with getting the kitchen and bathroom appliances and equipment delivered to Whitney's Island. He and Liam were glad that the cabin was completed and with a few more features, like an extensive security system, it would be ready for occupancy a full week ahead of schedule. Grandaunt Althea was making meals which would be frozen and stored in the freezer at the cabin along with dry goods so that they could make simple meals, like pasta.

He had to keep secret the fact that Tucker's parents and grandparents were giving the bride and groom a sailboat as a wedding gift, a skipjack. It would be moored on the island when the newlyweds arrived. All of these details were taking up precious time that Brian wanted to spend with KiLe.

"Brian? I don't think I have your attention," said Avilla.

He shook his head. "I apologize. What did you want to talk with me about?"

"You should prepare yourself."

"O-kay." He nonchalantly shrugged.

"Do you recall the reporter who wanted to interview you at the bowling alley?"

"Vaguely, I do, yes, but I refused to be interviewed."

"According to witnesses, he went away pretty steamed at you."

"I didn't pay attention to his behavior. I was there to bowl and have a good time with my family and friends."

"That was also the night that Molly Montgomery sat on your lap and kissed you."

Brian nodded and quickly checked his watch. "Yes, it was, but she was just being a kid."

"Yes, however, the reporter has pictures of you and her kissing."

Brian expelled a frustrated breath. "Okay, so what does he want? Money to not publish the pictures?"

"Oh, no, he fully plans to publish. What he wants is a statement from you about Molly's claim that she's pregnant and that you're the father of her child."

KiLe came down the steps in the Georgetown house just as she heard Brian and Avilla Montenegro talking in the library. She was about to enter when she overheard the allegation that Brian impregnated Molly Montgomery.

Shocked about what she heard, she took a step back, and then another. Before she realized it, tears flooded her eyes and she sprinted up the stairs as fast as her legs would take her. Just as she turned the corner on the stairwell, she ran into Roland Harrington, nearly bowling him over.

"KiLe? Are you crying? What's wrong?" Righting himself and concerned as he dropped his duffle on the floor, he took hold of KiLe's arms to hold her upright.

Unable to speak, she fell into his arms weeping. He took her into her bedroom and listened to a tearful recitation of what she overheard.

"You need some time to clear your head. Why don't you pack a bag and come with me for the weekend? I'm on my way to the airport now."

She did need to get away, so she packed a bag while Roland made additional travel arrangements.

CHAPTER 22

Once the Richardson private jet landed, Brian realized that he should have talked with KiLe before he left the house. However, he was so steamed, he just wanted to get to Monroe County and Molly to clear his reputation. He didn't want any of his cousins or KiLe under the impression that he would have sex with an underage girl. The entire flight, he wondered why Molly would tell such a ridiculous lie involving him. Regardless, he would get to the bottom of it. Keying a number into his phone, he waited impatiently until it was answered.

"Uncle Seth?"

"Hello, Brian. I know why you're calling. Where are you?"

"I just landed at Monroe County Municipal Airport."

"Okay, meet us at my place. I'll call the others."

"Thanks, Uncle Seth. I'm on my way." Brian disconnected the call. Turning to Avilla as they walked to the waiting, chauffeur-driven car she ordered, he said, "You don't have to come with me. I'll drop you off at Point of View North."

"No, Brian. I brought this to you, so I need to follow it through. If this is misinformation—."

"*If?!*" he demanded stridently, interrupting her. "I do not molest children, Avilla!"

Tense silence hung between them while they fiercely regarded one another. Finally, Brian opened the rear car door and Avilla climbed in before him.

"Of course, based on all the data I've discovered about you, something like this would be out of character for you. You have to admit...*Maldita sea!*"

"What?" he asked.

Avilla shook her head. "It's nothing."

"It must be something if you just cursed me in Spanish."

"It's not that…" frustrated, she released a sigh.

"Then, what is it?"

She looked at him and said, "Look, Brian, I know this is completely unprofessional, but you're an extremely handsome and virile man. I've only seen you smile and you're not just handsome but beautiful when you do it. However, when you're angry, you're drop-dead gorgeous."

Confused and surprised so much that he was unsure about how to react, he continued to frown at her. "What the hell…?"

"As I said, it's unprofessional, but I have to admit that more than a few times, I've entertained the thought of sleeping with you. No strings attached, but I'm aware that you're involved with KiLe Hakamora. Your usual MO is that you don't sleep around or sleep with more than one woman at a time. I've interviewed the women you've been involved with, except KiLe, of course, and not one of them has an unkind thing to say about you. In my experience, at least one or more women would be willing to bash a former lover. However, not true for the women you've been involved with. In fact, they tell me that you're a gentleman who is well endowed and with unbelievable stamina; that sex with you is off the chain exciting; and every one of them would welcome repeat performances because you care about their complete satisfaction before your own. You make loving fun because you pay attention to a woman's needs and fulfill fantasies. I admit those qualities turn me on."

He shook his head, his brows still beetled, and looked away from her out the side-view window at the passing scenery. With his elbow on the window of the door, he dragged his left hand down his face; a sure sign of pure frustration. "I'm not open to this type of discussion, Avilla. Especially not now when my reputation with my family is on the line."

"I understand that your primary concern is not only for your family, but also for KiLe. However, you should be aware that her parents will never allow her to stay in the states or have a relationship with you."

"So what? Are you suggesting that, because her parents are being difficult, I should disregard my commitment of fidelity to KiLe in order to assuage your curiosity about my sexual prowess?"

She snorted a laugh. "If only. However, that's not it. You see, KiLe has been promised to one of several men. Each one is a Yakuza man with standing in the Japanese criminal culture. Have you heard of the Yakuza?"

"Yes, I have. They're a transnational organized crime syndicate originating in Japan. Why are the Hakamoras involved with them?"

"KiLe's paternal grandfather is Yakuza. He pledged his first grandchild to the syndicate in exchange for the funds for his son, KiLe's father, to start his biofuel company. Now the company is very successful and KiLe is the first grandchild. She's beautiful and brilliant, elements held in high regard in Japan. She can talk effectively about the biofuel industry and because of her American education, she can reach out to American corporations and speak their language. With her doctorate, she can teach at the college level in Japan, as does her mother. KiLe would be the best salesperson for her father and through him a prize to her grandfather.

"However," she continued, "each Yakuza man vying for her hand in marriage is expecting her to be a virgin. You see, the Yakuza are notorious for their strict codes of conduct, their organized fiefdom nature, and several unconventional ritual practices which I won't go into now. Suffice it to say that this group is still regarded as being among the most sophisticated and wealthiest criminal organizations in the world."

"If she is not a virgin, then what?" Brian asked, concerned for her safety.

"There could be dire consequences for her family and for her."

"The whole 'losing face' factor," he surmised. Yet, he couldn't regret KiLe's and his action. He wouldn't want her trapped into a marriage with a Yakuza criminal. "Does KiLe know that the men she is expected to choose from are members of the Yakuza?"

"She does not. Her family has kept her sheltered from the facts. You see, KiLe's mother is from a high-society Japanese family who is royalty. The Imperial House of Japan is also referred to as the Imperial Family or the Yamato Dynasty. The Dynasty comprises those members of the extended family of the reigning Emperor of Japan who undertake official and public duties. KiLe is a shooting star in the Yamato Dynasty. However, her father and his family are from the Yakuza working class.

"KiLe's parents met in college in England. Their marriage was considered scandalous at the outset, but KiLe was on the way, so, they had no choice other than to marry. The families negotiated a settlement protecting KiLe's mother's wealth. Her parent's marriage was successful until KiLe left for college in the states. Both of her parents had an affair, which led to an unexpected pregnancy, divorce, and a second marriage. Now her parents both recognize that their divorce was a mistake and are now carrying on an affair with each other behind their current spouse's back."

Brian rolled his eyes. "I'm not going to ask how you learned all of this."

"It's all in a day's work for Richardson Investigations and Security. However, circling back to the topic at hand. Perhaps you can understand that this Imperial Family princess would not be permitted to live a life of her choosing. Through no choice of her own, she has awesome obligations. She's the link between Japanese society extremes. She's not your Notting Hill East romantic story between an American rancher played by you and a Japanese princess played by KiLe, who happens to be among his cousin's close friends."

Brian was beginning to see the vast number of difficulties his relationship with KiLe could involve. With this greater insight into the pressure which could be brought to bear on her, he would have to talk with her as soon as he cleared up this dilemma involving Molly. Fortunately, they were just arriving at Seth Montgomery's home. From the number of cars parked in the yard, everyone was in the house. When he entered, his expectation was realized; everyone was there. That included his paternal grandparents. However, he was surprised to see his Grandaunt Althea in the same room as Molly's mother Arabella. Though he was greeted warmly, everyone seemed on edge about the allegations.

He looked around the large gathering room, but didn't spot Molly among the family members. He turned at the sound of more family arriving. When his parents came in, they immediately went to him forming a solid wall of support.

"I didn't—." he began, but was immediately cut off.

"You don't have to tell us that, son," said his father.

"I would be disappointed if you thought we believed any of this," his mother chimed in, her brows furrowed in censure.

At that moment, Brian couldn't be more proud of the parents who raised him. As he looked around at the other faces, he saw nothing but unqualified love, trust, and respect. He released the breath he held as emotion churned in his chest. However, he knew that his family expected him to take the lead in solving whatever this was about. "Where is Molly?" Brian asked looking at Arabella.

"Brian," she exhaled a breath, a plea in her quiet voice.

"Where, Arabella?" he asked more forcefully.

"She's in her room," Liam spoke up before his mother could.

Brian nodded and turned to Avilla. "I'd appreciate it if you would come with me."

She nodded and followed him out of the expansive living area. She overheard Althea say that she would make coffee.

Brian knocked on the door decorated with teenage paraphernalia. "Molly, it's me, Brian. May I come in?" When he received no answer, he knocked again and then opened the door.

She was sitting on her queen-sized bed, a white teddy bear held tightly in her arms. Her cheeks were mottled with tears streaming down her gamine face. Brian thought that she looked about ten years old with her long, black, thick curly hair in two ponytails.

Without a word, Brian crawled onto the bed to sit to her right. He held up his left arm and without hesitation, Molly tilted until she was securely in his embrace. She emitted a keening cry, which caused Brian to tighten his hold on her and kiss the top of her head.

Moments passed while Avilla unobtrusively found a comfortable seat on a sofa across from the bed where Brian sat holding onto his distraught cousin.

When Molly's tears and wails began to subside, Brian pulled tissues from a box on the nightstand to his right and passed them to her. She took them, but stayed wrapped in Brian's embrace. "So, other than the horror story of becoming my baby mama, how was the rest of your day?"

"It was the best of times and it was the worst of times." She recited the Charles Dickens' quote and then rested her head against his chest.

"So, how soon am I going to become a father?" He still held on to her.

"Seven months," Molly said and exhaled a shaky breath.

"Did we plan this or was it an accident?"

She shrugged in response.

"Come on, Molly Wally," he teased using the nickname he called her when she was a little kid. "Tell your Bean what's up," he questioned, using the name she used to call him because she couldn't pronounce Brian with her two front teeth missing. That got a laugh out of her.

"The condom broke," she said on a sigh. "We didn't know it at the time and I didn't think anything of it until I missed my period…twice."

"Are you going to tell me who this undeserving young guy is who deserves a beat down?"

"No, not until you tell me who my father is."

"Molly, it's not my place—."

"You know who he is, Brian," she interrupted. "You know who my father is. So, until you tell me, I'm not telling anyone that you're not my baby's father. No one in the family is going to believe it anyway, but a newspaper reporter promised me a lot of money if I let him print the story and claim that you're the father. I can't stay here any longer where everyone knows who my father is except me. I want you to take me to your cabin in Maryland to live with you."

Well, that put him back on his heels, good and proper, Brian thought. He would do almost anything to help solve this situation, but he didn't think running away ever solved anything. Rather, it would only delay a discussion. They needed to solve this now, not later. When he happened to look up, he caught Avilla's nearly imperceptible nod toward the door. He gave her a slight nod in return. "Okay, Molly Wally, I'm going to speak with your mother," he said, lifting his arm from around her and sliding to the side of the bed.

"You're coming back, right? I mean, you're not going back to Maryland without me, right?"

"I'm not leaving until we straighten out a few things."

Momentarily mollified, Molly relaxed against her headboard and grabbed the white teddy bear to hug.

Once outside the bedroom door, Brian moved with Avilla further down the wide, dark hallway. When they were sufficiently far enough away from

Molly's bedroom door, Brian bent toward Avilla to listen to what she had to say.

She whispered. "I know who the father of Molly's baby is and I also know who her father is. If you want, I could be the go-between to help settle this right away."

Not as surprised as he should have been, Brian said, "I want to know who impregnated Molly."

When she whispered a name, Brian's anger rose. "You've got to be shitting me!"

Avilla shook her head. "What do you want to do about it?"

"I want to destroy him, but that won't solve any of this. It has to be Molly's responsibility to divulge the name of her baby's father. All I can do is help with one part of her demands." So, he went back down the stairs to talk with Molly's mother.

Once he and Avilla entered the gathering room, all conversation ceased and all eyes focused on him. "Molly is all right." Brian noted that everyone gathered seemed to let out a noticeable sigh of relief. Walking toward Arabella, he asked, "May I talk with you for a moment?"

With all eyes on them, Arabella looked around before meeting Brian's eyes. She nodded once and led the way to a home office. Once inside, she wrapped her arms around herself in a protective gesture and walked toward the unlit fireplace. Placing both hands on the mantle, she leaned forward, dropping her head to look into the dark maul of the unlit firebox. "What does she want?"

"She asked me to take her to live with me in Maryland."

Arabella sharply turned from the fireplace to regard him. "Why, Brian? There is no question in anyone's mind that you would not and did not have sex with my daughter, but she won't tell anyone who the father is. Now she wants to run away as if moving to live with you will solve anything?"

"She's using blackmail to solve the question of her parentage, Arabella." Brian's voice was a plea for understanding. "You've denied her the truth, that in my view, she is entitled to know. I'm no shrink, but she's retaliating in ways which are not emotionally healthy for her. She's young and I am concerned that her behavior could only get worse over time. It's my belief that you have to tell her."

"She will hate me if she knew." Arabella's voice was anguished, her beautiful face contorted in fear. "You know who her father is. If you were in her shoes, how would you feel?"

"Like an adult. Like the person Chuck and Vivian raised me to be. Like someone my family loved, respected, and trusted to handle the truth. I recently found out some things about my parentage that I didn't know, but no matter how shocking, I feel the better for having learned who I came from. However, I'm not in Molly's shoes and this isn't about me, Arabella. Your daughter is pregnant and hurting. You need to be there for her the way Chuck and Vivian have always been there for me."

At the knock on the door, both Arabella and Brian called out, "come in." Chuck stuck his head in and asked them to come back into the living area. When they did, Seth held Molly in his arms and both had tears tracking their faces.

"I've told Molly the truth; that I am her father." Seth looked to Arabella for a reaction. "I know that you were afraid to tell her for fear that she would be angry because I'm sleeping with my deceased son's wife. I cannot watch my daughter suffer because I fell in love with her mother, a woman I never should have touched, but there it is." Staunchly, he regarded everyone in the expansive room. "As everyone in the room knows, Brian is my grandnephew by love, but I love, trust and respect him as if he was born to my nephew by blood. He doesn't need to be made to feel as if any of us questioned his commitment to this family. My nephew and niece-in-law raised a fine man in Brian and we couldn't be prouder of him."

"Wait! Does that mean that the little imp is not only our baby sister, but also our aunt?" asked Danny. "You know how bossy Molly is, but I'm not calling her Aunt Molly or taking any orders from her."

However, one look at the Montgomery brothers' faces let Brian know that David was going to have a few very painful days ahead of him. For Molly's sake, that broke the ice for the time being. It caused everyone to laugh including Molly, but emotions were still running high. When Arabella stood regarding her daughter, Molly crossed the room and went easily into her mother's arms.

"Mi bebè. Mi bambina," cried Arabella, her native tongue pronounced. *"Ti amo. Ti voglio molto bene."*

"I love you a lot, too, Mama," Molly choked out.

No one much noticed when Seth and Brian left the living area for the in-home office. Seemingly, everyone was focused on Arabella and Molly. Once inside the office with the door closed, Seth wasted no time asking the salient question.

"Who impregnated my child, Brian?"

"Uncle Seth, perhaps it would be better coming from Molly."

"Yes, you're right, it would be best. However, whose ass am I going to have to kick?" Seth persisted.

Brian sighed. "According to Avilla Montenegro, it's David Turner."

For humming moments, Seth just stared. "You mean my deputy David Turner?"

Brian nodded. "That's what I understand."

"What the fuck?! He's nearly twice her age!" he thundered.

"Uncle Seth, I shouldn't have to remind you that you've been in a long-term relationship with a woman who is nearly half *your* age. I'm not condoning what happened between Molly and David, nor am I passing judgment on your relationship with Arabella. Still, you're going to have to take it down a notch. Any show of anger could potentially tip the scales in the wrong direction."

Seth stuck his hands in his pockets and paced the office. "Again, you're right. I can't even be righteously indignant. Do you think they're in love?" he asked skeptically.

"I don't know. I didn't ask that question because I didn't want to know the answer, but if I had to guess, I'd say that she was experimenting. I have no clue what David was thinking. I've met him only a few times, so I don't have a clear view of the type of person he is. You'd know more about that than I would. You work with the guy."

Seth nodded. "I would, yes, but only what I hear when the guys are ragging on one another. I know he likes his women young, just over the legal age. I heard him commenting on what a *'sweet'* piece KiLe is. I believe he was interested in her, particularly when he showed up to re-interview her at Point of View North. He didn't have a legitimate reason for contacting her again."

"I've been told that he's a bit of a social climber, which may be a part of the reason he was interested in KiLe and/or Molly. The information came from a reliable source, but that's pure conjecture. Before you say or do anything, I'd suggest that you have a father-daughter conversation with Molly to determine her feelings and expectations. She didn't even say to me whether she told David that she was pregnant."

"Geez Louise," Seth huffed out. "What a mess. I had sons, so I only had to make sure that they didn't get somebody's daughter pregnant."

"Well, now we only have to give her moral support to get through this. However, you may have to put a lasso around her brothers. They've got blood in their eyes."

Seth stopped pacing and looked at Brian. "Are *you* all right, son?"

"Yes, I'm fine, Uncle Seth. It's just that I've been trying to reach KiLe, but my calls keep going to voice mail."

"If anything happened to her, I'm sure that Whitney would have called you."

Brian nodded. "Yes, you're right." He perked up and asked, "If I'm off the hot seat, I'm going to head back to Maryland."

Seth clamped a hand on Brian's shoulder. "Yes, we're not pulling out the shotguns and making arrangements for the church wedding on come-to-meeting Sunday service," he joked.

"Thanks, Uncle Seth." He embraced his granduncle with a manly hug. "I'll probably see you sometime before Whitney's graduation."

"Okay, son. Have a care and, again, thanks for dropping everything and coming up right away to deal with this."

"You're welcome." Brian left the office. In the living area, he got his father's and mother's attention. "I think it's safe to leave now. Just let me say goodbye to Molly and everyone else and I'll head back with you."

"Take your time. We've got heavy weather coming up the coast. The pilot suggests that we not try to return tonight. We'll stay at Point of View North and head back in the morning early."

Disappointed, Brian could only agree, but he was still concerned about his inability to reach KiLe. However, Andy snagged his attention.

"Do you have any idea whether Claudia is involved with anyone?"

"Claudia Shaffer?"

"Yes, is she seeing anyone that you know of?"

Brian shrugged. "I haven't a clue. However, Dr. Mark Brooks was her physician when she was injured and hospitalized in Germany. He makes a point of coming to see her whenever he comes to visit the hospital dad, he, and others built. It seemed a little more than professional to me."

"Yes, she's mentioned him to me."

Brian's brows rose in surprise. "You're interested?"

Andy nodded. "I am, yes. Very much. I like her boys, too. I think she likes it here and may be interested in transferring to your ranch up here."

"Really? You know this because?"

"We've been out a few times on a date since she's been here working on her canine security system for you. She trained someone, a guy to work with her dogs in Maryland."

"I know. He's been doing a fine job, too." Just then, he caught his father's nod toward the door. His parents, Avilla, and his Aunt Althea were making the rounds to the aunts, uncles, and cousins of the Montgomery clan. He turned back to Andy. "Look, pal, if she wants to relocate, I'll support it."

"Thanks." Andy reached up from his wheelchair to embrace Brian.

They hugged in a loose, clasped hands shoulder bump fashion before Brian turned away to bid the rest of his family farewell. *Would wonders never cease*, he thought. *Andy and Claudia? He sure didn't see that one coming, but if it worked, they'd be the better for it.*

It was too late to call Whitney, Brian thought, looking at his watch. Tucker's parents and grandparents were in town, as were Whitney's parents and siblings. So, he knew she was busy entertaining them, preparing for graduation and her wedding. In any event, he had left several messages for KiLe already. He couldn't imagine why she hadn't returned his calls. He'd make a point of stopping by the Georgetown house in the morning. There had to be an explanation for this radio silence.

CHAPTER 23

It was morning in the small town of Cherry, in Traverse County, Minnesota. The night before, when they left Washington, DC, the flight landed in Illinois at Chicago's O'Hare Airport. They had to race through the sprawling airport to another concourse to catch another flight to St. Paul, Minnesota, and then a commuter flight to Traverse County. After landing there, they caught yet another flight, this time on a crop duster, to a field with a bare strip of land. The pilot owned the field where they landed without lights after dark. A pick-up truck waited to drive them to the pilot's home and then on to the Harrington farm ten miles away.

KiLe felt a little uncomfortable squeezed into the center of the bench seat, trying to avoid getting in the way of the drive shaft. Every time Roland's father reached to change gears, his arm grazed her left thigh. She felt even worse when he kept looking at her with a frown on his craggy, weather-beaten face. Through the long drive, other than the talk radio station spouting about the farm reports interspersed with commercial ads for fertilizer or farm equipment, the truck was dead silent for the whole ten miles along the rugged road. KiLe could feel Roland's discomfort, too.

When they arrived at the twenty-two-thousand-acre Harrington Family Farm, many trucks were parked in the yard. It seemed that every light in the two-story farmhouse was set ablaze. Entering the house, his family had banners and home-made streamers strung everywhere and loud voices raised the roof proclaiming their pride in Roland's accomplishments. Then, dead silence fell the room when she came into view. It was as if someone turned off a light switch into total darkness.

Awkwardly, Roland introduced her, but his family and friends just stared with barely an acknowledgment passing between them. Shortly after the meal was served, people began to leave. Ronald explained that all of his family and friends were farmers and rose very early in the morning to start their chores before they left to work at other jobs.

Dressed and ready to make the best of the experience for the day, KiLe started toward the kitchen when she heard Mrs. Harrington ask, "What does she eat?"

"Maw, she eats whatever anyone else eats," Roland answered, a whine in his tone.

Overhearing that part of the conversation, KiLe smiled and stayed out of sight. She started to turn around and go back to the bedroom and not eavesdrop on Roland's and his mother's conversation until more of the conversation reached her ears.

"You sure she doesn't eat like fried dog or some such thing? You never know what them Chinese put in that chopped suey stuff. What is suey anyway? My granddaddy used to call the pigs and the hogs by yelling 'suey.' I mean them foreigners; they don't eat regular stuff like pork chops or fried chicken steak. Mabel said they eat everything with those sticks. Even soup. I don't have sticks to give her."

"Mom, settle down. First of all, KiLe is Japanese, not Chinese. She's been in America for over four years and she sits down to eat breakfast, lunch, and dinner with the rest of the housemates using regular utensils like a fork, spoon, and knife."

Exasperated, Mrs. Harrington primly folded her kitchen towel and put it down on her new Formica countertop. "Why did you bring a girl like her here, Roland?" she asked not looking up at her son. "She doesn't fit in here. When you come home, I thought that you'd take up with Peggie Sue, the Landers' girl. You used to be sweet on her. She's a school teacher now and she teaches Sunday school at the Baptist Church. She would make you a better wife."

"Maw, I'm not planning…well, you see, I've been offered a position with a very good law firm in Washington, DC. It's one of the best in the country. It has a great reputation and I'll be working for Mr. Thomas Ashton Marshall. He's of counsel to the Alexander, Carter, Chandler law partnership and they're going to expand their role in international law. That means I may get a chance to travel all over the world and argue cases before

The International Court of Justice, which has its seat in The Hague in the Netherlands. It's the principal judicial organ of the United Nations. If I work hard and smart, I could make junior partner in five to seven years and maybe a full partnership before I'm forty." Roland's enthusiasm was rising and a wide smile covered his face.

Mrs. Harrington's brows drew together. "Washington, DC? You've been there for three years, Roland, and I've never heard of this hag place. I don't even know where this Neverland place is," she said, her concern and frustration growing. "Is that where that singer Michael Johnson died?"

"The Netherlands is a country in Northwestern Europe and borders Germany to the east, Belgium to the south, and the North Sea to the northwest…never mind, that's not important. I have an Atlas in my room. I'll show you where The Hague is located. The singer you're thinking about is Michael Jackson and his Neverland Ranch in Santa Barbara County, California, but that's not important to this conversation either, maw."

"Roland, you could come home now, work on the farm with your father and your brothers. Now that we don't have to help with your tuition and room and board, maybe we can buy the old Higgins farm when it comes up for auction next month. You can live there, fix it up and also make a real good living working for the Corn Huskers Consortium in their human resources department. You could bring in more money to help the family instead of traveling all over hither and yonder with some little girl who can't fit in. I hear they use lawyers over there at the Consortium. The manager told your father they would hold a position for you with them on a count of all the business your father and brothers do with them. They buy up our produce every year for a good price. Mr. Puckett said they'd start you off with a real good salary…"

"Maw, I'm going to be practicing international law working with one of my classmates, Whitney Alexander. I told you about her, right?"

"Yes, yes," she said testily. "She's the one whose father is the Air Force General and her mother is a Navy Admiral. Lands sake, is she the one who put all of these foolish, highfalutin ideas in your head? Them Alexanders, they have seven children, don't they? Why would a woman want to be an Admiral anyway? I want to know? She should be home tending to her children 'stead of trying to boss men around. Don't her husband make enough money to support her and their children? I hear tell that the Army pays good money to take care of the troops." Shaking her head and cleaning an already spotless countertop, she continued, "You never thought like this before when everyone chipped in to send you to that fancy college and law school."

"Maw, the Alexanders aren't in the Army. They're …"

KiLe heard the surliness in Mrs. Harrington's voice and the resignation in Roland's voice before she turned away. She'd heard enough and headed back to the bedroom, where two of Roland's nieces still slept. The little girls couldn't be more than five years old and were doubled up in one single bed to make room for KiLe to sleep in the other single. As she sat down tailor style, she compared how she had been welcomed in the Alexander homes to how she was treated here among Roland's family and friends. She wasn't naïve enough to think that everyone would welcome her, but she didn't think she was ever disliked on sight around people who didn't even know her name. Those who spoke to her did so in a loud voice as if she were deaf. They thought that she couldn't speak English so they spoke loudly so she could understand. She had to shake her head at that. Then when she answered, they looked surprised and pleased that speaking loudly had worked. What irritated more was that they called her Kell Lee.

Palming her face and sighing, KiLe wondered whether it was wise to even come on this trip with Roland. She left so fast, she didn't get a chance to let Whitney know she was going out of town with Roland. Then, when they arrived, she realized that they didn't have cell service here in Cherry, Minnesota. She couldn't even check her voice mail, but, then again, she didn't want to know how Brian had betrayed her trust and had sex with Molly Montgomery. They were even having a baby together. Somehow it was worse than what Payton had done with Stephany. She had real feelings for Brian, more than she ever had for Payton.

Still, both had disrespected her to the point that she was beginning to believe that maybe her parents were right. She would do as they instructed and go home to Japan for the summer to be paraded around like a prized painting on an auction block and then select a husband and become engaged. In the fall, she would go to England to complete her education. The fact that her heart wouldn't be in it wasn't important. She had only a few more weeks until Whitney's wedding in South Carolina. After that, she would leave with her family for Florida and then… She couldn't stop the tears that suddenly flooded her eyes. She would never see Brian again.

Quickly, at the soft knock on the door, she brushed away the tears and conjured up a smile from somewhere as Roland stuck his head inside the door.

"Good morning. I'm glad you're already up. Breakfast is ready."

"Okay, thanks. I'll be down in a few moments. I just need to freshen up."

He nodded and retreated, closing the door behind him.

Thank goodness the room was still dim and he couldn't see her tears. When he was gone, she went into the little attached bathroom and bathed her face in ice-cold water.

As soon as breakfast was over at Point of View North, Brian, his parents, and Avilla Montenegro headed for the airport. Brian and his parents boarded an Adventurer Executive Airline jet headed to the county municipal airport near their home in Maryland, while Avilla's jet headed to a Washington, DC, airport. The flight was mercifully short and within the hour, they were landing again. His brother, Vincent, who, with his twin sister, Geneviève, was a year younger than him, waited to take them to the ranch, which was less than five miles away.

Once they arrived, Brian started toward the barn garage before Vincent snagged his attention.

He noticed that Vincent waited until their parents were out of earshot, so he asked, "What's up, Vincent?"

"I need to talk with you."

"Okay, is it something quick or can it wait? I want to get into DC, and catch up with KiLe. Then later, I have to go up to do a final inspection on a project near Maine."

"I know you're busy, but it's important, Brian. It's about Eve. Something happened to her. She resigned her commission with the Coast Guard and came home, but she won't tell me what's wrong. She made me promise not to tell dad or mom, but she didn't say that I couldn't go to the top of the sibling food chain and talk with Linda or you. Linda's about to have her baby any day now and she's working on her Broadway show, so, tag, you're it."

That set Brian back on his heels. This, whatever it was, had to be monumental. If her twin couldn't get information out of Eve, Brian knew he would have to. Geneviève or Eve, as the family was prone to call her, loved her position as a commissioned military officer who flew helicopters for the Coast Guard. She had been with them for three years and was assigned to an area which included northern Maine to Lake Champlain and from Western Massachusetts to Rhode Island, Cape Cod, and the islands, like Martha's Vineyard. She liked it because it was close enough that she could fly home frequently enough to attend weekend family gatherings. Eve was also a strong, no-nonsense, young woman and steady as a rock. So, this behavior was way out of character for her.

Checking his watch, he resigned himself to finding out what was going on with his sister. "Where is she?" Brian asked Vincent.

"When I left to pick you and the parental units up, she was at the child care center."

"Okay, I'll head over there. Where are you off to?"

"I've got a med school lecture I want to attend at Georgetown Hospital, but I can get someone to video it for me if you need me to stay."

"No, you go ahead to your lecture. I'll find out what's up with Eve."

"Yeah, I know," said Vincent with a knuckle bump before he headed out to the barn garage.

Brian headed in the opposite direction and decided to walk the half-mile or so to the children's school. On the way, he noticed his father striding off down the driveway toward his medical office across the single-lane road. The I-shaped shopping area was wood framed and resembled the Cracker Barrel chain of restaurants. Alex-Mont owned and operated those properties, too.

His father's long-term nurse, Judy, had recently married the man whose family had managed the general store for over one hundred fifty years. The couple was in the mid-sixties and the marriage was the first for either of them. They lived above the general store and relished sitting on their deck in the evenings when the workday was over. They chatted with each other like magpies and would often be found stealing kisses because they worked next door to each other. *Brian wanted that type of forever love with KiLe*, he thought as he continued his walk to think.

As he neared the school, he could see his sister sitting on top of bales of hay, her booted legs pulled tightly to her chest. The little children were feeding the animals in the petting zoo adjacent to the school. His youngest brother Charles Patrick, who they called Patty, was the first to spot him and squealed a greeting with both hands full of straw he was using to feed the Shetland ponies.

"Bri! See, Bri! I fed him! I fed my pony! See?"

"Yes, Patty, I see. You're doing a good job, too, while your big sister is being lazy."

"She's sad, Bri. Eve is sad," he said, frowning up at Eve.

"I think I can fix that. She needs to work like you are, Patty. Then she won't be sad anymore."

"Kay," the toddler said and continued feeding the ponies assured that his big brother will make his big sister happy again.

Brian held up his hand to Eve. "Okay, sister mine, let's go. We've got work to do." After a humming moment, she uncurled her long, shapely body and took his outstretched hand to climb down the bales of hay. Once she was on the ground, his right arm circled her shoulders while she automatically clamped her left arm around his waist. They were quiet as they walked matching steps toward the horse barns.

"Hello, Mary Pat," Brian said to the horse trainer.

"Top of the mornin' ta ya, Lad, and looka here," Ireland whispered through her voice. "We have our own sweet Eve come to visit the horses."

"Hi, Mrs. Todd," Eve acknowledged, monotone, and then walked to the first of thirty stalls where horses stuck their heads out over the wooden fencing.

Mrs. Todd frowned and eyed Brian. When she started to speak, he shook his head at her, indicating not to worry. Her expression was of concern, but she shrugged and nodded her understanding.

"Which of the horses haven't been washed yet?" Brian asked.

"We haven't gotten to the ones on this side yet."

"Okay, we'll start there," Brian said and went to get the buckets and brushes. When he returned, Eve was leading two horses to the horse shower stalls.

They were into the third horse when Brian felt a shower of water drench his back. When he stood and turned around, he couldn't see Eve over the horse's back, but he waited and when she peeked up, he blasted water at her waist under the horse's belly and down her jean-clad legs. The water battle was like a paintball contest for a good fifteen minutes until they misjudged the other and both stood at the same time. However, it was their mother who was walking past between the horses and got the brunt of the spray from both sides.

"Ooops!" Brian and Eve said in unison while they tried unsuccessfully to control their laughter.

Vivian's left eyebrow hiked up an entire inch, Brian thought, as she surveyed her two older adult offspring.

Vivian, as drenched as she was continued to the next shower stall and unbeknownst to Brian and Eve, grabbed two hoses, blasting them both. Then the water battle was on!

Later, as the three sodden people trudged toward the house, Chuck walked up the driveway, stood and flicked up his Stetson with his thumb and forefinger regarding his wife and children. He shook his head, repositioned his hat low on his face, and said: "Uh, uh, I don't even want to know what you three have been up to." No one had to see the little grin on his face as he preceded them into the house. He knew his wife would head for the shower in their bedroom. He came home a little early for lunch because Vivian was working from home today. He planned to spend his lunch break, making love to his wife, so this was perfect timing.

Showered and dressed, Brian and Eve went to have lunch in the sunroom. They sat at a table near the indoor/outdoor swimming pool and chowed down on full plates.

"So, obviously, my womb mate told you something was up with me," Eve commented and then bit into her hoagie.

"Why do you think that?"

"Come on, Brian. Are you saying that Vincent didn't talk with you?"

"He did, yes. Are you ready to tell me what happened to make you resign your commission?" He dug his spoon into a bowl of thick and creamy tomato and basil soup.

Eve sighed heavily. "I have been dating this man, a fellow officer in my squadron for the last two years."

That raised Brian's eyebrows and halted the next bite of his hoagie. "You never mentioned that you were seriously seeing anyone. Why?"

"You know how it goes in this family, Brian. We bring someone around the family only if the relationship is likely to result in marriage. I wasn't sure that I was ready for that type of commitment yet. You see, he was my first lover. Before him, I was still a virgin."

"Okay," Brian nodded. "I can understand that. The first isn't always the best indication of a long-term love affair. So, what happened?"

"We were together in bed one night and I had just had this incredible screaming orgasm…"

"Uh, you can skip that part," Brian interjected and winced.

"Anyway," she stressed, "we're cuddled up when he casually mentioned that his wife found out about our affair and he was going to start divorce proceedings so that he can marry me. I'm not believing what I'm hearing, so, in all my naked glory, I jump out of bed and ask him why he didn't tell me he was married. He tells me it's because he knew I wouldn't sleep with him if I knew about his wife. Whereupon, he tells me that I'm making too much over the situation and wants me to get back into bed for another round. When I disagreed, he tried to force me back between the sheets."

"Uh, oh, don't tell me, let me guess. He's dead and stinking and you've cut up his body into little pieces you fed to the sharks at sea?"

"Not quite. I clocked him and broke his jaw."

"Okay, after lunch, we'll find the bastard, cut him to ribbons, and then feed him to the sharks."

"See! That's why I didn't want to say anything. If I told my brothers, you guys would have guns loaded and locked. He wouldn't know what hit him."

"I noticed that you didn't mention his name because you knew what his fate would be."

"That's why you're one of the sharpest knives in the drawer, brother mine. I feel stupid enough. I know I have to tell the family, particularly our sisters, because it's a good lesson learned. Trust, but always verify."

"Smart. I've always liked that about you," Brian said, pushing his empty dishes aside and leaning his elbows on the table. "So, if you want to work the ranches, there's plenty for you to do."

She shrugged. "I appreciate that, but I've been offered a couple of positions. One with the FBI in Washington and the other with the DC Police Department working for my former Coast Guard training officer. I'll let you know when I decide."

"Okay, but are you sure that you don't want to give me his name?"

"Brian, insanity does not run in this family."

CHAPTER 24

"So, I've decided to leave with my parents right after Whitney's and Tucker's wedding. I'll go home to Japan after we visit Miami, Florida," KiLe stoically said while pacing the library at the Georgetown house.

Brian leaned his butt against the library table, his hands in his pockets, his left hand fingering a small grey box, and his feet crossed at the ankles. His eyes tracked KiLe as she paced back and forth, but his face wore a mass of confusion. "So, you reached this decision on an extended weekend trip to Minnesota with Roland Harrington?"

"I did, yes. I needed to get away for a while. I haven't done much traveling since I've been here these past four years. You were very busy, so I didn't want to bother you. It is my decision to follow my parents' and grandparents' instructions. You said that you would respect any decision I made. So, I have told my parents and grandparents that I will meet the men they have selected and choose one of them to wed. So, that's why I think that we shouldn't see each other anymore."

Nodding, Brian stood. "As you wish," he said without expression and turned toward the closed library door. He stopped and regarded her again. "KiLe," he said and waited for her to turn. When she did, he said, "It was an honor and a privilege to have known you. I wish you well." He slipped his hand into his left pocket around the small grey box and left the library, quietly closing the door behind him.

Ten seconds later, KiLe covered her mouth and her stomach to hold back the keening cries racing to her throat. Dropping to her knees, she bent to the floor and cried out her misery in racking sobs.

"Where is KiLe?" Vivian asked, smiling as the family was loading up to go to the airport.

"She's not with me, mom. She dumped me."

Vivian's eyes narrowed. "Dumped you? That's not possible, Brian. KiLe is in love with you."

He nodded in agreement. "I know. I'm in love with her. I learned from Whitney that KiLe's visa will expire at the end of the month. As a result, she must leave the country. However, if she married an American, she would not be forced to leave."

"Oh, I can take care of the visa problem with one phone call. However, you bought the ring and left home yesterday with the intention of asking her to marry you. What happened?"

"I never got to that part of our discussion. When I arrived, she had this stock speech ready and worked so hard to deliver it that I just let her get it all off her chest. She tells me that she's going home to Japan to choose one of the men her family selected for her to marry, and then to finish her education in England at her parents' alma mater. I wished her well and left."

"Why, Brian? Don't you think that she might have agreed to marry you if you proposed, showed the beautiful ring you selected for her, and explained the benefit of marrying an American citizen?"

"Perhaps, but she has to want to be with me, Mom, more than she wants to adhere to her parents' and grandparents' dictates. I can't fight her battles if we aren't fighting together on the same team. I'm willing to face her relatives and plead my case to get their agreement for the marriage. However, if KiLe isn't strong enough, doesn't have the confidence that we can make a marriage work, doesn't love, trust, and respect me enough, then, perhaps, it's not to be."

"You're not giving up, are you, son?" Vivian placed a comforting hand on his arm.

He shook his head. "No, not on a bet. I have the next eight days in Summer County during the family reunion to convince her to marry me and stay here for the rest of her life. However, I may have to bring out the big guns to help with other aspects of my plan."

Vivian grinned at her son and gave him a warm hug. "Let's go get you married," she confidently teased. "We've got your back, babe, big guns and all."

"All right, let's head 'em up and move 'em out. We're burning daylight," Chuck called out to his wife and multitude of children. When Brian walked away to hurry his siblings along, Chuck took Vivian into his arms and soundly kissed her waiting mouth. "Is he ready for what's ahead of him?"

"He's our son, babe. We raised him to plan his work and to work his plan. He's ready."

"Good. Let's go celebrate our good fortune and another addition to our posse."

"By the way, did Kenneth find out who the man is who hurt and humiliated our Eve?"

"He did, yes."

Vivian nodded. "Good. Once Eve is ready to tell us officially who he is, I plan to have a come-to-justice discussion with him."

"We'll both have that conversation," Chuck said and ushered her up the steps and into her seat next to him for the ride to the airport. Just as he looked around to do a headcount, he thought, *oh, well, we're going to need a bigger bus,* and smiled.

KiLe had never seen so many people who were related to one another by blood or by love, but there they were. Her parents and grandparents were similarly overwhelmed by the sheer number of those gathered on the first day of the reunion to hear the oral history of the Alexander family in America.

"Gather around, family, to hear our history as told by the eldest Alexander," Bernard Alexander, Vivian's father announced, stepping aside to let his uncle take his place.

"The original members of the colony were from Alexandria, a small pharaonic town founded by Alexander the Great, hence the name that survived through the generations of our family. An ancestor from

Alexandria, Egypt, on the Mediterranean Sea, was a privateer and he and his five sons owned ships that raided slave ships, freed the captives, looted and then stole or sank the vessels. The father-and-sons team hunted the Atlantic Ocean in packs.

"One of the sons spotted an English Man of War sailing vessel attacking a passenger ship off the coast of Barbados and attacked the British galleon. A storm overtook them and our relative lost his own ship and got separated from his father's and brothers' ships in the battle. He was but a teen of less than twenty years when he and his crew of similarly young sailors managed to save the Barbadians and their ship. Among the passengers was a young Barbadian girl of only about fourteen or fifteen years old, who was said to be beyond beautiful. She was being sent by her father to a wealthy Greek merchant in exchange for horses and other livestock. Though they could not speak a word of each other's language, our relative fell instantly in love with the young Barbadian girl.

"Because the Barbadian ship was severely damaged in the battle and storm, they had to sink her off the coast of what is now known as South Carolina. The Egyptian sailors and Barbadians hid from other British ships, which were hunting for them and other pirates in the area. They went into the deep woods and swampland and formed a colony living in harmony with the Indigenous Americans in the area and then intermarrying with them. The Egyptian and Barbadian sailors never saw their homelands again, but lived here in isolation avoiding slavery and helping enslaved people escape their captors. The Underground Railroad made a path through the dense woods and great swamp to the colony and then moved north or west from there. Some of the enslaved stayed in the colony and raised families intermarrying with the Barbadians, Indigenous Americans, and the Egyptian sailors. Many years later, around the late eighteenth, early nineteenth century, that colony became Summer County.

"Most of the people who live in Summer County descended from those early settlers and the Indigenous Americans who inhabited these lands before they were invaded.

"June nineteen, eighteen sixty-five, is known as Juneteenth Independence Day or Freedom Day; an American holiday that generally commemorates the announcement of the abolition of slavery. The name of the observance is a portmanteau of 'June' and 'nineteenth.' It is the emancipation of enslaved Americans of African descent throughout the former Confederate States of America, outside Native American lands. The Alexander family chose Juneteenth to come together in celebration of our family history, in reunion with our relatives living both near and far, and to affirm our collective vision and plan for our future.

"For the next ten days and nights, our observance will include public readings, singing traditional songs and reading of works by noted writers. The celebrations will include rodeos, a county fair, cooking contests, park parties where our young people will entertain us, historical reenactments, and the Mr. and Ms. Juneteenth contests. The Mascogos, descendants of Black Seminoles of Coahuila, Mexico, are also here to join with us in celebration of Juneteenth. We will sing, we will dance, we will educate, we will listen, we will eat, we will play, and we will pray. We will also rejoice in the young people who have chosen to wed on this occasion before all family and friends gathered here on Saturday, June nineteen, beginning at eleven o'clock. On June twentieth, the Sunrise Service will begin at six, Farewell Breakfast at seven, and Departure Blessing at nine. Remember all; what happens in Summer County…"

"Goes with us until we meet again," the crowd answered amid loud cheers.

"Hello, Whitney," said Avilla Montenegro. "I know you've just completed taking the bar exam and you're really busy with last-minute wedding plans, but may I have a word with you in private?"

"Sure." Whitney shrugged. "I thought you concluded your investigation involving Point of View North."

"I have, yes, however, there is one detail that I believe you are uniquely positioned to handle."

"Okay, what does this detail involve?"

"It's who it involves. Your cousin, Brian, and your friend, KiLe."

"Yakuza?" KiLe whispered, her fears mounting. "You believe that my grandfather is a Yakuza?"

Whitney nodded in the affirmative. "It is my understanding that the men selected for you to marry are also all Yakuza."

KiLe shook her head in denial and disbelief. "That can't be so, Whitney. He is an honorable man who is always gentle with me."

"You and I both know boys we went to private school with who were Yakuza. We also know that male members are often heavily tattooed all over their bodies and wear slicked-back hair. Think about it, KiLe. Have you ever seen your grandfather without his shirt on?"

"No," she frowned. "That would be disrespectful. Until I was with Brian, I had never seen any man without his shirt on."

"Except for my father and brothers, remember. When we went to the beach, my dad and brothers wore only swimwear."

"I did not look. It would be considered rude."

"I understand, but the point is, are you willing to marry a Yakuza?"

Frowning and fretful, KiLe's fears rose.

All during the week of activities, Brian made sure that he was in KiLe's line of sight though he pretended not to notice her or her family who persistently surrounded her. Some men were apparently bodyguards constantly trailing the extended family. The Hakamoras participated in the activities and seemed to have a great time. They even enjoyed the variety of food choices. Anything they didn't understand, Whitney, her mother or father, who all spoke fluid Japanese, explained. Eating barbecue ribs and corn on the cob with their fingers instead of chopsticks seemed to be a particularly enjoyable experience. They chatted amiably as they walked through the fairgrounds. KiLe's father and both grandfathers even went on stage to sing a few popular Broadway tunes. They were all overwhelmed to meet Whitney's cousin, prima ballerina Linda Lewis, known worldwide as The Black Swan. Every opportunity they got, they wanted to pose with the tallest men in Whitney's family, her nearly seven-foot Uncle Chuck Montgomery, a basketball icon, and renowned basketball star Gregory Alexander, known as Alexander the Great in the annals of sports. Baseball being very popular in Japan, the Hakamoras wanted many pictures with World Series Champion Will Hamilton, Linda's husband.

Chuck and Vivian rolled out the red carpet for the Hakamoras at their ranch, Point of View South, for a hot afternoon swim and luncheon where they served traditional Japanese cuisine prepared by the former high-fashion model, Angelique, now the wife of Brian's uncle. Whitney's parents did the same thing and invited him to come. At The Summer House, the bed and breakfast where the Hakamoras stayed for the week of activities, they were given the royal treatment by Brian's cousin Satarah, owner of the facility, and her husband Douglas Johnson, the Summer County Fire Chief. One night after dinner, Douglas gave the Hakamoras a ride to the carnival on the fire trucks with the sirens blaring. When they arrived, their eyes were aglow.

On another occasion, Brian's grandfather, Bernard Alexander, and the Dean of the Summer County Academy, Ambassador Emeritus Jefferson Logan, a star in the international arena, gave the visitors a private tour of the campus. They were introduced to students who came from around the globe to attend the school. Some were even from Asian countries and impressed KiLe's mother and step-father, both educators, with the international flavor of the programs.

Brian appreciated that his family, both the Alexanders and the Montgomerys, showed up and pulled out all of the stops for him. They never let KiLe forget the great times she had with them and Brian. They provided a picture album to her recounting all of the experiences she had in Pennsylvania and Maryland. He loved these family times, too and hoped that one day soon, KiLe would enjoy the camaraderie as a member of the family and wear the family's gold chain around her neck.

KiLe tried to catch glimpses of Brian without making her family and their bodyguards suspicious of her action. She had to sit quietly and stoically during the rodeo, where Brian competed in the team roping, calf roping, rough stock riding, and barrel racing contests. She wanted to get up and cheer for him, but remained still and composed.

Brian's sister Dena was a star in the riding and roping contests, but Brian won several of the events. As a result of her parents' and grandparents' excitement over being at the rodeo, they went to the shops and little nooks. They bought an extraordinary number of clothes to wear at the upcoming events. Yet, KiLe was just excited to see Brian, even at a distance.

Her family was awed by the beautiful art created by Brian's family members, Whitney's Grandmother Helen Greene and Uncle Russell Greene. The Greene mother-and-son accomplished artists had just returned from a successful art tour in Spain. The Hakamoras asked whether the Greenes would be willing to do a show in Tokyo during their next tour. Of course, they agreed to put Tokyo on their schedule. After all, Stacy Greene Alexander was a U.S. Navy Admiral stationed in Tokyo with her husband, five-star Air Force General and Astronaut Benjamin Alexander. Both were military diplomats, members of the U.S. Joint Chiefs of Staff, and Whitney Alexander's parents.

Still, the biggest guns had yet to arrive.

CHAPTER 25

"Air Force One just touched down." After checking his watch, General Benjamin Alexander turned to his wife and regarded her near nudity with pleasure as she put lotion on her skin. "We're down to T minus three hours and counting before…" Not hesitating, he sat on the bench beside her and watched the tears slide down her beautiful gamine face, with beguiling light, crystal brown eyes. "What is it, babe?"

Stacy leaned her head against her husband's solid bare chest. "You're my hero, Benny. Not because you're a five-star general or because you're an astronaut, but because you're a good man. You're everything that's wonderful and right in my life. You're everything that I've ever needed. From the very beginning, when you hit on me in the Pentagon cafeteria at ten o'clock at night, you changed my world for the better."

He grinned at her. "You are still that sleek, sexy woman who made me work hard for the honor of you deciding to take me to your bed. You held me off for longer than any other woman had. That made me know that you were special. I knew from the moment I touched you that there would not be another woman as important to me as you are in my life. I don't know how or why I've been so lucky to have you, but you're my *shero* too, babe."

Stacy wrapped her arms around his waist and just breathed him in. "You're the reason this day, the day our daughter will marry the love of her life is possible. I wanted to have an abortion…"

"Shhh, babe. You didn't and now we can celebrate the first of our children take a step into building a life with her own family. I'm so enormously proud of her and what she's accomplished. She's brilliant, just like her mother."

"You deserve all the credit, Benny. When I disappeared the day after Whitney was born, you raised her alone. You never let her down or disappointed her. She loves you fiercely."

"You were honor-bound to do your duty as a military officer and I didn't question whether you loved us for the years you stayed away. Throughout all of your deployments, since you returned to us, you've worked to protect and serve all of us. We have seven children you've given us, despite the hard and often dangerous duty you've no doubt had to perform."

She looked up at him now, love shining in her eyes. "Well, maybe we need to do a recount on the children we have in about seven more months."

The grin on his handsome face still made her blood warm. When he easily lifted her in his arms and took her back to bed, she didn't release the lip lock she had on her husband's mouth.

"Are your parents going to make it on time?" KiLe sat at the table in the kitchen with Whitney finishing an early breakfast. "They haven't come down to eat yet."

Whitney lifted her head, frowned while listening. "Yes, they'll make it with time to spare. They've been making love for the last forty-five minutes or so."

KiLe laughed. "You have incredible hearing ability. In this house, I can't even hear when your sisters or brothers get up."

Whitney pushed her empty plate away and turned to KiLe. "What's wrong, KiLe. You're trying so hard to be cheerful and upbeat. We've been friends since we were six years old. I know your moods. Something is bothering you. What is it?"

"Brian and I aren't involved anymore."

Whitney's brows beetled. "What? Why? How did that happen?"

"He's involved with Molly."

Whitney's confusion grew. "Molly? Who is Molly?"

"Molly Montgomery."

Whitney just stared at KiLe before she rose from the table to pick up their dishes. "The hell you say, KiLe. She's a child. Brian doesn't go after children."

"She's a beautiful teenager and she's pregnant, apparently by Brian."

Whitney laughed and shook her head before opening the dishwasher. She began inserting the dishes on the racks and cleaning up the kitchen. "If you believe that type of foolishness, you're lunar."

"I heard him and Avilla Montenegro talking about it in the library."

Whitney turned from her tasks and looked at the sadness on her friend's face. "Did you ask Brian about what you overheard?"

"No, I ..."

"Just assumed and went away with Roland for an extended weekend, right?"

KiLe nodded with tears forming in her eyes. "You don't believe that he has been with her?"

"Hell no. Not on a bet. I know, love, trust, and respect my cousin, KiLe. He may look like every woman's fantasy, but he respects himself and any woman he's involved with. You don't know him if you think he would do such a thing and you're wasting your tears. If you think he would touch Molly Montgomery, you're off the rails." Whitney huffed out a frustrated breath. "Look, KiLe, call Brian and talk with him. If he's not interested in you or he's interested in some other *woman*, he'll be honest and tell you the truth. Until you hear it from him directly, trust and believe he would never do something like what you think you heard. Now, I'm going to go shower and dress for my wedding which will start in T minus two hours."

KiLe remained in the kitchen ruminating over her friend's absolute unshakable belief that her Brian would not, indeed, could not have sexual relations with any woman under the age of consent, including the pretty, young Molly Montgomery. After hearing Whitney's comments, KiLe didn't know what to do or what to feel. She had known Brian intimately for only a matter of months, not even six months. Somehow, she believed in her gut that maybe she misunderstood what was going on in the conversation she overheard.

Still, she had broken off their relationship and Brian had not raised any argument against their separation. When he left the house on that fateful night, he did not try to contact her. Not the way Payton continued to encourage her to renew their relationship. However, Payton made it clear that unless or until she slept with him, they could not have an exclusive relationship. He would continue to sleep with other women until she agreed, but he would be discreet? She shook her head at that bit of insanity. How he thought that would be okay with her was beyond her understanding of what a committed relationship entailed. She admitted to herself that she was beyond that now. Brian opened her eyes to what could exist between lovers, but it was all academic now. Though her heart ached anytime she spotted him during the festivities that led up to this day, they were over with now. In a few hours, after Whitney's and Tucker's wedding ceremony, she would leave with her parents never to see Brian again.

Batting away the tears, she rose from the kitchen table to help Whitney get ready to have a forever kind of love with a man who loved and cherished her.

Once the President of the United States stepped up on the platform under an arbor of pretty pink and purple Bougainvillea blossoms, the crowd on the south lawn quietly stood. Brian's and KiLe's voices began and blended beautifully with the song "When You Know," a duet written by Whitney and Tucker on their first official date nearly two years earlier.

Before their first date was over, they admitted that their strong feelings for each other would last for a lifetime. As she sang, KiLe remembered how Whitney and Tucker looked at one another. There was no mistaking how much love and excitement for each other resided in their gazes. Much in the same way she sang and looked into Brian's eyes.

She looks so sad and so beautiful, thought Brian, as he sang the duet with KiLe. The words to the song meant so much to him as he sang for Tucker and Whitney, but from his heart to KiLe.

You can look for a lifetime and never really find that special
Someone who fits into your life just right and that tight
But when I met you, I knew in an instant you were my Mr. Right
The man who would light up my life. The man I want to reach for each night
The one who held me and kissed me just right.
My love, I want you and need you for the rest of my life.

I knew at the first sight you would be my Mrs. Right. Because
When that feeling grabs you in your heart, with might, that's when
You know it's right. I'm giving you all that I've got
Because you, my love, put an end to my lonely nights.
You will hold me tight and I will always love you just right.
Love isn't a game for us. It's what we'll have for the rest of our lives.
It's a forever kind of love

KiLe could feel the words Brian sang deep in her soul. She wanted to cross the expanse between him and her, but she stayed in place as Whitney and her parents approached the platform from the right and Tucker and his parents approached from the left.

The President held up his arms and looked first toward Tucker. "Who gives this man, Tucker Duncan Cavanaugh, into marriage?"

"We do, his parents, Leland and Aurora Adamson Cavanaugh."

Tucker, resplendent in his white dress military uniform, embraced his parents and joined the President on the platform taking his hand. Then the President looked toward his Goddaughter and asked, "Who gives Whitney Ivy Alexander into marriage?"

"We do, Benjamin and Stacy Greene Alexander, her parents."

Whitney, with her perfusion of golden-brown corkscrew curly hair piled artfully on the crown of her head and wreathed in a cloud of white Baby's Breath flowers, smiled radiantly. She fiercely hugged her parents, exchanging kisses and words of joy. In a slim, sleeveless, floor-length column of virginal white, she regally raised her head, and walked up to take the President's outstretched hand.

"It is said, in One Corinthians that: *Love is patient, love is kind. It does not envy, it does not boast, it is not proud. It is not rude, it is not self-seeking, it is not easily angered, it keeps no record of wrongs. Love does not delight in evil but rejoices with the truth. It always protects, always trusts, always hopes, and always perseveres. Love never fails.*"

As the ceremony continued on the platform and Brian and KiLe listened, their eyes never strayed from one another. Fifteen minutes later, after the ceremony, when the President announced Tucker and Whitney to be husband and wife, KiLe and Brian sang *Endless Love*. As the newlyweds left the platform hand-in-hand, they passed through a saber arch tunnel. The honorary arch of sabers was held up by members representing all branches of the military. Their parents followed and then proceeded to the huge white tent where the reception started. Changelings, Tucker's band members, serenaded the couple's first dance with the song "No One."

It was clear to KiLe that her performances at the wedding displeased her parents and grandparents. At the reception, they would not permit her to mount the stage to sing with Changeling. So, after the meal, of which she ate very little, she said her goodbyes and followed in her family's wake toward the waiting black vans with darkly-tinted windows. Her head was down and didn't immediately notice that the path was lined on both sides with Brian's family members. She finally looked up when she heard them singing, "Let's Give Them Something to Talk About."

The tears she had tried to hold at bay fountained up and overflowed her tremulous smile. When her grandmother noticed that she was lagging behind, she grabbed her wrist and pulled her along as the bodyguards fell in behind her.

"Come! You must go now!" her grandmother hissed in Japanese and yanked on her arm even harder.

When her grandfather turned with consternation written on his face, she snatched her arm away from her grandmother and stood her ground. "Honorable Grandfather, why must I leave to marry a man I do not know?"

"You do not question my will!" he sternly said and began to turn away from her.

"Honorable Grandfather, are you Yakuza?"

That stopped him in his tracks. When he turned back to her, the fierceness on his face and of demeanor froze KiLe's blood. She started to back away from him as he reached out to force her toward the vans, and the guards placed a firm hand on her back.

Low, menacing growls emanated from the black Labradors, Starsky and Hutch, causing the guards to step back away from her. Even her grandfather did not approach her as the dogs continued to shield her. Dropping to her knees, she buried her face in their warm fur and held on. When she looked up, Brian stood at the end of the row, feet apart with his arms across his firm chest watching. She knew in that instance that he was waiting for her to stand up for herself…and for him.

Rising to her feet, she screamed his name running to him and leaping into his arms.

Brian caught KiLe on the fly and swinging her up to clamp her legs around his waist, fused his mouth to hers.

"I'm in love with you, Brian. I don't want to go away and leave you," she cried, her tears flooding her face.

"I'm here for you, KiLe Hakamora. I'm in love with you, too, but I will not disrespect your parents and grandparents, nor will I ask you to choose between us. Will you stand here with Starsky and Hutch while I speak with your family?"

She nodded stupidly and then whispered something in Brian's ear, which caused him to stop and stare at her.

"Are you sure that you want this? That you want me?"

Again, she nodded, palmed his face and kissed his mouth slowly and thoroughly.

"Okay." He nodded and slowly backed away to go to speak with her family. His Uncle Benny and Aunt Stacy joined him and stood at his back to translate his words. His parents came to stand beside him, as did the President of the United States. However, none was persuasive until his cousin, Donald Dixon, his family's lawyer, stepped up and whispered something in KiLe's grandfather's ear. Whatever it was, had the older man bowing repeatedly and nodding yes to the questions Donald asked.

In less than an hour, KiLe and Brian stood before the President on the platform under the arbor holding hands as they were pronounced husband and wife to the cheers from the family gathered on the bright, sunny June nineteenth day.

EPILOGUE

On Monday morning, after the wedding, Brian woke violently aroused. His wife of only two days was somewhere in the sleeping bag, busying herself with providing for his pleasurable morning wake-up call. He moaned and his breath caught in his chest before he reached for KiLe and brought her up into his arms.

"Good morning, Honorable husband," she impishly grinned at him as she wrapped around him to snuggle into his warm embrace.

"My Honorable wife, is up to her usual tricks early this morning. Why don't I make breakfast and then you can have your way with me?"

"Okay, but I'm not sure that I can keep anything on my stomach." She rolled on top of him, stacked her hands on his broad chest, and placed her chin atop them.

He ran his hands up and down her naked body enjoying the feel of her soft skin against his palms. "Are you experiencing morning sickness?"

"I don't know. Your father told me what to expect when he confirmed that I'm pregnant."

"We're pregnant, KiLe. We're in this together."

"I know. At first, I didn't know what was happening to me. I was sleepy and tired all the time and my appetite was off. When I realized that I had missed two periods in my cycle, it occurred to me that I might be pregnant."

"Yet, you were willing to leave and go back to Japan without telling me?"

"I planned to go to England early for the summer school session and, if I were pregnant, I would have my baby there. I wasn't sure how you would feel about becoming a father. I needed to have time to think."

"If you had told me what you suspected, I would have married you right away. I planned to propose to you on the day that you dumped me. I had the engagement ring in my pocket."

"I didn't want to trap you into marriage against your will. I didn't know how you felt about me. We never said the words. Then, I thought that you had betrayed me with Molly."

"I would never do that, KiLe."

"I know that now, but until you explained that she was trying to coerce you into telling her who her father was, I didn't understand her motivation."

"Are we all clear now?"

"We are, yes."

"Good."

"Still, there is just one more thing I need to know."

"Okay, what is it?"

"What did your cousin, Donald Dixon, say to my grandfather to make him change his mind and agree to my marriage to you?"

"I have absolutely no idea. I don't speak Japanese yet. However, I told your family that I'm in love for the first time in my life."

"I told them that I'm in love for the last time in my life."

With that, the honeymoon grew brighter in the Pennsylvania Poconos in a tent by a mountain lake where they planned to spend two weeks and begin to build their retreat before their baby was born at the end of the year.

About the author...

Ann Jeffries, the critically acclaimed author of the Family Reunion—Wisdom of the Ancestors Series, is a native of Washington, DC. As an only child, she enjoyed the benefits of a private school education at Allen in Asheville, North Carolina, and a public education at the University of Maryland. Ann began writing fiction for her own amusement.

Ms. Jeffries is the recipient of many awards for leadership and public service. A keynote speaker at colleges, universities, conferences, and conventions, she has extensively traveled the North American continent, Asia, and Europe. Among other endeavors, she is an entrepreneur, an avid supporter of public television, a genealogist, and a voracious reader.

Her pride and joy are her family, particularly her Fabulous Four grands. She lives in Maryland and South Carolina.

Follow Ann on her website: www.annjeffries.net, Facebook: @ Ann Jeffries, on Twitter @Ann Jeffries and her publishing house site: www.newviewliterature.com. Her novels are available in e-book, paperback, and audiobook formats. Her autographed copies can be found through www.annjeffries.net and also unautographed on Amazon.com and barnesandnoble.com.

Audiobooks are also available through her webiste, Audible, iTunes, and Amazon. For bulk sales, contact Ingram Book Group Distributors.

www.ingramcontent.com/pod-product-compliance
Lightning Source LLC
Chambersburg PA
CBHW030147100526
44592CB00009B/163